Haven't We Been Here Before?

JOHN NOTT

First edition published in Great Britain in 2007
By
Discovered Authors Diamonds

ISBN 978-1-905108-49-7

Available from Discovered Authors Online
All major online retailers and available to order through all UK bookshops

Or contact:
Books
Discovered Authors
50 Albemarle Street, London
W1S 4BD

+ (44) 207 529 37 29

books@discoveredauthors.co.uk

Printed in the UK by BookForce Ltd.

BookForce's policy is to use papers that are natural, renewable and recyclable
products and made from wood grown in sustainable forests where ever
possible

BookForce UK Ltd.
Alma Park,
6 Woodlands Drive
Grantham, Lincs
www.bookforce.co.uk

*To Miloska, my wife
and my six grandchildren,*

*William, Thomas, Saffron,
Siena, Tabitha and Freya*

Haven't We Been Here Before?

JOHN NOTT

First edition published in Great Britain in 2007
By
Discovered Authors Diamonds

ISBN 978-1-905108-49-7

Available from Discovered Authors Online
All major online retailers and available to order through all UK bookshops

Or contact:
Books
Discovered Authors
50 Albemarle Street, London
W1S 4BD

+ (44) 207 529 37 29

books@discoveredauthors.co.uk

Printed in the UK by BookForce Ltd.

BookForce's policy is to use papers that are natural, renewable and recyclable
products and made from wood grown in sustainable forests where ever
possible

BookForce UK Ltd.
Alma Park,
6 Woodlands Drive
Grantham, Lincs
www.bookforce.co.uk

*To Miloska, my wife
and my six grandchildren,*

*William, Thomas, Saffron,
Siena, Tabitha and Freya*

CONTENTS

ACKNOWLEDGEMENTS

This book would not have been possible without the availability of several outstanding contributions to the history of the periods concerned. Having decided as late as October 2006 that the experience of my forebears, my wife and myself in relation to the news stories of today merited an early book, I had no time for research into original sources.

This meant that to some extent I came to rely on the research and scholarship of others. This book contains several extracts, interlaced with my own experiences and writings, from several other authors. I name them here:

Peacemakers:
The Paris Peace Conference and its Attempts to End War
Margaret MacMillan (John Murray, 2002)
Reprinted by permission of John Murray Publishers
© Margaret MacMillan, 2002

Ploughing Sand: British Rule in Palestine, 1917-1948
Naomi Shepherd (John Murray, 1999)
Reprinted by permission of John Murray Publishers
© Naomi Shepherd, 1999

Empire of the Plains
Leslie Adkins (Thomas Dunne Books, 2004)
Reprinted by permission of Harpercollins Publishers
© Leslie Adkins, 2004

I also drew on several articles in the *RUSI Journal* (the journal of the Royal United Services Institute) by Dr Paul Robinson and Dr Correlli Barnett.

I found all of these books and articles outstanding in their various ways.

I was fortunate also in being introduced to the publishers, Discovered Authors, by a friend of mine. It is situated in the premises of John Murray in Albemarle Street and John Murray personally has been a valuable guiding friend. Discovered Authors, together with my excellent editor, Richard Collins, have produced a book in a very short time.

I had to get a book into circulation whilst Afghanistan, Palestine, Iraq and Bosnia are in the daily news, aware that the fiftieth anniversary of Suez occurred in 2006 and the twenty-fifth anniversary of the Falklands War falls in 2007. I could not wait to join the queue and fit in with the lists of larger publishers.

In the foreword to the book I make no claim to be an expert in any of the issues which I cover – and, by the very nature of time and space, readers must go to the authors mentioned for an in-depth study of these issues. But, I hope that readers will feel that the chapters are topical and relevant and provide a fresh insight into the news stories which engross us day by day.

FOREWORD

'Is it really twenty-five years since the Falklands War?' A young friend asked me recently. 'I remember watching it on television as a schoolboy and I can't believe it was so long ago.'

Neither can I.

The world has changed in so many ways over the past quarter of a century as technology – notably the internet, mobile phones, the BlackBerry, iPods – has come to dominate the lives of most people below the age of sixty and changed the way we communicate. Technology has certainly transformed the battlefield.

The Falklands campaign of 1982 was largely fought with ships, aeroplanes and weapons of the Second World War, although there had of course been a step change in military capability to meet the challenge posed by the Soviet Union. Nuclear submarines and heat-seeking missiles were the products of the Cold War. This had been a war, no less for the fact that the two superpowers, the United States and the Soviet Union, stopped short at annihilating each other, and us.

Methods of fighting were different in 1982 as well. Soldiers were compelled to yomp with their heavy haversacks up to 100 miles of bleak landscape because all the troop-carrying helicopters had gone down with MS *Atlantic Conveyor* when it was sunk by the Argentinians. Field-Marshal Erwin Rommel once said, 'Before the battle is fought, it is decided by the quartermaster'. During the Falklands campaign the quartermaster came up trumps in the extreme circumstances of a war fought 8000 miles from home, an astonishing achievement when you think about it.

And think about it I did.

At the time, as a member of the War Cabinet, closeted alone with the Prime Minister Margaret Thatcher I expressed my doubts about the logistic viability of a war fought on the other side of the world near an Antarctic wilderness. Why did I have those doubts? Partly because I remembered the sorry tale of Suez and, even more poignantly and pointedly, the circumstances surrounding another logistic nightmare in my own family history.

My ancestor Major-General Sir William Nott GCB commanded the 1st Division of the 'Army of the Indus' which, 10,000-strong, marched in 1838 for about a thousand miles across the deserts and plains of northern India into the mountains of Afghanistan with a baggage train carried by 30,000 camels and 40, 000 thousand camp followers.

For three years between 1839 and 1842 he fought the Afghans around Kandahar and in Helmund province, where British forces operate today. He emerged one of the few heroes of the First Afghan War. The Afghan Medal bearing the inscription 'Kandahar, Ghuznee and Kabul' forms an integral part of the Nott family coat of arms.

Surely some lessons should have been learnt about fighting Afghans from my ancestor's story and from the experiences of countless others who fought in that inhospitable terrain? The Russian generals who fought and lost their campaign in Afghanistan between 1979 and 1989 with an overwhelming force, far beyond anything this country can put in the field, are wont to ask – have the British learnt nothing from their history?

In the chapter on Afghanistan I describe how William Nott was obsessed with his lack of 'carriage'. Carriage in 1840 meant camels and he never had enough of them to carry his fight to the enemy. I read that British troops fighting around Kandahar today lack sufficient carriage in the form of helicopters. *Plus ça change.* In most respects the basic requirement of every war – good logistics – remains the same.

In recalling the story of my ancestor in Afghanistan, I realised that when I wrote my memoir, *Here Today, Gone Tomorrow*, in 2001, I skated over the experiences of my grandfather, the great-great grandson of General Sir William Nott. Major Lewis Nott accompanied General Allenby in the conquest of Palestine in 1917 and became Governor of Gaza, and then Nablus, up until 1926. This period – after the Balfour Declaration of 1917 proposing a 'national home' for Jews, in Palestine – still dictates the conflict between Jew and Arab today. Trying to reconcile these two communities has been described as 'ploughing sand'. Major Lewis Nott, a fluent Arabic speaker, became, for all his goodwill, exhausted and frustrated by his task in Palestine. The parallels to be drawn between this good man and other men and women in contemporary times are, as can be seen in the chapter on Palestine, all too apparent.

There is no doubt too that in this same period, at the conclusion of the First World War, the British betrayed the Arabs. Iraq was created by the British out of three former provinces of the Ottoman Empire: Basra, Baghdad and Mosul (Kurdistan). None of these provinces had much in common with each other. There was no Iraqi nationalism because Iraq did not exist, only Arab nationalism, which was already stirring. My grandfather, an Arab specialist, was close to King Abdullah of Transjordan, the great-grandfather of the present king. Abdullah was made ruler of this new country, Jordan, at the same time that the British made Faisal king of the new Iraq.

The problems of Iraq today stem to a great extent from British policy in 1920.

Having pondered on the lessons we might have learnt from the experiences of my own relations – over a broad span of time in Afghanistan, Palestine and Iraq – and my own experience as Defence Secretary during the Cold War and as a member of the War Cabinet during the Falklands campaign, I then began to consider who else within my family had been involved, albeit peripherally, in some other dramas of the twentieth century.

Although there is a sort of peace in the Balkans at the present time, and the tragedy of Bosnia seems largely to have been forgotten, it nonetheless contains an explosive mixture in the very heart of Europe.

Did we get this one wrong as well?

Yugoslavia, created as a state for the southern Slavs following the collapse of the Austrian and Ottoman empires, never had much coherence with its mix of peoples and religions – Muslim, Serb Orthodox and Catholic. I might have forgotten the problems of former Yugoslavia had it not been for the experiences of my Slovene wife, Miloska. Brought up as a Catholic, a child of the former Austro-Hungarian Empire, schooled in Nazi-occupied Yugoslavia, educated as a Communist under Tito and then as a student in Catholic Italy – her story, related in the chapter on Yugoslavia, explains why she has devoted the past fourteen years of her life to assisting the destitute Bosnian Muslims around the town of Srebrenica, in 1995 the scene of the worst massacre in Europe since the Second World War.

In this book, therefore, when I reflect on all those places that we read about every day – Afghanistan, Palestine, Iraq, former Yugoslavia – I have tried to draw briefly on their history in an attempt to understand the problems that exist today. I have quoted quite extensively from my own memoir, where I rather skated over my family connections with these places. It would have been impossible to pass over the coming Falklands anniversary in April 2007 – that was trouble – and the Suez crisis of 1956, really the end of an era in British history. In attempting to comment on the difficulties we face today neither conflict – not least the former, of which I had direct experience – could be ignored.

I make no claim to be a specialist in any of the several dramas that I attempt to cover but, having spent a lifetime reading about the experiences of my relations in earlier wars, and having been Defence Secretary during the Cold War, I wanted to put it all down in writing. This is not a family history but it does shed light on events and experiences in the life of a family which has been involved, one way or another, in a number of key episodes of British history over the past 150 years.

THE FALKLANDS –

A PERSONAL CONNECTION

1982

INTRODUCTION

In a leading article in the *Sunday Times* (18 October 2006) Simon Jenkins (former editor of *The Times*) gave his opinion that the 'political conduct of the Falklands war was near impeccable'. Jenkins had studied the war from Whitehall and his journalist colleague Max Hastings was seconded to the Task Force, to the 2nd Battalion, the Parachute Regiment, as part of the British press corps reporting the war. Their book *The Battle of the Falklands* was published with commendable speed in 1983, and still gives a fair summary of the campaign.

I am bound to say that the conduct of the war in Whitehall and Westminster did not seem 'impeccable' to me. But then I was, perhaps, too close to it to form a judgement at the time. The tensions between the Foreign Office and the Prime Minister, and with me representing the interests of the Ministry of Defence, were acute but always, I believe, good mannered. There were many upsets and several cliff-hangers which I describe in the following extract from my memoir.

But it is certainly true to say that it was a remarkable episode in our long military history; probably our last colonial war; my ancestors, as this book records, had fought or participated in several others. The military behaved with great courage and loyalty towards the political decision to wrest the island back from Argentina. The aftermath of the Falklands War was wholly beneficial to the standing and prestige of this country overseas.

I do believe that Margaret Thatcher's conduct of the campaign was near 'impeccable', not least because of the several disagreements we had with her along the way. She emerged from it as a great war leader, determined, courageous and direct. It was *her* war and at the conclusion of my extract I ponder whether any *man* would have carried it off with her conviction.

The article in the *Sunday Times* that I have cited was, in part, to compare the conduct of the war in the Falklands with Iraq and in particular to comment on the unfortunate criticism of it made in autumn 2006 by General Sir Richard Dannatt, the Chief of the General Staff. He will be forgiven for his naivety but, perhaps, he should remember the words of Napoleon Bonaparte, who said of war that the 'moral is to the physical as three to one'. Any public criticism of the political conduct of a war by a serving military officer can hardly fortify the morale of soldiers fighting on the ground. This book is full of criticism of the justification and conduct of earlier wars; it is full, too, of invective about the Foreign Office. Perhaps, therefore, I am being unfair not to recognise the frustrations of an admirable general, but there we go.

Before the outbreak of the war in 1982 I had already told Margaret Thatcher of my wish to retire from politics at the next election. She told me in her inimitable way not to be so silly. So, in a way, my weariness about the excitement and emotion of it all can partially be explained. As soon as the war had ended, I went back to her to confirm my decision to retire. 'But you can't go now,' she said, meaning, I suppose, that politicians don't retire after a success, always following failure. And Enoch Powell's remark that 'all political careers end in failure' has a measure of truth in it. I was persuaded to stay on for a few more months to oversee an examination of the military lessons of the campaign and publish them in a White Paper. The Franks Committee subsequently examined the circumstances leading up to the crisis. It let the government off quite lightly.

Virtually the only criticism of the Franks Committee was directed at me for announcing the forward scrapping of HMS *Endurance*, and I deal with that incident quite fully later in the chapter. Of course, with the benefit of hindsight, the scrapping of *Endurance* should have been postponed again, for the umpteenth time. History is about hindsight – and historians and journalists have the luxury of not experiencing in real time the realities of life for politicians and generals. Everything is different in the cauldron of events than it seems thereafter. So, when, in a later chapter, I am critical of my former colleague Douglas Hurd for his approach to the Bosnian war, I hope he will appreciate that now I write with a different perspective, as a commentator and historian. I have myself been in the cauldron of events in government – where policy-making is the by-product of many conflicting factors which crowd in on ministers every day.

I remember being particularly annoyed with Max Hastings, an inveterate journalist if there ever was one, for his accusation in *The Battle of the Falklands* that the Ministry of Defence had hazarded the lives of the soldiers at a Goose Green by leaking. It was, of course, a ridiculous assertion since the other criticism throughout the book was that we were obsessed by censorship. After so many years of peace, few reporters were possessed of any knowledge of military affairs and therefore had little respect and trust from Service officers. The British press at home found it difficult to set aside the normal requirements of competitive journalism in response to the demands of war. The communications systems of the Task Force were ill-equipped to handle operational requirements and journalistic copy so it was not just the newspapers and the television that were often short of news in real time; so was I. This meant that the BBC in particular filled the gap with propaganda from Argentina: not exactly helpful in time of war. I was also annoyed with the armchair generals and former politicians who could not resist forecasting the next moves of the Task Force. And now I have myself become an armchair general.

***

Last year I booked a cruise to Antarctica with my wife, and I had arranged to start the journey in Chile because I was uncertain whether I would get a friendly reception in Argentina.

One day I was in the kitchen at home when my wife said that I was wanted on the telephone. 'Oh, no,' I said, 'it will be someone trying to sell us something. Why don't you take the call?' 'I think you had better do so,' she replied. 'Who is it?' I asked. 'He calls himself Jack Straw.' 'I don't know anyone called Jack Straw,' I replied. 'Yes, you do,' she said. 'I think he is the Foreign Secretary.'

I went to the telephone. 'Hello, Jack,' I said, 'what can I do to help you?', although I don't think I had ever met him. It was twenty-three years since I had left politics. 'We hear,' said Jack, 'that you are going to Antarctica on a cruise and that the ship embarks in Ushuaia in Argentina. It is entirely up to you, but I wonder if you want to go through Argentine immigration?' It was very courteous of Jack Straw to call me personally.

I would have spent two hours in Argentina during my transfer from Chile, but I decided not to go – overcautious, I am sure. I did not want to end up like General Pinochet

When I asked Jack Straw what things were like in Argentina, he merely said that the reconciliation that had taken place with President Menem, who was anxious to gain the goodwill of the islanders, had been replaced by a more strident policy towards the Falklands by the new President, Nestor Kirchner, who was seeking re-election in 2007. He has indicated that he will take a hard line on Argentina's claim to the Malvinas – and has charged Britain with bad faith in failing to enter substantive talks on the future of the islands, over which the two countries went to war twenty-five years ago.

So the outlook for the Falkland Islands is clouded once again, which is somewhat sad when we tried to settle the future in 1981, before the war began. Self-determination for the islanders meant that 1000 men died to enable them to have the government of their choice. Now, having won the Falkland Islands back by force, they will have to be retained by force. This residual responsibility from our colonial past requires the presence, perhaps indefinitely, of a deterrent military force.

It is in the interests of Argentina to win the goodwill of the islanders, but that now seems distant. .

When our survival in Britain was threatened by the Soviet Union in the Cold War, the thought of keeping a constant garrison in a state of readiness, 8000 miles away from home, seemed distressing but not impossible; that remains the case today. Will we be there for ever? The answer lies with Argentina as much as with the British citizens of the Falkland Islands whom it is our duty to protect.

My memoir now records what the war was like in real time in 1982.

'King Philip of Macedon said to his son, Alexander: "You see the glory, but war is above all else horror. It is blood, sweat, excrement; it is dust and wind; it is thirst and hunger, unbearable frost and unbearable heat. Let me face all this for you, for so long as I am able. Stay here [with Aristotle, your tutor] for one more year."'

(Valerio Manfredi, *Alexander: Child of a Dream*)

THE FIRST WEEK

I hate war; the thought of sending young men and women away to fight is repugnant to me. Yet on the night of Thursday 1 April 1982 I agreed, with my immediate colleagues, that we had no option but to do so; and we sent them to the other side of the world, at huge risk, across 8000 miles of ocean. It ended in triumph and tragedy – 255 British lost their lives and many more were wounded.

Those who had experienced war – Admiral Terry Lewin, the Chief of the Defence Staff, William Whitelaw, the Deputy Prime Minister, and Francis Pym, the Foreign Secretary, my colleagues in the War Cabinet – must have felt as I did. Margaret Thatcher, as a woman and a mother, must have been just as deeply affected as us men. But all of us managed, in the crisis which engulfed us, to conceal these feelings from each other. Sometimes Francis, in his determined quest for a negotiated settlement, perhaps allowed his emotions to show a little; but it was his job as Foreign Secretary to seek a diplomatic exit – an exit to a situation that had vexed successive governments ever since the Second World War.

Whitelaw, Pym and I, as members of the Cabinet Committee under Margaret Thatcher's chairmanship, had all agreed to an earlier proposal by Nicholas Ridley to attempt a negotiated settlement with Argentina, based on a long-term leaseback of the Falkland Islands, but this proposal had been sabotaged by a cross-party alliance in the House of Commons. When a gun is pointed at your head, diplomacy has a tendency to veer towards appeasement. Yet appeasing the fascist junta in Argentina, once they had invaded British territory, was not on our agenda. There were only two choices: war or surrender. As circumstances later showed, there was never an honourable negotiated settlement in between.

Throughout the Falklands conflict Margaret Thatcher was at her best, showing great courage and determination. I had some disagreements with her when I urged restraint, and occasionally I aligned myself with Francis Pym, not entirely to Margaret's liking. But generally there was a remarkable sense of unity among us – and that was surprising, given the rather diverse personalities involved. There were only five of us as politicians: Thatcher, Whitelaw, Pym, Cecil Parkinson and myself. We were later joined by Michael Havers, the Attorney-General.

There were strong differences of opinion on the handling of the negotiations, which were being conducted by Francis Pym; but generally, the atmosphere was good. There was none of the hectoring or personal antipathy which had characterised our debates on domestic economic policy. Fortunately, on Harold Macmillan's advice, the Chancellor of the Exchequer was excluded from the War Cabinet so that money was never mentioned and the institutionalised negativism of the Treasury was avoided.

The handling of the Falklands crisis was a personal triumph for Margaret Thatcher and for Admiral Lewin – and both of them deserve their high place in military history.

My great-grandfather's experience of war in Afghanistan and his insistence, as a general, was that it was the job of politicians to set out the objectives and the framework of activity, but that it was for the commanders in the field to decide the 'manner' by which they put those directions into effect:

> The Envoys and Ministers – will state to you from time to time the services which they may wish the troops to accomplish; when the 'manner' of performing and carrying them into full effect must depend entirely on your judgement ... (General Nott to Lieutenant Colonel Wymer, commanding a detachment – Kandahar, 1840)

My experience as a soldier was limited to my time with the Gurkhas in Malaya, but I had seen how things can go wrong, particularly if consensus overrides command. Someone must be in charge; war cannot be waged by a committee; nor for that matter must its conduct, in today's conditions, be unduly influenced by press and television.

Napoleon had said: 'Nothing is so important in war as an individual command ... Long discussions and councils of war ... will terminate in the adoption of the worst course which in war is the most timid, or, if you will, the most prudent. The only true wisdom in a General is determined courage!'

As we see in the last chapter of this book on the war in Bosnia, the European Council of Ministers is ill-equipped to be involved in war. Thankfully I had agreed and implemented, not many months before, a change to the status and authority of the Chief of the Defence Staff. I had placed Admiral Lewin in charge *de jure* and his outstanding personality guaranteed that he was also boss *de facto* within the MoD. Lewin scrupulously consulted daily with his principal colleagues on the Chiefs of Staff Committee but ultimately his decision was paramount before he presented it to the War Cabinet. Each day he and I had a private meeting to ensure that we were in accord in presenting the military options to the War Cabinet. Terry Lewin himself established the shortest chain of command directly from the War Cabinet through him to Admiral John

Fieldhouse, the Commander in Chief, down to Major-General Jeremy Moore on the battlefield and Rear-Admiral Sandy Woodward in the Fleet.

I will also explain in a later chapter how the shambles of Suez had influenced me. It was not just the interminable time that it took for the British forces to reach the Canal Zone, but the deception which the senior politicians practised in Whitehall in order to ensure secrecy about their intentions. I know that Whitelaw, Lewin and I, in the early stages, thought 'Suez, Suez, Suez' in many of our waking hours. Not least, we needed the support of the Americans.

If you go to war you have to trust the system – the relevant parts of the bureaucracy must be kept informed. This was one of the principal failures of Suez. It means widening the circle of information and consultation far beyond what is wise; but in an emergency the key people must be made to feel part of a team, for exclusion breeds resentment. In the early days several of my parliamentary colleagues were a real threat to national morale and good order, not least because of their incestuous relationship with the parliamentary press, but with difficulty (as I shall explain later) we managed to neutralise the worst speculation and gossip in the newspapers.

Margaret Thatcher had discussed with me personally how I wanted to present the military intelligence and advice to the War Cabinet. I had no hesitation in saying that I thought this function would be better deployed by the Chief of the Defence Staff rather than by me. Richard Hill's biography of Lewin, *Lewin of Greenwich* puts the matter accurately:

> John Nott had early decided, and cleared with the Prime Minister, that the military voice in OD (SA) [the War Cabinet] should be that of the CDS and not the Defence Secretary. He himself might sometimes take on the role of devil's advocate if he thought political sentiment was getting too hawkish, but generally he would keep a low profile.

General Bramall, who was Chief of the General Staff/head of the Army, describes it rather differently in his book *The Chiefs*, but he puts the position of the Defence Secretary in time of war with clarity:

> John Nott played a well-judged and significant part. In war, the position of a Secretary of State for Defence, who is not also Prime Minister, can be anomalous. There has to be a direct relationship between the Prime Minister and the Chiefs. Nott cast himself as something of a devil's advocate in his discussions with the Chiefs within the Ministry of Defence, ensuring that political requirements and military planning were co-ordinated, and that realism always prevailed.

I had an uncomfortable time – not as uncomfortable or as dangerous as the sailors, soldiers and airmen that we sent to war – but difficult nonetheless. I was the spokesman for our forces in the House of Commons and had to explain and answer for events over which I had very limited control. I had to agree statements that were, by necessity, based on the shortest and flimsiest information from the Fleet whilst at the same time the world media, led by the BBC, was pumping out contrary Argentinian propaganda. I had to argue against the Foreign Office, which frequently wished to postpone military activity when it conflicted with diplomatic negotiations. I had a particularly difficult time with some colleagues – alternately doubting and frenetic – in the House of Commons. Sometimes I had to disagree with a bevy of admirals on how and when we would issue statements about casualties and losses to the Fleet.

Others had equal problems, and even today, nearly twenty years-five after the event, I have nothing but praise and admiration for everyone in the MoD and in Northwood, the command headquarters. No one, of course, deserves greater praise and admiration than the Chief of the Defence Staff himself. Terry Lewin, with whom I had a very close and good working relationship throughout, was an excellent man. I have read his account of the Falklands and I am sad that he is no longer with us to read mine.

When I stepped down as Defence Secretary at the start of 1983 I wrote an account of some of the key events of those times. I did not keep a diary – I was too busy – but my record of events is reasonably contemporaneous. I cannot guarantee the accuracy (including the chronological accuracy) of every memory, and of course my opinions will be disputed, but it is not my intention to fight the war yet again. Many others have done that before me. This is primarily a book of recollections, as well as a work of history. The most accurate and full historical record of the Falklands is, in my view, contained in the two chapters of Margaret Thatcher's memoirs (*The Downing Street Years*, 1993), an excellent section, which I am sure she wrote herself.

***

Throughout March 1982, the month preceding the Argentine invasion on 2 April, I had been preoccupied with the typical round of events that fill the days of a Defence Secretary. There was a state visit by the Sultan of Oman – important for Defence as we were trying to establish ourselves as a major supplier of equipment in the Gulf. There was a one-week NATO war game, in which I had to participate. I was trying to make a start on the reorganisation and privatisation of the Royal Ordnance factories, then one of the largest businesses in the country. I was trying to agree with the Army the number of armoured personnel carriers – costing nearly £1 million apiece – that we intended to buy. British industry, in the form of Sir Robert Hunt and Sir Austin Pearce of British Aerospace, were at me, rightly, to get British offset work for Trident, following my statement to Parliament on 11 March of our intention to purchase the American nuclear system. It was a busy time, but not unusually so.

On 19 March I attended an Anglo-German summit at Chequers, and it was on that same day that I was shown the Defence contingency plans to meet any emergency in the Falkland Islands. I took this paper with me down to Cornwall where I had constituency engagements for the weekend of the 20th and 21st. It was on 20 March that we heard of the Davidoff landing on South Georgia and the hoisting of the Argentine flag, together with a message from the Governor (Rex Hunt) requesting that we despatch *Endurance* to South Georgia.

I read the contingency plans over the weekend and they seemed to me to be very negative. I said that I couldn't clear the paper without a meeting with the Naval Staff, which occurred on the Monday morning just before my departure that day to the United States. After a discussion, in particular about the deployment of our submarines, I agreed the paper. As I departed, news came through that the Argentine flag had been taken down and that a party of only twelve Argentinians had been left behind. So when I arrived in Colorado Springs for the bi-annual meeting of NATO's Nuclear Planning Group, the Falkland Islands were not at the forefront of my concerns. It seems odd to say so after the event, but even up to ten days before the Argentine invasion I was preoccupied with the problems of Trident.

The added firepower, or, to be precise, the greater number of warheads on Trident II, was causing considerable difficulty with our European allies. It had been discussed at the Anglo-German summit the previous week. The Germans, whilst favouring the British nuclear deterrent in principle, were nevertheless carping at its impact on the nuclear arms reduction programme. They took the view that our choice of system was excessive. I had to explain to all our European allies in NATO, without disclosing the full extent of our knowledge of Soviet developments, why we needed more sophisticated accuracy, penetration and decoy capabilities in order to maintain the credibility of our deterrent in the eyes of the Soviets. Although NATO intelligence briefings to our allies were frequent and wide ranging, only we, the British, shared the full intelligence picture with the United States.

The main parliamentary debate on Trident was due to take place on the following Monday, 29 March – four days, as it happened, before the invasion – and I had to avoid any rash press comments by our European allies that might strengthen the opposition to it, which was already very strong in the Labour and Liberal parties. The Germans in particular, with their Social Democratic coalition, were a constant problem to me at this time – and they remained so throughout the Falklands conflict.

I succeeded, however, in getting not only Trident on the agenda, but a statement agreed by all the Social Democratic coalition countries of NATO that Trident was necessary for the defence of Europe. To get the Germans, Danes, Dutch and Belgians with their coalition governments to be unanimous about anything positive was something of a triumph. I also managed to agree a valuable degree of offset work for British industry on both the American and British Trident systems, with the ever-helpful and friendly Caspar Weinberger, the US Defense Secretary.

There were many defence journalists in Colorado Springs. The BBC had a team of around fifty people, though ITN did a rather better job with six. I was asked about the situation in South Georgia but the questioning was relaxed. I was in touch with Jerry Wiggin, the Parliamentary Under-Secretary, back in London about the deployment of RFA *Fort Austin* to replenish HMS *Endurance* and the proposed doubling of the Royal Marine contingent on the Falklands. Even so, there was little sense of the impending crisis.

I returned from Colorado Springs direct to Cornwall, the RAF VC10 dropping me off at RAF St. Mawgan, near Newquay, on the Friday morning. After a short snooze I attended my constituency surgeries in Penzance, saw a pile of correspondence and attended the St. Ives Conservative Association annual dinner in the evening.

It was not until Saturday morning, 27 March, that I opened my red boxes for the weekend work; as soon as I did so I could see that the South Georgia situation was worse than I had expected. It had been discussed at the Cabinet meeting on Thursday in my absence. I had not been sent the intelligence reports, which arrived later on Saturday. These indicated that Argentine warships had been despatched to intercept *Endurance* on her passage to South Georgia. But even without them there was sufficient information to give grounds for concern. On Sunday I telephoned the Navy Duty Officer at the MoD and asked to see the First Sea Lord first thing on Monday morning.

I met Henry Leach and the Naval Staff as soon as I arrived in London. I wanted them to put some frigates on standby and to discuss again the deployment of a nuclear submarine. A number of our nuclear submarines were operationally deployed in the far north and others were not suitably equipped for a passage to the Falklands. However, he went away and returned later in the morning to say that *Spartan* might be available, but that it would take two or three days to equip her with the necessary weapons, provision her for a very long mission and fit her out with the right torpedoes.

Quite by coincidence the Prime Minister's Private Secretary, Clive Whitmore, had telephoned mine, David Omand, to say that Margaret Thatcher and Peter Carrington had come to the same conclusion on a journey that they were making to Brussels – and their concern gave added urgency to the despatch. We also agreed that whatever the detriment to other operational activities, a second submarine should be put on standby. Equally important, we agreed that RFA *Fort Austin* should not only be provisioned for *Endurance* but she should carry the maximum amount of stores in case we decided to send frigates subsequently. I sent a telegram to Brussels to tell the Prime Minister what was happening. In the afternoon we had the Trident debate in Parliament, which we won by 297 votes to 147.

After the debate, I returned to Admiralty House, where I was living. I did not sleep well. Next morning, Tuesday the 30th, I returned to the office and asked the Naval Staff to prepare the second submarine. I then asked to see the acting Chief of the Defence Staff, Air Chief Marshall Beetham, because I wanted to be sure that we could not land reinforcements of the Parachute Regiment with Hercules aircraft. He confirmed that as we could not risk a military aircraft being diverted to a South American country in the event of problems, this could not work. Even with refuelling the Hercules it would have been at the limit of its range – and therefore only able to carry a very small team. It had to be ruled out as an option.

In the meantime I was not consulted or involved in the diplomatic negotiations over the Argentine landings, which were being conducted by the Foreign Office. If I had been asked I would have agreed that any overt military reaction by us at this stage would have been very foolish, as it would have precipitated the very action by the Argentines which we were trying to avoid. 'We believe it would not have been appropriate to prepare a large task force ... before there was clear evidence of an invasion' was how the Franks Committee later put it. With the benefit of hindsight, I should, of course, when I saw the Chief of the Naval Staff the week before my departure to the United States and we discussed the situation in South Atlantic, have pressed the question of an early submarine deployment. I knew, however, that at that particular juncture no suitably equipped submarines were available. In any event, such a submarine could hardly have reached the South Atlantic in time, as it took around fourteen days to get there.

But the more interesting 'what if?' question is this. What would we have done if a nuclear submarine had been on station and we had disclosed its presence? Would it have deterred an Argentine invasion? Knowing the subsequent problems that we had with the rules of engagement, I find it a little hard to believe that, at that moment, we would have given it orders to sink approaching Argentine merchant ships in the area. Moreover, even if we had done so, it could hardly have prevented the landing of sufficient forces to overpower our Royal Marine contingent on the islands.

In the debate on the Franks Report on 25 January 1983, David Owen claimed that deployment of a nuclear submarine in 1982 would have averted the crisis. Later he said that for this reason 'the Falklands was an avoidable war'. It led to a public disagreement with Lord Lewin who had, by that time, retired. All war, thankfully, is avoidable; but the Falklands War was never avoidable by the earlier deployment of a nuclear submarine.

The Franks Committee made an exhaustive independent study of the internal papers and the circumstances which preceded the invasion on Friday 2 April, so I will not repeat them here. Its conclusion vindicated the government. Nevertheless, criticism persisted that the invasion had been encouraged by my announcement in June 1981 that HMS *Endurance* was to be withdrawn from service.

The cost of running *Endurance* was about £3 million a year – not an intolerable amount of money, but that was not the issue. I had taken a decision, which had been endorsed by the Cabinet, to cease mid-life modernisation of surface ships, using the savings to bring forward more building of the new Type 23 frigates. I was closing Chatham, Gibraltar and part of Portsmouth dockyards. HMS *Endurance* had been listed for disposal ever since the Labour Defence Review in 1974. She had been reprieved repeatedly; but she was getting very old, had no defence capability of any real consequence, as events subsequently showed, and she was overdue for a refit costing up to £30 million – and this at a time when I was stopping this very practice. We were, moreover, desperately stretched for funds.

More important, the Royal Navy had themselves listed *Endurance* near the top of their list for disposal at the outset of my Defence Review. In pure defence terms they were right, as, although she was a symbol of our continuing interest in the Antarctic dependencies and the Falklands, she had little deterrent value whatsoever. Having cut the Royal Navy's frigate force from sixty-four to fifty, with all the controversy that this had caused, I did not feel justified in taking on the Naval Staff once again over an ageing and expensive ship, albeit one that had symbolic importance in the South Atlantic. In my final minute to Lord Carrington, dated 3 February 1982 , I had observed, 'I think there would be considerable depth of feeling in the Royal Navy if further inroads had to be made on the Naval Programme to make room for *Endurance* which, quite frankly, is a low priority in defense terms.'

Again with the wisdom of hindsight I regret that I so stubbornly refused Carrington's pleas for a reprieve, but at the time I had no suspicion of any kind of a threat to the Falkland Islands. I had agreed that we should jointly approach the Treasury to see if she could be retained on a non-defence vote or out of the contingency fund; but the Treasury would never have found the money. Nor was *Endurance* the only 'symbol' of Britain's rather relaxed approach to the South Atlantic. The Labour government had showed no great resolve when the Argentines landed on Southern Thule in 1976 ; the Treasury had rejected Lord Shackleton's recommendation made that year to strengthen defences in the islands, by lengthening the runway; and an earlier government had refused to extend, without conditions, British citizenship to the inhabitants of the Falkland Islands.

Possibly the weakening of our stance went as far back as the Defence Review in 1966, when decisions were taken to withdraw the Commander in Chief South Atlantic and the frigate on station in the area, and in 1974 to terminate the Simonstown agreements and our naval base in South Africa. If I can be accused of some guilt for the announcement of the withdrawal of *Endurance*, I share it with a very large number of my ministerial predecessors of both major political parties right from 1966.

In any event, having agreed to the despatch of two submarines to the South Atlantic – and having convinced myself that it was impossible to reinforce the islands in short time – I decided to carry on with my programme.

On Tuesday I was due to leave London early in the morning to visit Marconi at Neston on Merseyside. I had postponed this trip on several occasions, but it was important as Marconi was responsible for building the Stingray torpedo and was about to gain the contract for the heavyweight torpedo, both contracts running into billions of pounds. I also wanted to do a Territorial Army visit following my reserve forces statement in Parliament, so I stayed the night with Lord Derby, the President of the Territorial Army Association.

That took me to the fateful Wednesday the 31st, when the crisis finally broke. However, as I was up in the north anyhow I had arranged to visit British Aerospace at Wharton. The industry was running out of work. Unless I took a decision to start work on the so-called advanced combat aircraft, which became the European Fighter, the whole of Wharton was going to disintegrate. I met the management and the unions, but I was not ready to make a decision.

I then flew back to Northolt in an HS125 and went straight to the House of Commons to vote. I had to see General Allen, the head of the United States Air Force, with Sir Michael Beetham; but my thoughts were on the Falklands, and I called a meeting in my room in the House of Commons at around 6.00 p.m. to be updated on the situation.

In the meantime there had been a meeting of the Defence Operations Executive, a creature of the Chiefs of Staff Committee; and it is clear in retrospect that, following the decision to deploy submarines to the South Atlantic and despatch RFA *Fort Austin* from Gibraltar, the Royal Navy began, on their own initiative, to run with the ball. Initially there had been some resistance to a diversion of effort and thought away from an important NATO exercise to meet a rather minor political incident in the South Atlantic, but the mood changed on the Monday and Tuesday. Although I had suggested it at the beginning of the week, I was unaware that Admiral Fieldhouse (who was to become the Commander in Chief of the Falklands Task Force, based at Northwood) had considered with the Naval Staff the option of despatching a contingency surface force should the problem escalate. Fortunately, a large part of the surface fleet was on the NATO exercise called Spring Train, off Gibraltar, so that a significant part of our naval force was already at sea. It may explain the confidence which Henry Leach displayed at the meeting with the Prime Minister late on Wednesday evening.

Unfortunately, although it was possibly too late to be relevant, Richard Luce, the Foreign Office minister, had made a statement in the House on Tuesday about the situation in the South Atlantic and had been given rather a rough ride. Later, at a private Conservative Party meeting upstairs, the Falkland Islands lobby had attacked him for the lack of any action by the government. In reply he must have hinted that the government had taken some action. I am sure that he did not specify, but a number of Tory MPs rushed downstairs to speculate with the parliamentary press among others that the government had despatched a submarine. Next day this speculation was all over the press, and the despatch of *Endurance* to South Georgia to take off the Davidoff scrap dealers clearly provoked the Argentine junta. The presence of *Endurance* was already causing more trouble than it was worth. Possibly the junta had already taken a private decision to trigger the invasion, but Wednesday's British press about the despatch of a nuclear submarine, together with the riots in Buenos Aires the day before, put pressure on them to act.

At my request a briefing team from the intelligence staff, led by Roger Jackling from the Ministry of Defence, assembled in my room in the House of Commons. Although the Falklands problem was beginning to escalate, I had no conception as late as six o'clock that Wednesday evening that a major crisis was about to hit us. They then produced a series of intercepted signals and other intelligence which left little doubt that an invasion was planned for the morning of Friday 2 April. We knew four things: that an Argentine submarine had been deployed to the area around Port Stanley (we were subsequently to learn that its task was to reconnoitre the beaches); that the Argentine fleet, which had been on exercises, had broken up into smaller units and seemed to be reassembling for an invasion; that an army commander had been embarked separately on a merchant ship and seemed likely to be the commander of an amphibious force; and, finally, that the fleet had been ordered to destroy all its documents.

I said to my Private Secretary David Omand that we must see the Prime Minister immediately. He telephoned No. 10. I saw Ian Gow, Margaret Thatcher's Parliamentary Private Secretary, and slowly we assembled in her room. I believe that this informal meeting consisted of Clive Whitmore, the Prime Ministers' Private Secretary, and Peter Blaker, one of my ministers in the MoD, Humphrey Atkins and Richard Luce, the two Foreign Office ministers, and Ian Gow. Margaret Thatcher herself suggested that Sir Antony Acland, the new Permanent Secretary at the Foreign Office, should join us, and I asked for Sir Frank Cooper, my Permanent Secretary, to come over from Defence. Our initial conversation was somewhat unstructured, but mainly concerned itself with how we could react diplomatically. A message was prepared for Margaret Thatcher to send to President Reagan asking whether he was aware of the signals intelligence that we had just received. David Omand was sent to ensure that our intelligence material had equally been received by our US counterparts. At this early stage it had not. A message was prepared to send to our Ambassador in the United States, Sir Nicholas Henderson, and to the Governor of the Falkland Islands.

At this juncture a secretary took me aside and said that Henry Leach, the Chief of the Naval Staff, was outside the Prime Minister's room and had asked to see me. After I had suggested to Margaret Thatcher that he should join us, Henry did so in full naval uniform. The sight of a man in uniform always pleases the ladies and Margaret, very much an impressionable lady, was always impressed by men in uniform.

She asked for Henry's views. With great assurance he said that it was possible to prepare a large Task Force. This would include *Hermes* and *Invincible*, together with the greater part of our destroyer and frigate forces, which were exercising off Gibraltar. He declared that the Task Force could be ready to sail early the following week, so long as he had authority to prepare it, with instructions to sail to follow later. This assertion greatly boosted the confidence of Margaret Thatcher; it was met by some scepticism by the rest of us.

Eventually the meeting broke up late at night and I was left alone with Margaret. I thought Henry had performed very well – and I have great praise for his supreme self-confidence and assertiveness. He had appeared, quite by chance, at a critical moment. Henry was a sailor in the best Nelsonian tradition: 'Sail at the enemy!' and do not hesitate about the consequences.

However, unlike his immediate superior Admiral Lewin, who was away in New Zealand, Henry was not exactly 'cerebral man'. Such an epithet might have been applied to Edwin 'Dwin' Bramall, the Chief of the General Staff, and perhaps, but rather less so, to Sir Michael Beetham, the acting Chief of the Defence Staff. I was pleased with Henry's performance, but I was not going to take his assurances just like that. The latest Defence briefing, such as it was, had indicated considerable uncertainty about our ability to recapture the Falkland Islands – and on Wednesday night I had my own doubts, not least about the logistics of fighting a war 8000 miles away without air cover from land-based aircraft. I had confidence in what I had seen of the Royal Navy's Harriers, but no one had briefed me on the capabilities of the Argentine Air Force.

The second chapter of this book is about the extraordinary logistics operation which saw the Indian Army, 50,000 strong with 30,000 camels, cross the plains of India and move into the mountains of Afghanistan, where it suffered one of the greatest disasters in British military history. I have also explained at some length the impact which the disaster of Suez had upon me whilst I was at Cambridge.

If I had had confidence in Henry Leach's judgement no doubt my hesitation might have been partially dispelled. But I did not have such confidence – there had been a full year of misunderstanding between us. So I expressed my qualms to Margaret Thatcher about the viability of such an operation. Reasonably enough, she has often reminded me of them. In particular, I recall the following exchange between us. She said, 'I suppose you realise, John, that this is going to be the worst week of our lives.' I responded, 'Well, that may be so, but I imagine that each successive week will be worse than the last.' It was not a helpful exchange at that particular juncture. Nevertheless, we gave Henry Leach authority to make preparations for a Task Force.

The following morning, Thursday the 1st, I went to the MoD at 8.15 for a meeting with a group of senior civilian and military personnel under the chairmanship of Michael Beetham. We discussed the whole situation, ahead of a Cabinet meeting which was due at 9.30. I was told that the Defence Operations Executive would meet later to advance planning on the military options and I suggested that Beetham and Leach should make themselves available for a meeting of the Overseas and Defence Policy Committee of the Cabinet (OD) after the main Cabinet was concluded.

At Cabinet there was a brief discussion of the Falklands. The Prime Minister described the situation as being very grave; but neither at that meeting nor at the subsequent meeting of OD, which concerned itself with our diplomatic proposals, did we reveal the intelligence information that had been received the night before. As was customary, signals intelligence of this kind (only revealed some nine months later in the Franks Report) was treated on a 'need to know' basis.

After the OD meeting concluded, I believe that we met the Prime Minister as a small group consisting of Beetham, Leach and Whitelaw, who had not been present the previous night. I have no record of the meeting, but I believe it took place.

When I returned to the MoD I was given a full Minute from Beetham, the acting Chief of Defence Staff, which had been prepared whilst I had been at Cabinet, laying out all the military options including the deployment of a full Task Force. Set out clearly, it indicated that a Task Force was a viable proposal and had a good chance of success, although the risks were to be studied further in the next few days. This gave me much greater confidence than I had felt the night before, as I knew that all three services had been involved in putting this advice together. There was a further proposal – to deploy communications equipment and some men to Ascension Island, in order to join up with RFA *Fort Austin* which was already on its way to the South Atlantic. Later in the day I was to have a further meeting to discuss the deployment of a team of SAS and SBS to join up with *Fort Austin* and the second nuclear submarine respectively. By the early evening I was much more fully briefed than on Wednesday night and my confidence was increasing. I also asked whether the Royal Marines on the Falklands could destroy the airfield, but I was told that they had already been dispersed around the island to await a possible invasion. I did, however, feel extremely foolish when I was told that there were, anyhow, insufficient explosives on the island to do the job.

At two o'clock I had to be on the steps of the MoD to welcome Mr. Hernou, the French Defence Secretary. In the circumstances, I was hoping that I could make it a reasonably short meeting. No such hope.

Mr. Hernou looked like a rather tubby French provincial mayor, which no doubt he may have been. I do not recall whether he spoke any English. I think not, and my French is inadequate, so everything had to be translated. Mr. Hernou, a good socialist, was nonetheless a great enthusiast for the French nuclear deterrent. He was benevolent and exceptionally voluble. He regarded this meeting as of great importance because he was very anxious to get closer to us on nuclear issues. I had been briefed that there were several areas where we could cooperate together; but there was very great reluctance to allow the French to get anywhere near our technology, which of course was of American origin. I wanted to discuss how we could do more together on the conventional side, but Mr. Hernou was not to be diverted and he talked with immense enthusiasm, almost obsessively so, for over an hour in French about what he was doing to improve France's nuclear capability. The more he talked the more uncertain I became about the effectiveness of the French nuclear deterrent – and the more relieved I was about our Trident decision. Unfortunately whilst Mr. Hernou's monologue continued, I could not help drifting off into thoughts about the Falklands. My guest was a charming man and he, Mitterrand and the French government were, as I shall explain, very helpful to us during the coming weeks; but I was relieved when I managed to say goodbye to him at five o'clock in the afternoon.

Margaret Thatcher, meanwhile, had called another meeting at No. 10 in the evening, but she did not want it to start until Peter Carrington, the then Foreign Secretary who resigned a few days later, had arrived back from a trip to Israel. Accordingly, it was ten o'clock by the time she, Whitelaw, Carrington and myself got together.

In many ways this was a smaller and more useful meeting than the night before. Peter Carrington looked exhausted – he had had a difficult time with the Israelis in Jerusalem. After a lengthy discussion, it was decided that he should speak to Alexander Haig, the US Secretary of State. I think it was on this occasion, rather late at night, that Haig told him that following a talk between Thatcher and Reagan earlier in the day the Argentine President, General Galtieri, had refused to take Reagan's call. Further intelligence came in late the same evening that sections of the Argentine forces had been ordered to rendezvous at 0600 hours the next day at a particular point off the Falkland Islands. Peter Carrington, new to the crisis, did not hesitate to say that we had no option but to put the Fleet to sea.

At this point we decided to ask Henry Leach to join us. Unfortunately he had been asked to be on standby and had been sitting for an hour or more in an anteroom at No. 10. He confirmed that the ships on exercise could be reprovisioned in Gibraltar and told to sail back to the UK, but turned south thereafter; such a deployment would not remain covert, because anyhow we needed *Hermes* and *Invincible* and other ships to sail from the UK. He said that if he had the authority to put the Fleet on alert, much of it could sail within three or four days. We were impressed. The speed with which the Task Force put to sea was critical and no one deserves greater credit than Henry Leach himself. It was a triumph of determination and executive will. Later in the campaign, he and the Naval Staff in Whitehall tended to pass several of their personnel and much of their authority to Admiral Fieldhouse in Northwood as the operational command; but, of course, they continued to play an important role in Whitehall. At about one o'clock in the morning Henry Leach left No. 10 in order to place the Fleet on alert; and we agreed, subject only to a Cabinet meeting the next day, to set it for sail at the beginning of the following week.

In his memoirs, John Major asserts that 'if the Cabinet had not sent the task force Margaret Thatcher would not have survived as Prime Minister'. He adds that 'she took a great risk, requiring huge nerve, but the alternative was certain catastrophe'. Actually, I do not agree with that judgement. I would not have survived, but I think Margaret Thatcher would have done so. But that is another 'What if' of history. Who can know?

***

Friday 2 April was a day of some confusion. The Cabinet met in the morning but there was not a great deal to report; it parted in some gloom. A statement was organised for 11.30 a.m., but we had no communication from the Falklands. There was a high-frequency system, interrupted by very bad weather; a Cable & Wireless telex, which had presumably been taken over; and a satellite link with *Endurance* which was on its way to South Georgia. Humphrey Atkins was not able to confirm that an invasion had taken place, but he did say that the Governor had been in touch with the Foreign Office some hours earlier, which was incorrect. Humphrey felt bad that he had given inaccurate information to the House – but it was not his fault. I never saw why he needed to resign with Peter Carrington. It was only around lunchtime that we heard via a British Antarctic Survey vessel that the Falklands had indeed been occupied.

We met in the Prime Minister's room, after Humphrey Atkins' statement, to decide what to do. Suggestions were made for a statement in the afternoon, because by this time the BBC and other stations were relaying from Buenos Aires that the Falklands had been taken. However, we had no corroborative information at all. We were all against another statement in the afternoon, but really bought off the protests by proposing an emergency debate on Saturday morning. It proved to be an unwise move. It would have been better to have waited until the following Monday.

One of the most constant aggravations was the inability of Parliament and the press to understand the nature of our communication problems. Huge amounts of technical effort were put into maintaining signals contact, even in a nuclear conflict; but whatever provision for redundancy you construct into your communications, they can go wrong. There was always the feeling among wide sections of the press that people engaged in conflict had nothing better to do than send messages back home for them.

Friday represented also the first spat between the Ministry of Defence and No. 10 about how many journalists should accompany the Fleet. Understandably the Navy fought against taking anyone, on the good grounds that the limited satellite facilities were needed for operations. I insisted that they should embark a number of journalists (six, as I recall) initially, each to cover a range of media outlets. The editors made their protests to Bernard Ingham, the No. 10 Press Secretary, who sounded off loudly at such a paltry number. Frank Cooper, who was in charge of the negotiations with No. 10, and I increased the number to up to fourteen, to be chosen by the Newspaper Publishers' Association. The NPA then nominated a team which excluded *The Times*, the *Sun*, the *Guardian* and other newspapers, so we had to add them. I had a disagreement with the Navy, but called rank and insisted that the key television channels and newspapers were included.

Bernard Ingham was a constant nuisance throughout the Falklands campaign – jumping up and down and causing no end of difficulty, criticising the Ministry of Defence on trivial issues. But Frank and I were determined to keep the press under the tightest Ministry of Defence control and, as far as possible, away from No. 10, with its obsession for background briefing and for spin. Margaret Thatcher in her memoirs has the temerity to claim that 'too much talk was giving the Argentinians warning of what we intended, though the fault did not always lie with the media themselves but also with the media management of the MoD'. In fact, we had a constant problem trying to prevent Ingham in No. 10 from adding his largely uninformed opinion to the No. 10 spin.

Even just one photograph took up an inordinate amount of satellite time, to the detriment of operations, and explains why I often had to make statements to the House of Commons based on a single terse signal. It was good military practice, but it made the job of keeping everyone on side really very difficult. The fault lay, of course, in the ships' limited communications systems, as they had never been prepared for a press contingent embarked at sea. Of course it was necessary all along to embark the press, but it did cause severe problems in handling the media at home.

Frank Cooper chose a Ministry of Defence official, Ian Macdonald, to be press spokesman. He spoke slowly and methodically, uttering each word as if he was savouring a delicious plum. He did it very well and no one ever questioned his integrity. It was painfully obvious to the whole world that Ian could only speak the truth. It was a huge contrast to all the lies coming out of Buenos Aires, but sometimes the Argentine statements were more lurid and therefore to the liking of the members of the British press. However, generally the press was very helpful. Only the BBC was quite appalling – seeing its role as requiring dispassionate even-handedness between their own country and its enemies.

About halfway through the campaign there was a well of growing criticism of Ian Macdonald's style. The Americans, in particular, were astonished at this strange Englishman, and PR smoothies worldwide, including Ingham at No. 10, demanded a change to a more professional style. Frank Cooper, in one of his better moves, said that he thought the way around the problem was to send Ian up to Glasgow for a weekend with his mum. In his place we put on parade a number of polished young officers to do the job. Sure enough, as soon as Ian was gone there was a surge of demand for us to reinstate him. Ian Macdonald was borne back to the world's screens in triumph. There he remained to the end.

At 7.30 on Friday evening the Cabinet met again and gave its backing to the despatch of the Task Force. Only John Biffen expressed some doubts, but without in any way opposing the move outright. I thought it was courageous of him to speak up in this way – no one else did so. Considerable discussion took place as to how we could get a resolution condemning the invasion in the United Nations, condemnation from our so-called friends in the European Community, and a freezing of Argentine assets.

Sir Anthony Parsons, our man at the UN, with Sir Antony Acland and Sir Michael Palliser, the present and former Permanent Secretaries of the Foreign Office, together with the legal adviser Ian Sinclair, were at many of our meetings. Parsons played a key role by obtaining Resolution 502 through the Security Council, demanding the withdrawal of Argentina. This was an absolutely crucial success and had required lobbying around the world to gather sufficient support; somehow Parsons managed to get an abstention from the Russians. Without Resolution 502, which gave us the moral authority for our actions, I doubt if we could have held international opinion over the next few months. We would have been in deep trouble, as well as making our task in Parliament infinitely more difficult.

Here I must interpose a comment about the Foreign Office. Throughout this book I have been critical of its attitudes and approach. Yet face to face in critical meetings about how to handle the long drawn-out negotiations with Haig, the Peruvians and the United Nations, Parsons, Acland, Palliser and, in particular, Sinclair, their admirable legal adviser, were helpful, pragmatic and constructive. Why is it that one can respect and enjoy the company of so many outstanding individuals when one holds their institution in such deep contempt?

Margaret Thatcher, recalling the events of Friday the 2nd, poses this dilemma very well:

> I received advice from the Foreign Office which summed up the flexibility
> of principle characteristic of that department. I was presented with
> the dangers of a backlash against the British expatriates in Argentina,

problems about getting support in the UN Security Council, the lack of reliance we could place on the European Community or the United States, the risk of the Soviets becoming involved, the disadvantage of being looked at as a colonial power.

It might have been the duty of the Foreign Office to warn of all these obstacles, which were very clear to all of us, but it is the never-ending feebleness of the institution and its demeaning role as a spokesman for foreign interests that rankles so deeply with Tories like myself. All of this was to break out in a ruthless attack by Tory MPs on Peter Carrington the next day.

I retired to Admiralty House on Friday night, after further meetings in the Ministry of Defence, bearing a draft of my speech for the emergency debate on Saturday. I glanced at it and, not unusually, realised that I had to bin it and write it myself. However, I was too tired to do so; I went to bed and got up at four o'clock to prepare it for myself.

The Saturday emergency debate (the first since the Suez crisis) has gone down as a famous event in parliamentary history. The House was full, worried and concerned; but there was an underlying ugly mood – a developing desire to find scapegoats for the national humiliation that had occurred. The Prime Minister opened the debate, wisely in a low key, and expressed the government's anger at what had happened. She announced the preparation of the Task Force and this somewhat mollified, albeit temporarily, the more hawkish members of the Tory Party.

Michael Foot, the Leader of the Opposition, could be relied upon in any crisis to make an emotive and impressive speech. With the passing of Iain Macleod, he was the last outstanding orator in the House of Commons. His principal attack was against the fascists in Argentina, but quite correctly he posed the question of how such an event could have been allowed to happen. How could there have been such a failure of British intelligence and diplomacy? So far, so good.

There were then speeches from Enoch Powell, who attacked the Royal Marines for surrendering, and Julian Amery, who fiercely attacked the Foreign Office. The most unpleasant contributions came from a predictable direction, namely from the Tory benches. Edward du Cann and Patrick Cormack both made contemptible speeches, dressing up naked self-advertisement in patriotic clothes.

As I was about to wind up the debate, the Whips asked for more time for backbench speeches. As a result, my prepared and reasonably balanced observations, intended to last half an hour, had to be compressed into a shortened timescale of fifteen minutes – always a problem, because the House feels that its concerns have not been answered. Rule No. I: be very wary of any advice coming from the Whips. However, the speech went quite well initially. I said that if, after the South Georgia incident two weeks before, we had sent a Task Force of sufficient size to the South Atlantic, it would not have arrived in time to perform its task. I added that 'certainly in deterrence terms, had it been successful [i.e. in strengthening our negotiating hand], that large task force would have had to remain indefinitely in Falkland waters, in detriment to its other tasks'. However, 'as my right hon. Friend the Prime Minister said in opening this debate, we were throughout seeking a peaceful solution through the United Nations and by other means'.

At this point things began to go wrong, because I tried to answer the criticisms of Jim Callaghan and David Owen. I was correct in what I said but it did not help:

The other option would have been the deployment of a small force insufficient to resist the Argentine Navy, as was done [by the Labour government] in 1977. May I comment first on this particular proposal, because there seems to be a difference of view between the then Prime Minister [Callaghan] and the then Foreign Secretary [Owen] about the events in 1977. The right hon. Member for Cardiff South-

East [Callaghan] said that this force in 1977 became known and that a diplomatic solution followed, whereas the right hon. Member for Plymouth, Devonport [Owen] said yesterday on the radio that it was done in total secrecy – (Interruption) – but he added that it gave him confidence in his negotiations, whatever that might mean – (Interruption).

At this point, one interruption followed another and Michael Foot joined in, noisily supported from the Labour benches. The description given by Alan Clark in his diary well captures the gathering drama:

> Poor old Notters was a disaster ... The *coup de grâce* was delivered by David Owen, who had spoken earlier. He forced Nott to give way and he told him that if he could not appreciate the need to back negotiations with force he did not deserve to remain one minute as Secretary of State.

Politics is a performing art and a politician is only as good as his last performance. This was a good example of that abiding truth.

I only had a few minutes left before the debate was curtailed at two o'clock. I now made the most serious error of my debating career – I attacked the Labour Party. It was foolish in the circumstances. I said:

> The military problems are formidable, but they are certainly not insoluble because of the professionalism, the preparedness and the quality of our defences, which for our nation's size are unique in the free world. I do not believe the claim that the new Labour Party, with its well-known and well-advertised anti-defence bias and lack of commitment to defence spending, would have done any better ...

There was uproar and calls for my resignation. The debate ended with the House in a very ugly mood.

Again, I resort to Margaret Thatcher's memoirs:

I faced a crisis in the Government. John Nott, who was under great strain, had delivered an uncharacteristically poor performance in his winding-up speech. He had been very harshly treated in the debate. He was held responsible by many of our backbenchers for what had happened because of the Defence Review which he had pioneered. This was unfair. The budget for conventional naval forces (that is excluding the Trident programme) was £500 million higher – and also higher as a share of the Defence Budget – than when we took office … But there was no doubt that the Party's blood was up: nor was it just John Nott they were after.

It was understandable that I should be the scapegoat for the whole affair. The Foreign Secretary was in the House of Lords; I was the spokesman for the government. The anger of the House was bound to fall on my shoulders – and I was expecting it. I had seen the House of Commons turn into a mob before. Or in Alan Clark's apposite words, 'Like the pack that they are they always smell the blood of a wounded animal and turn on it.'

Immediately, with hugely long faces all around, with a general feeling that I had made a complete cock-up in the debate, we moved back into the Prime Minister's room behind the Speaker's chair. I am an excitable person by nature, though normally I get excitable about little and unimportant things. But in a major crisis of this kind, for reasons that I do not quite understand, I go extremely calm. When we arrived in the Prime Minister's room, I was indeed the calmest person there. Willie Whitelaw, not unusually, was in a frightful flap.

At that moment Michael Jopling, the Chief Whip, arrived and said that the party was in a state of chaos, that many people were saying that they wished to resign the whip, that the government had been humiliated; the lobbies, he added, were seething with press and discontented Conservative Members; and he declared that he could see no other choice but to call an immediate meeting of the party, which he suggested that

Carrington and I should address. Peter had had an easy ride in the House of Lords and I don't think he realised how bad it was. He shrugged his shoulders and said, 'Oh dear, well yes, we'd better go up and talk to the party.'

I quote from my near-contemporary record:

So he and I went upstairs to the Party meeting and Peter made a short speech which was met by an element of cat-calling, derision and jeers from the assembled Members. I suppose there must have been about 150 to 200 Tory Members there – it was a very full meeting. I then made an intervention which was received marginally better than Peter's, because I made it clear that we intended to sail the Fleet and, if necessary, we intended to use it. It was easier to play the hawk in a private meeting of the Party than it had been in the House of Commons, where I had to justify and explain the government's policy up to then. Whereas in the Party meeting upstairs I was able to sound the note of a forthcoming war, which, in a way, responded to the mood of the Party, Carrington was there for the first time in front of the Party and he was on the defensive. It was his policy on the Falklands which was under attack, and all the resentments of the Party now came to the surface about what had happened in Rhodesia and the election of Mugabe and a long, long history – going back over ten, fifteen years, going back to the Heath Government when Carrington as Minister of Defence, I remember it very well, had been under attack for his policy in Northern Ireland. Several of the more elderly backbenchers felt that Carrington was a consensus man, and the whole fury against the Foreign Office came out more against him than against me. Mind you, there were many Members there who were determined that I should go. I had, I would say, ten or so bitter enemies in the Tory Party as a result of my Defence Review and there were sufficient numbers of people in the Party who were gunning for me. Although the Defence Review was all finished and behind us, the memories of it were fairly recent. The Party meeting, which went on for two and a half hours, developed more into an attack on the Foreign Office than on me, and I emerged from it slightly less under total siege than I had emerged three hours earlier from the debate in the House.

Alan Clark's version is as follows:

> After the debate we all trailed up to Committee Room 10. Carrington and Nott were both present. Thirty-three Members asked questions and, with the exception of three heavy-weight duds (Patten, Kershaw and van Straubenzee), every single person was critical. I asked a long, sneering question about the failure of our intelligence. I made a point of addressing it to Peter Carrington whom, with my very long memory, I had not forgiven for snubbing me at a meeting on Afghanistan in December 1980 in the Grand Committee Room. As my irony developed, people in the Committee Room started sniggering, but poor Notters was still so rattled and blubbery that he leant across and answered it, while Carrington sat staring at me in haughty silence.

As Peter Carrington and I left the meeting on our way back downstairs to tell the Prime Minister how it had gone – we could not give her much encouragement – he said to me, 'You know, I really think I must go. I don't think that I can possibly stay. The Party regard it as being all my fault, there is no way that I can sustain my position and I shall tell the Prime Minister that I intend to go.' To which I replied, 'Peter, I think that you must stay. You can't leave at this particular moment. We've got to see the next few days through and it would be a catastrophe if you left now.'

It seemed to me then – and still does now – that it was the party meeting that did him in, not the newspapers that called for his resignation. The sadness was that Peter Carrington, being in the Lords, did not know the characters in that party meeting – whereas I could say to myself, 'A' is an idiot, 'B' always talks nonsense, 'C' is a pompous twit, you only need to be bothered about 'D' and 'E' who carry some respect among their colleagues. Peter possibly saw them all as having equal relevance.

Having reported back to Margaret Thatcher – and leaving Peter Carrington with her (I never saw him again as a ministerial colleague) – I escaped back to the Ministry of Defence. I was conscious that I had responsibility for a Task Force which was due to sail in two days' time. Whilst the political war had been raging in the House of Commons, the Chiefs of Staff had been planning for the real war in the South Atlantic. By this time the MoD had got itself into top gear and confidence was building everywhere.

One of the earliest problems lay in the status of Ascension. Although the island was British we had entered into an agreement with the State Department, placing the airfield totally under American control. The use of the airfield was an absolute precondition to our getting the full complement of provisions, equipment, ships and men to the South Atlantic. It was by no means certain at this stage that the State Department would not be obstructive. When the Fleet sailed on the Monday, it was in the knowledge that a host of additional equipment would have to be shipped by air to join the Task Force at Ascension. The island also, along with Dakar in Senegal on the west coast of Africa, became the essential air bridge for flying extra RAF Harriers to the Fleet. Dakar was important because refuelling there enabled the Hercules supply aircraft to carry heavier loads on their way to Ascension.

It was at this very early stage that the immensely close military relationship between the Ministry of Defence and the Pentagon proved its value. The Royal Navy and the US Navy were extremely close. The intelligence agencies of the two countries virtually worked as one, while the recent negotiations on Trident and co-operation in NATO meetings had brought the two ministerial teams together. Weinberger was splendid from the outset. Ignoring the jealousies and rivalries in Washington, he ordered his staff to give maximum and urgent support to the British.

We needed additional fuel supplies in Ascension, which the Americans supplied with their tankers. Certain valuable weapons systems, in particular the Sidewinder air-to-air missile, supplemented and upgraded the capability of the Harriers, and a host of other incremental stores were all forthcoming without cost ever being mentioned.

Looking back on it, this all seems rather academic and unremarkable; but anyone who has dealt with Washington will understand the incoherence of the United States' government system. The Washington agencies work independently of each other and often in contradiction, so you could never expect too much. The State Department at this time was dominated by the Latinos who saw President Reagan's Latin American policy going down the drain. Mrs. Kirkpatrick, the US Ambassador to the UN, dined with the Argentinians on the evening that they invaded British territory.

For all Margaret Thatcher's friendship with Ronald Reagan, he remained a West Coast American looking south to Latin America and west to the Pacific. Sometimes I wondered if Reagan knew where Europe was – although he was certainly conscious of the Russian 'Evil Empire'. It took weeks of determined diplomacy by Sir Nicholas Henderson, our Ambassador in Washington, before the White House was prepared to declare itself wholeheartedly on the side of the British. Moreover, it did so, I suspect, only because Congress and American public opinion had come down heavily on our side. By doing so, it destroyed the support of the South American dictators for Reagan's anti-Communist crusade in Central America. It would have been impossible in those crucial early days to muster support from the US Administration; where it was forthcoming, wholly independently of the State Department and the White House, was from Weinberger and the Pentagon.

Many influential Americans, furious at Britain's later unwillingness to support the US invasion of Grenada, have claimed that we could not have recovered the Falklands without American support. Certainly the use of Ascension – a British island – was essential. In Weinberger's memoirs, *Fighting for Peace*, he says: 'Some said later that the British could not have succeeded if we had not helped. This is not so – I believe the decisive factor was Mrs. Thatcher's firm and immediate decision to retake the islands, despite the impressive military and other advice [in the Pentagon] to the contrary.'

I too believe that we could have succeeded without US logistic and equipment back-up – though certainly the whole operation would have been infinitely more extended and hazardous. We would not have succeeded if the Americans had positively turned against us, as they had at Suez. But for those, like me, who oppose our political integration into Europe, do not imagine that the United States is in some way 'an alternative' to Europe. It is not.

On Sunday morning, the 4th, I attended my first meeting of the Chiefs of Staff Committee. Terry Lewin was still away in New Zealand and there was great hesitation about where I should sit. The Secretary of State did not attend these meetings normally; his forum was the Defence Council. I was offered, out of courtesy I imagine, Mountbatten's chair – Mountbatten being the first Chief of the Defence Staff. I insisted that Michael Beetham chair the meeting, so this awful high-backed chair – Mountbatten's chair – was shifted to his right and I was forced to sit in it. Two days after the invasion there was a host of decisions outstanding. We had, for instance, to decide whether to charter or requisition civilian ships. We chose the latter course, requiring an Order in Council, and action was put in hand to acquire the *Canberra*. We had to agree contingency plans, which in the event were not needed, to evacuate the thousands of British nationals living in Argentina.

We also had to establish procedures for considering the rules of engagement – the basis which set out the limits of action by the military.

Each day this question became one of the most difficult decisions for the War Cabinet. What authority were we to give the forces if civilian aircraft and merchant ships were used to spy on the Fleet? How was the Task Force commander to react to Russian vessels, submarines and fishing boats, equipped with listening and reconnaissance devices? What was to be done about South American scheduled aircraft overflying the Task Force and passing back information to the Argentine Navy? The rules of engagement, setting out the degree of response, defensive or aggressive, towards the Argentine Navy, were rather more straightforward; not least in the case of the aircraft carrier whose aircraft could easily be within striking distance of our ships. We had no hesitation in recognising the danger to the Fleet posed by the *Belgrano*.

The rules of engagement for our submarines posed rather different problems. As the submarines moved fast and submerged underwater, they only emerged infrequently to send and receive burst signals from satellite; so with two submarines fast approaching the Falklands, forethought was needed about what orders they should have when they encountered Argentine naval shipping or merchant vessels supplying the invasion force. It was this discussion which led to the recommendation for a maritime exclusion zone, which I announced in Parliament the following Wednesday.

One of the most vexing questions, extraordinary as it seems, was whether we could say that we were at war. Evidently not; we were strongly advised by the excellent Foreign Office lawyers not to declare war but to act entirely under Article 51 of the United Nations Charter, which gave the right to countries to act in their own self-defence. This legal distinction caused no end of puzzlement in the Ministry of Defence – and when asked the question in the Commons, I said, 'No, we are not at war', which caused some mirth.

On Admiral Lewin's return the Chiefs of Staff meetings settled down into a regular routine throughout the conflict. After the first meeting on the

Sunday, I expressed a wish that I should not attend the full meeting, which really agreed the military plans that later came forward for consideration by the War Cabinet. Terry Lewin saw me after each meeting to brief me on the outcome and then went on to a gathering of senior officials who, in turn, briefed their ministers in advance of the meetings of the War Cabinet.

On most days, however, I did join the meeting for the first few items on the agenda. Each day General Glover, the Deputy Chief of Defence Staff Intelligence, gave a briefing on the deployment and state of the Argentine forces; then we heard where the Soviet forces were operating and the extent to which they were gathering intelligence, either by means of satellite or from their ships in the area. We had several scares about covert Argentinian plans to attack Gibraltar dockyard with special forces. And in the early days, before our nuclear submarines arrived on station, we were informed of the situation of the Argentine Navy, which was all at sea between the Falkland Islands and South Georgia. After the *Belgrano* incident the Argentine Navy, which was not insubstantial, largely stayed in port – but up to then it posed a very major threat to our forces.

We had landed reconnaissance teams on the Falkland Islands long before the Task Force arrived – and some of the most effective, Spanish-speaking sections from the SAS, dug into holes in the ground near the Argentine trenches, reported back to their HQ in Hereford on a daily basis the state of morale of the Argentinian forces around Port Stanley. We learnt where the regular forces were positioned and where the poor Argentine conscripts were located. The conscripts were being brutalised by their officers, were short of food and clothing and generally suffered from very low morale. 'In war', said Napoleon, 'the moral is to the physical as three to one.' And so it proved. On occasions General Glover gave us a run-down of the Argentinian menu for the previous day and what the soldiers in the trenches were saying about their food – or lack of it!

There was then a briefing about the disposition of our forces, where the long, strung-out Task Force was located, and other information about the need for stores and weapons. The problem of what to do with *Endurance* kept on coming up. In the days preceding the invasion of South Georgia she had been ordered from one place to another, first in order to avoid provocation and then to escape the attentions of Argentine submarines. Once the conflict happened she had little relevance in a military sense; but she remained an important political symbol, and so the captain of *Endurance* was given orders to avoid all Argentinian shipping and hide himself in the ice south of South Georgia.

Another item on the agenda of the Chiefs of Staff was the press. I normally stayed for the discussion about how much we could release to the press and in what form. Frank Cooper, as Permanent Secretary, was in charge of the 'D' Notice system and discussed with the editors the way in which we might voluntarily control the flow of information from the Task Force. We knew that we were going to encounter severe communication problems; and censorship of press copy sent back from the Fleet. The communications overload was much more severe than we had anticipated, possibly because we embarked too many media representatives in the first place.

We received a report from the Americans, I think at the first meeting, about the likely reaction of other South American countries to the invasion. With the single exception of Chile, they declared their support for Argentina. If we had been able to use a South American airfield, even for a diversion in an emergency, it would have made the whole operation easier. The importance of Chile, with its long-standing rivalry and fear of Argentina, was therefore very great. We wanted to use their airfields for stationing our Nimrods, the maritime patrol aircraft, so that they could hunt down the Argentinian submarines, which were a real threat to the Fleet. They would also have been valuable to monitor the movement of the Task Force. For reasons of NATO priority, we had no satellite coverage at all of the South Atlantic and, even later in the campaign, we had considerable difficulty persuading the Americans to divert satellite coverage from NATO tasks to ours. I don't think we ever expected that the Chileans would allow us to station combat or support aircraft on their soil, though as they wanted to buy some maritime patrol aircraft from us, we tried to do a deal. We were never successful, but in several respects the Chilean link proved very valuable to us later.

***

I return to the account which I dictated not long after the Falklands War was concluded, picking up the story on the morning of Sunday, 4 April:

> I did not stay to the end of the Chiefs of Staff meeting because I had made arrangements to appear on *Weekend World* – one of the influential current affairs programmes at that time. After my disaster the previous day, Brian Walden had personally asked if I would be prepared to go on his programme and, after some heart-searching, I agreed to do so. It was, I think, a very valuable occasion for me and I am still very grateful to Brian Walden for giving me the opportunity. I do feel that, as we were friends, it was not just topical news; he also had some sympathy for the way in which I had been treated in the House and wanted to give me a chance to have my say. I went on the programme and took a very hawkish stance. I said we would not be sending the Fleet to sea unless we were prepared to use it. As soon as I had left the television studio I was deluged with a great volume of telephone calls from my Parliamentary colleagues, congratulating me on my performance and saying that it had greatly raised everybody's morale and confidence. Rather cynically I recall that at least two of the people who congratulated me were the very same people who'd been

rushing around like madmen the day before demanding my immediate resignation. That is the nature of politics. The Prime Minister also passed a personal message to me at lunchtime – saying that she had watched the programme, how well it had gone and how delighted she was that the thing was beginning to turn back. That *Weekend World* programme, which had a very large audience that Sunday morning, began to restore confidence in the Conservative Party, which had totally collapsed as a result of the invasion and the Saturday debate.

I then hurried from the studio to the City heliport and took a helicopter straight down to Portsmouth to visit the Fleet. Over the weekend, apart from the hectic efforts of the Royal Navy and all the dockyard workers, effectively the whole of the Army in southern England had been mobilised to move the war reserves to the Fleet. The Territorial Army, in particular, played a key role in transporting equipment and stores to Devonport and Portsmouth. Without the Territorial Army we would have been hard put to it to get the Fleet away on time. My visit was, in a way, very difficult but, at the same time, an emotional occasion. My visit was well-publicised and led the national news. I was met by the Port Admiral when I arrived off the helicopter – the same man who had handled my earlier visit to Portsmouth when we had been besieged by rioting dockyard workers who had heaved these enormous steel bolts at me and smashed the windows of the Headquarters building.

As I was about to go on board *Hermes*, I saw a group of the same dockyard workers standing on the dockside and I went up to speak to them. During the course of the next two hours I met several groups of dockyard workers and I had a word with each of them. I think it was one of the most poignant memories that I have of the whole Falklands affair, because these were the very same men whom I was putting out of work. Several of them had received their redundancy notices a few days before; but in spite of that they'd all rallied around over that weekend, working day and night, and had done a splendid job. I must have been a real nightmare to them, but they nevertheless spoke to me with courtesy – not with any enthusiasm, but there was no rudeness, there was no attempt to be abusive. They made their feelings very clear about the dockyard measures, but at the same time they behaved with great dignity and restraint.

I cannot read this record of events even today without a great sense of sadness - and the feeling of what a wonderful country we live in and the greatness, yes the greatness, of our fellow countrymen and women.

My account continues:

I went on board *Hermes* where there was an enormous amount of activity going on. It was tremendously impressive. The Harriers were flying in from Yeovilton and landing on the deck. I took the opportunity, which was a rather unique one for me, of meeting more of my naval constituents on *Hermes* than I had ever met in one place before in my sixteen years in Parliament, because a very large number of men came from RNAS Culdrose, which is in my constituency in West Cornwall; they had flown on to *Hermes* with their Sea King helicopters the day before.

I went around the ship and, to my intense astonishment I must admit, in spite of repeated questioning of the chief petty officers, those responsible for the radar, the weapons systems, the stores, I could not get a single chief petty officer to say that he was short of any spares or of any of the supplies which he considered to be necessary for the deployment. Having in the earlier months discussed with the Admiralty Board the problem of where we were to make our reductions in supplies and in stocks, I was surprised but very impressed by the fact that there was no major shortage in the key stocks and spares which were necessary for this deployment. It says an enormous amount for the Royal Navy that, living the life they do, constantly ready to put to sea, their logistics were brilliant. I had my disagreements with the Royal Navy on their strategy but I have to admire their readiness, which showed itself so clearly on that Sunday.

I went down to the engine room of *Hermes* to find that her boilers had been completely defective three days before and a team had worked all day and all night to get them repaired. By the time I got there on the Sunday they were confident that they'd done a sufficiently adequate job for her to be able to go to sea the next day.

It was an enormously encouraging visit and the astonishing part of it all, looking back on it now, is that although I had been in the centre of a major row, a very emotional row, about the future of the Royal Navy over the preceding six to nine months, and although there must have been a number of officers on board who felt that I was responsible for having taken totally wrong decisions about their future, nevertheless none of this came out at all during my visit.

There was an intense feeling of unity between all of the people on board and I sensed the reaction that they did not see me as a visiting politician, but acknowledged that I was there as the Minister of Defence; that the nation had a crisis and that we just had to all work together to put on a good show. And that feeling did pervade itself through all the Services, and between the Navy and myself throughout the Falklands conflict. It shows how much this country does come together in times of crisis and in a quite astonishing way.

I left *Hermes* and took a helicopter straight back to Windsor. We had some difficulty in finding the rendezvous in Windsor and we flew round and round the town but eventually we found the place to land. The colonel commanding the Blues met me on the barrack-square and drove me up to the Castle, where I was met by Robin Fellowes, the Queen's Deputy Private Secretary, and a number of other Palace staff whom I knew. John Biffen, Francis Pym and I attended a Privy Council meeting where the requisitioning arrangements for civilian ships were agreed as an Order in Council. After the short Privy Council meeting, the Queen offered us a glass of sherry, a most unusual act of generosity, and we had a little chat, dwelling somewhat on polo ponies and their Argentine grooms!

Monday was another day of drama. I was in my office with Frank Cooper and David Omand preparing a number of organisational matters when Jerry Wiggin telephoned me from Brize Norton. He had been with Richard Luce to meet the returning Royal Marines from the Falklands, who had flown back from Uruguay by an RAF VC10. Jerry Wiggin told me that Peter Carrington was about to resign and that Richard Luce and Humphrey Atkins had decided to resign with him. Was I aware of it? I knew that everybody was trying to persuade Peter otherwise, but no one had told me that he had been in to see the Prime Minister earlier in the morning and insisted on tendering his resignation.

Imagine my consternation when I received this call – not having heard anything at all from No. 10 – when I, with him, was regarded as the principal culprit for the whole affair. It seemed to place me in a totally impossible position. Although I had not been responsible for policy over the Falklands, I was depicted as having been so, equally with Peter Carrington. For him to resign and insist upon it, and for me not to tender my resignation, would make him the 'honourable man' and me the 'dishonourable' one who wanted to cling to office. I was astonished that no one had told me. I could not understand how the polished Whitehall system could work in this way. I had also heard a few minutes earlier that the Chief Whip had advised that if Peter Carrington were to resign, I should not be told in advance. No doubt he did this with the best of good intentions, thinking that if both of us went it might have been the end of the government. It was no doubt a passing remark and was not in any way intended to let me down, but it was reported to me nonetheless and I was very angry.

I said to Frank Cooper that I must resign immediately. Frank said he didn't think that was necessary, but I insisted. I told my Private Secretary to ring the Prime Minister immediately. David Omand spoke to Clive Whitmore and said I wanted to talk immediately to the PM. She came on the line. I said, 'Prime Minister, I have just heard indirectly that Peter Carrington is about to resign. I cannot understand why I have not been told. Indeed, I am appalled. My own resignation is already on its way.' Indeed, having heard the story, I had sat down and written out my letter of resignation, going over the drafting with Frank Cooper and David Omand in Frank's room. The letter had been despatched and I told her so. She said, 'John, you cannot resign. I will not allow it. There is no possible circumstance under which this is your responsibility. I insist that you do not send your letter over. Tear it up and the matter must end there.' I said, 'Prime Minister, I understand your position but I am afraid I cannot do so. You have my resignation. If you wish to refuse it, then you must say so publicly. I cannot be placed in the position where Peter Carrington is said to be the "honourable man" and I am the "dishonourable" one. I do not want to stay in office. As you know, privately I have told you, I no longer intend to fight the next election and, in my view, I should go with Peter in view of the public outcry.' 'I will not accept it,' she said. I replied, 'Well, I have sent it over.' And that was that.

When the call was over, I thought about it less emotionally and I asked my Private Secretary to speak to Clive Whitmore again. I said to Whitmore that the only way in which I could be persuaded to remain was if my letter was published, so that the whole world knew I had tendered my resignation with Peter Carrington. If the PM wished to refuse it, then she should publish her rejection of my offer, so that the whole world could see the full position. Clive Whitmore said she was calling in Willie Whitelaw to consult him immediately. Within ten minutes I had a call back from Ian Gow to say that there had been a great misunderstanding. There was no question of hiding Peter Carrington's resignation from me. No. 10 had just not had time to tell me, but certainly the PM would publish my letter of resignation and her reply. And he read out her reply to me. It could not have been more generous. As I did not feel responsible for what had occurred, I did not feel the necessity to press my resignation as Peter had done.

Peter Carrington's resignation was on the one o'clock news. Passing mention was made of my resignation and of the refusal of the PM. The news came as a bombshell to the Party. Many of those people who had called for his resignation had joined in the hunt at the Party meeting on Saturday and now deeply regretted what they had done.

For all the fact that he was criticised for being a real Foreign Office man, and had often been accused of appeasement, for instance on Rhodesia, there was not a soul in the Party, except for a few of his enemies, who did not recognise that, although he was a diplomat through and through with all that that implied, he had marked up many achievements for the country. I have to confess that I did not agree with his politics or with his policies, particularly those on the European Community, as I had often felt him not to be strong enough, not to be emphatic enough; but I could not deny that he had added greatly to the prestige of the government. Most people felt likewise and were deeply ashamed at the witch-hunt the previous Saturday. From a personal point of view, I too regretted Peter's departure, but to some extent I could not help reflecting that it made my position easier. It would clear the air. Blood had been shed. Peter had gone. A victim had been offered up for sacrifice and the funeral pyre had been lit.

Almost every decision in the MoD needs political authority. Many of the actions we took came near to flouting the letter of the law, but in the chaos of the past few days the Whitehall system had been hit below the solar plexus. A great tangled mass of coordinating committees, Cabinet sub-committees, the great panoply of bureaucratic checking and double-checking had been completely flattened. The horrendous way in which Whitehall ensures that it retains control through an excess of coordination means that nothing happens with any kind of urgency. The whole system had been caught with its trousers down. It was partly due to the fact that Whitehall was virtually in suspense, shell-shocked and useless, that no obstacles arose in getting the Fleet to sea. The shackles of bureaucracy just fell off. I felt a blessed sense of relief that all the committees, which were always there to prevent anything being done, were not there to frustrate us.

On Monday, as well as Peter Carrington's resignation the news was full of the sailing of the Fleet. I prayed that they would come home safely. I had been accused of wishing to ruin the Royal Navy. The charge was totally untrue. Changes that I had proposed were for the best for the Royal Navy. They were not just my whim. They were also the best advice that I had available from the Defence Staffs and the Intelligence Staffs. Several of my Party were quite unable to understand that money must always be a constraint on the Defence programme. We were greatly over-programmed and we had to claw it back.

As the Fleet sailed, like everybody else I had tears in my eyes. It was a great achievement. The Royal Navy had done a magnificent job.

The RAF too had played their part and the Army, as I have said, helped to get everything to the dockside on time.

There is one other event that I remember that day, and it will remain in my memory for a long time. It was the *Panorama* interview given by Peter Carrington that evening. I had been asked the previous Saturday if I would do *Panorama* on Monday night. Knowing that they were an unpleasant bunch, knowing that whatever one said they would twist it, knowing that the BBC was anti-patriotic, was out of control, using opinions rather than facts, I decided that I would not go on *Panorama*. Beside the quality of ITV and, in particular, ITN, the BBC is a disgrace.

The interview with Peter Carrington was a classic of its kind. It was handled by Robert Kee, who was rude, combative, totally inaccurate and badly prepared. Peter Carrington batted the questions well, but his exasperation at the futility and asinine nature of the questions came through. It was, I think, a classic interview because it showed the low depths to which the BBC descended throughout the Falklands campaign.

Tuesday was a less hectic day within the Ministry of Defence and I was able to spend some time in the House of Commons, concluding with a meeting with my awkward squad – the Conservative backbench Defence Committee. They were a strange bunch under the chairmanship of Anthony Buck, who had once been a Parliamentary Under-Secretary for the Navy and I was never allowed to forget it. Tony was rather a sad figure and I fear that he liked the bottle. Other members included Victor Goodhew, Winston Churchill, Julian Critchley and Alan Clark. I had a very difficult time holding them together over the Defence Review; but I had taken the trouble to invite all the Tory backbenchers to my room to brief them on Trident, and my relations with the backbenchers generally were rather better than with the Defence Committee zealots.

Although I maintained a friendly, if somewhat tense, relationship with the officers, they were always a potential source of trouble.

Fortunately I was well served by two excellent men: the person responsible for Defence in the Whips' Office, Bob Boscawen, and my Parliamentary Private Secretary, John Wilkinson. Bob is a Cornishman, the brother of Cornwall's then Lord Lieutenant, Lord Falmouth, and he had been the Conservative candidate for Falmouth & Camborne when I was first selected for St Ives. We worked together quite closely; I won my seat and he unfortunately could not shift the Labour man from his. Throughout my Defence Review and the Falklands, Bob did a wonderful job calming the more frenetic members of the Party; he had been a brave soldier during the Second World War, which helped, and he was greatly respected by his colleagues. John Wilkinson, a younger man, had doubts about my reductions to the Naval Programme, but he too reported back to me when trouble was brewing. Both of them attended all our ministerial meetings in the MoD, so they were well informed of what was happening. They were loyal, constructive and ready to criticise where appropriate.

To understand the flavour of these feverish days, I cannot do better than recommend a reading of Alan Clark's second published set of diaries, *Into Politics, 1972–1982*. I knew Alan well and enjoyed his company, but we were never close. A great part of his diaries describes his determination to replace Buck as chairman of the Defence Committee. Why this mattered to him so much is beyond my comprehension, because I do not believe that the Committee had any influence except, perhaps, that the chairmanship was seen in some quarters as a rung on the ladder to promotion. But I do not even believe that.

What I find valuable about the diaries is the way they illustrate the dangers of the parliamentary lobby, members of which spend their whole life cohabiting 'off the record' with disaffected MPs. Every piece of tittle-tattle finds its way as gospel into the newspapers – so it was damaging to read that the Harriers were no match for the Argentinian Mirages (untrue), that very few Harriers would reach the Falklands due to attrition on the way (luckily untrue), that it was suicide to attempt an opposed amphibious landing without air superiority (luckily also untrue), that the Army's boots were no good (true).There was an endless stream of damaging gossip from the Defence buffs and Bob Boscawen, John Wilkinson, my ministerial team and I had to spend an inordinate amount of time correcting it.

Typical examples from Alan Clark's diaries include:

Hermes was suffering from mechanical trouble and her propellers were seizing ...

Michael Mates dwelt at length on the prospects of very heavy casualties and how we ought to warn the public, etc ...

Callaghan ... said it was the most frightful situation and fraught with danger, that it was important to find a way out, short of a full-scale amphibious assault with all the casualties that might accompany it ...

It was not just in the corridors of the House of Commons that this kind of speculation was rife – and certainly some of it had a degree of truth – but a few MPs and even some ministers were indiscreet at dinner parties in foreign embassies. I was kept informed of the conversations which took place around the dinner tables of foreign ambassadors in London, which must have given considerable joy to President Galtieri.

The armchair generals – the retired senior officers of the three Services constantly on television to give their expert opinion – did no harm but became something of a bore. I learnt that you cease to be an expert in anything the day you step down from Whitehall or the military. The very day you leave you are a goner, and you had better know it.

John Major's memoirs (*John Major: The Autobiography*, 2002) record how one day he 'overheard a washroom conversation in which two Cabinet ministers denounced the expedition as "ludicrous" and as "a folly" due to the lack of air cover for the fleet'. This 'gave me a glimpse of the tension that existed at the heart of the government'. I know who they were – and neither spoke up when the matter came before the Cabinet. On another occasion I happened to drop into the Chief Whip's office to find two Cabinet colleagues denouncing Thatcher and the whole government response.

Finally, I leave Tuesday with this extract from Alan Clark:

> People who should know better are striding up and down the Smoking Room corridor telling anyone whom they can apprehend that the *Invincible* is sailing without her radar operative; that many of her weapons systems have already been removed, that the Sea Harrier cannot land on deck in a rough sea, that many of the ships in the task force have defective power trains, etc., etc.
>
> It is monstrous that senior Tories should be behaving in this way. It is only on occasions such as this that the implacable hatred in which certain established figures hold the Prime Minister can be detected. They oppose government policy whatever it is …They are within an ace they think of bringing her government down. If by some miracle the expedition succeeds they know, and dread, that she will be established for ever as a national hero.
>
> So regardless of the country's interests they are determined that the expedition will not succeed. The greater the humiliation of its failure, the more certain will be the downfall of The Lady's Government, the greater the likelihood of a lash-up coalition … One angle from which [it] can be attacked is via the so-called 'expert' opinion, which is that we just do not have the equipment to launch and sustain an expedition of this magnitude.

Just imagine how this kind of thing must have encouraged the Argentine junta in those early days. No wonder that they were not prepared to make any concessions in the diplomatic negotiations.

'Nothing except a battle lost can be
half so melancholy as a battle won.'

(Wellington's despatch from the field of Waterloo, 1815)

LANDING AND VICTORY

The first meeting of the South Atlantic sub-committee of the Overseas
and Defence Policy Committee of the Cabinet OD (SA), usually known
as the War Cabinet, took place on Wednesday, 7 April. I had discussed its
composition with Margaret Thatcher at the same time that I recommended
the full membership and participation of Terry Lewin. I was nervous
about its political balance. Suspecting that Francis Pym, as the newly
appointed Foreign Secretary, would be likely to take a very cautious
line, and knowing that Pym and Whitelaw were politically close and
were former members of the Chief Whips' club, I proposed the selection
of a fifth political member. I am not a hawk by nature, far from it; but
as Defence Secretary, with the responsibility of giving every possible
support to the military, I was concerned that Margaret and I would find
ourselves opposed by a combination of Pym and Whitelaw. She and I
discussed who the fifth member might be and agreed on Cecil Parkinson.
As the Chairman of the Conservative Party, and as a keen and adept
performer on the media, he seemed a good choice. Cecil, who had been
my deputy at the Department of Trade, proved to be a valuable addition
when it came to putting forward the government's case on television.
In retrospect I need not have worried about political balance because
Whitelaw – who always supported Margaret Thatcher anyhow, whatever
the merits of the issue – became with Margaret herself the most hawkish

political voice in the War Cabinet. And Michael Havers, who attended nearly all our meetings in his capacity as the government legal adviser, proved to be more of a pragmatic former Fleet Air Arm officer than a typical, pernickety, nitpicking wordsmith of a lawyer. We also had no Chancellor of the Exchequer.

Francis Pym therefore found his determined efforts to achieve a diplomatic solution somewhat frustrated by the balance of sentiment in the War Cabinet. But it was important to understand his position and help him with it. Margaret Thatcher was not good at conciliation with her colleagues. She preferred the bludgeon to the rapier.

She and Francis approached the negotiations for a diplomatic settlement from opposite directions, and there was a frequent clash of wills. Both took an entirely honourable position but they were in fundamental conflict. Francis seemed to want to avoid an ugly and dangerous battle at all costs; I think he was genuinely upset at putting all these young soldiers and sailors – at very great risk – into an opposed amphibious landing without air superiority. He had seen war himself. Moreover, on his several visits to Washington he must have been increasingly influenced by Haig and other US military opinion to the effect that this whole exercise was beyond our capability.

Nicholas Henderson's excellent published diaries make this clear:

> … the facts disclosed the scepticism of the US Navy at the outset about the prospects for the success of the British Task Force. Britain was ill-equipped to fight a war in the South Atlantic. They lacked air surveillance; their satellite communications were inadequate. They were short of an effective air-to-air missile for the Harriers. They had no base in the South Atlantic.

Later, he quotes Weinberger admitting that 'we all knew of the enormous military odds against Britain'. Weinberger's own memoirs say:

Our military leaders advised that lack of shipping made Mrs. Thatcher's position and plans impossible to carry out. Also they noted that the UK's lack of air transport, the length of time the Argentinians would have to prepare defences against the British and all the normal difficulties inherent in making an opposed landing, not to mention the difficulties of doing that after an 8,000 mile trip with no real intermediate bases – all of those factors led our military leaders to conclude that the UK action could not succeed.

As a former Defence Secretary, Francis Pym *may* – and I emphasise may – have been horrified at the likely financial cost of garrisoning the Falklands against a subsequent military threat from Argentina. He knew, as I knew, that we were insufficiently resourced to meet the threat to NATO, let alone future threats 8000 miles away in the South Atlantic. Francis wanted to do a deal and was flexible in his approach to achieving this objective.

Margaret Thatcher had, I believe, made up her mind from the outset that the only way we could regain our national honour and prestige was by inflicting a military defeat on Argentina. She was sufficiently pragmatic to understand that if the negotiations could bring about a total withdrawal of the Argentinians and the restoration of some kind of British administration, then her Cabinet would accept it. A myth grew up about Margaret Thatcher that in some way her word was law. It was never the case in my day; she was very well aware that she had to keep her Cabinet, her parliamentary supporters and the party in the country with her. The painful and endless negotiations for a diplomatic settlement produced the only significant personal clashes of the war. The only positive thing that can be said of them in retrospect is that they filled a horrible vacuum, whilst the Task Force made its long, long voyage towards Antarctica – as far laterally as Hawaii.

The first clash between the military imperatives and the requirements of diplomacy came on Wednesday 7th, only five days after the invasion.

Spartan, our first nuclear submarine, was approaching the Falklands, and we needed to decide on the appropriate rules of engagement for its captain. The Chiefs of Staff, by now headed by the returned Terry Lewin, had recommended the imposition of a 200-mile maritime exclusion zone (MEZ), the principal purpose being to stop further Argentinian supplies reaching the troops embarked on the Falkland Islands. I had to get this through the War Cabinet and announced as soon as possible. In the end I agreed to announce it at a debate in the House of Commons on the Wednesday, the first major debate since the debacle on the previous Saturday. I wanted not only to give this support to the military, but also to show to the world after the sailing of the Task Force that we really meant business.

From the beginning of the week the position of the Americans was becoming clear: they stopped arms sales to Argentina, but were unwilling to take more effective economic measures. Nicholas Henderson, our Ambassador, reported back that the Americans were not prepared to 'tilt' too heavily against Argentina; to do so, they said, would deprive them of their influence in Buenos Aires. They did not want Galtieri to fall – whereas we saw him as an outright fascist dictator and aggressor. Galtieri was for the Americans a central pillar of resistance to communism in South and Central America, and all of Reagan's and the State Department's efforts were concentrated on the crisis in El Salvador. The United States did not wish to choose between Britain, their principal NATO ally in Europe, and their interests in Latin America. Apart from Weinberger and the Pentagon, the Americans were very, very far from being on our side

Al Haig was due to commence his mediation – although we resented his use of such a term – on Wednesday, but because of the debate it was postponed until the Thursday. The War Cabinet met for the first time that Wednesday morning and again in the evening. My 1983 record describes the drama that occurred at that evening meeting, for me one of the most important of the war:

It took place informally at seven o'clock in Margaret Thatcher's room in the House of Commons. It had been decided that we should meet to confirm the declaration of the maritime exclusion zone. We had discussed this in detail that morning and it had been agreed that, subject to any second thoughts, the declaration of the exclusion zone should be included in my own winding-up speech [due to be made later that evening]. It had been a struggle to get it agreed but I had done so at a meeting of the War Cabinet that morning, subject to final decision in the evening. I heard, as I was sitting on the front bench – nervous, of course, at my approaching speech – that the Foreign Office was now absolutely determined, and passionately so, to avoid the declaration of the MEZ that evening. Their reason was that Haig was coming to London and that it would be a slap in the face to ask him here as a negotiator and an intermediary and then, just before he arrived, to declare the zone, an act which was hostile to the Argentinians. I was absolutely horrified. The whole thing was on course and the Royal Navy needed it. It was the central part of my speech. It was a climb-down at a critical moment when our resolve needed to be shown to the whole world. It was typical of the Foreign Office. Margaret Thatcher was on the bench beside me listening to the debate. I whispered to her that I was deeply upset at this change of plan.

It was clear to me as we sat down in her room that Margaret, who had just appointed Francis Pym as Foreign Secretary, was not going to come out against him. She did not agree, but she felt having just appointed him that she had to back him up. I think she must have realised that this made my position very awkward indeed, but at the same time I knew that she was not going to back me up. Francis opened the discussion by saying that he thought there was no question, now that Haig was coming, of going ahead with this declaration. It would make Haig's mission impossible and he could not agree with it; he realised what a foolish decision we'd made that morning. I said that I could not disagree more strongly. In fact, although I never said so, I felt that I could hardly stay as Defence Secretary if the decision went against me. I knew that Whitelaw would be likely to back up Francis, as was

Margaret. Cecil Parkinson was my only hope. I said that I fundamentally disagreed. If Haig came to London and we had not already started on military measures, we would be in balk thereafter. How were we ever going to take a necessary military measure if, every time he came, we were concerned about upsetting him? I said that it was absolutely vital that we now showed our determination to the Argentinians; this would improve the peace process, the negotiating process, it would help Haig. We could not declare it after he arrived, and it was urgently necessary now that our submarines were approaching the Falklands to get on and show that we meant business.

Margaret did not come down on my side. She wondered whether we could not declare it the next day. I said that was impossible. It was the last day before Parliament went into recess. Why, if there was a speech by me in one hour's time, would we not have declared it but waited till the next day to make a statement? The following day was Good Friday. We could not make the statement on Good Friday. If we waited till Saturday, it would seem very odd that when we had had a major debate on the subject, we had deferred a decision until Saturday. And, anyhow, by Saturday Haig would be in Buenos Aires and we could not send him back there to negotiate a settlement and than announce a maritime exclusion zone when he was there. Willie Whitelaw came in, concerned not so much about the substance of the matter but about parliamentary opinion. I could see a Chief Whip's mind grinding through. The parliamentary situation was very difficult, he said. This was the time to announce it, and yet he saw how difficult this would be for Francis. He was worried that if we did not announce it now, it would look as if we had been frightened out of doing so. Cecil Parkinson then came in. He too said he thought it was very difficult. We were reaching a stalemate in a decision. I knew that I had to plough on. I once again protested that the submarines were there; the Fleet had put to sea; the public and international recognition of our resolve following the passing of Resolution 502 was absolutely crucial; the Party would not stand for any weakness; this was the last occasion on which we could do so before Parliament left for the Easter Recess. Haig would place us in balk. We had no choice. The argument went on and on and on – but gradually, slowly, I pulled it round my way.

We then discussed whether we had to tell Haig in advance. I said I did not mind informing him, but it must be information and no more. About an hour and a half had passed when, somewhat to my surprise, Francis, who saw that the argument was going against him, suddenly said well, he would accept it. It was one of the most relieving moments of the crisis. We agreed to inform Haig, and the statement, which had already been prepared by the Foreign Office lawyers, was re-incorporated in my speech.

I made the statement right at the beginning of what I had to say. It completely transformed the atmosphere of the House and met with universal agreement from the Labour Party, Callaghan and the rest, and brought great cheers from our side. I believe it was one of the most important decisions that we took throughout the crisis. We indicated to the world that we meant business. Haig, when he arrived the next morning, knew that we meant business. The Argentinians now realised that we were not fooling around, and at least it made possible my political recovery from the disastrous speech I'd made the previous Saturday. I had not had time to prepare my wind-up, but David Omand and others had put together a rather boring, flat and dull speech for me.

As it turned out, the House was in a much better mood. It allowed me to speak. I was unprovocative. For the first time since I had done the Defence Review the House actually listened to what I had to say about the Royal Navy. I was able to explain that we were spending more, not less, on the conventional Navy. As I sat down the House was appreciative. Margaret and Willie and Francis beside me were genuinely relieved. It had been a difficult occasion. Afterwards Miloska, my wife, and I went round to Margaret's room for a drink, and the mood was very different from the previous Saturday's. I could now carry on with my work.

***

I have dwelt on that single occasion at some length because it illustrates the problem of managing the intricate relationship between military and diplomatic requirements. If we had not given priority to the military on this first occasion when the clash of interests arose, I doubt whether the resolve to support the Task Force against all the diplomatic, international and parliamentary pressures could have been sustained. Thereafter, I don't think there was another occasion where such a problem went against the military imperatives. It had been a close-run thing, but it set the right precedent for the future. The maritime exclusion zone itself took effect from the early hours of Easter Monday morning, 12 April.

The Haig-led negotiations were interminable – and it would be tedious to go over again all the twists and turns that encountered us. If Washington had been in the hands of the East Coast WASPs (White Anglo-Saxon Protestants) instead of the West Coast Americans, with their overriding concern for the Americas, it might have been different. The State Department, the White House security staff, led by Judge Clark, and Reagan himself were never wholly committed to our case, although they came out publicly in our support on 30 April. Even thereafter the Americans gave every assistance to the Peruvians, the United Nations and every other mediator – Brazilian, Mexican and the rest – to bring about a negotiated settlement, on terms which would have been seen as a surrender by political, press and public opinion in the United Kingdom. In the closing stages, when we had already lost many ships and men and were already safely back on the Falkland Islands, the Americans leant heavily on us, backed up by telephone calls from Reagan to Thatcher, to find some way of saving Galtieri's face. 'Magnanimity before victory' became their watchword. Fortunately the military, apart from Terry Lewin, were kept largely ignorant of the hesitations of the wider Cabinet and the considerable international pressures on us to call it a day, not least from Germany, Ireland, Italy and Spain. Only Mitterrand and the French remained staunch allies to the end. Bravely Margaret Thatcher held firm

– and it needed a massive exercise of will to resist these pressures, but she did so.

When Haig and his party returned from Buenos Aires after their initial talk with us, there was a classic demonstration of how Whitehall's undoubted skills can be unhelpful. After various talks on the morning of 12 April, we all gathered in the Cabinet Room to discuss the draft proposals that he had brought back with him. Unfortunately Robert Armstrong, who performed a valuable role as the Secretary of the War Cabinet, had included several senior civil service colleagues in the meeting. The meeting was far too big.

Haig talked and talked, speaking up for his proposals with some vigour and skill. Margaret Thatcher, Whitelaw and I resisted him. The civil servants (Robert Wade-Gery, a Foreign Office man, among them) started passing amendments up and down the table. We reached the point where they were trying to broker a drafting compromise between us and Haig – typical Foreign Office practice but thoroughly unhelpful. At one stage, with the assistance of these Whitehall draft writers, we had nearly reached a stage where we were being asked to withdraw 4000 miles to Ascension whilst the Argentinians were withdrawing 400 miles to their mainland. I protested and it was taken out. Eventually, after some eleven hours of discussions, we had reached a sort of compromise: the Argentinians would withdraw to the mainland; we would position a naval force the same distance from the Falklands; and there would be a joint United States–Argentine–British administration acting in conjunction with the Falkland Islanders, who would agree for one or two of the Argentine resident population to join the Executive and Legislative Councils. It was a nonsense, but we were under great pressure to agree something positive with the Americans.

Haig departed, saying that the Argentinians would never accept the final draft but that he would put it to them. When he arrived back in Buenos Aires he was met by organised riots in favour of the occupation, and his discussions with the junta, which was deeply divided, were chaotic. As soon as one point was agreed there were protests from senior officers of the Services and the position was rescinded. So it went on.

The final drama of the Haig negotiations occurred almost a fortnight later, on Saturday 24 April. By this time, Haig was getting nowhere very fast between the intransigent Argentine junta and the determined Margaret Thatcher.

Francis Pym returned from one of his visits to Washington with an amended set of American proposals. There is no need to give the details – the text is available in several other memoirs of the time. But by the time the War Cabinet was called to consider them that evening, Francis was advocating acceptance with some vigour. I quote from Margaret Thatcher's accurate record:

> Francis Pym's document [brought back from his latest negotiations in Washington] ruled out the possibility of a return to the situation enjoyed by the Islanders before the invasion. We would have gone against our commitment to the principle that the Islanders' wishes were paramount... Did Francis realise how much he had signed away?
>
> Francis put a paper to the War Cabinet recommending acceptance of these terms ... I asked Willie Whitelaw to come upstairs to my study. I told him that I could not accept these terms.

At the meeting itself, there was a long discussion which led to something of an impasse. The Foreign Office representatives were in favour of acceptance, but the rest of us were not. Margaret again:

> It was John Nott who found the procedural way forward. He proposed that we should make no comment on the draft but ask Mr. Haig to put it to the Argentinians first. If they accepted it we should undoubtedly be in difficulties: but we could then put the matter to Parliament in the light of their acceptance. If the Argentinians rejected it – and we thought that they would, because it is almost impossible for any military junta

to withdraw – we could then urge the Americans to come down firmly on our side, as Al Haig had indicated they would as long as we did not break off the negotiations. This is what was decided.

And so a great crisis passed. I could not have stayed as Prime Minister had the War Cabinet accepted Francis Pym's proposals. I would have resigned.

I am always surprised when support for me comes from unexpected quarters. To receive praise from a senior Foreign Office mandarin, albeit one for whom I had considerable respect, came as a real bonus. In his account of this critical episode, Nicholas Henderson describes my 'brainwave' as 'a finesse of which Talleyrand would have been proud'! The Argentinians did not respond in favour of the American proposals, and in consequence the United States announced their support for the United Kingdom on 30 April – nearly one month after an armed aggression on the territory of their closest NATO ally.

Before I finally leave the subject of the negotiations and return to the more important subject of the war, it is worth mentioning the meeting which took place at Chequers on 17 May.

By this time the peace negotiations had passed to the United Nations. Our support remained quite fragile among our allies, and we were concerned that the whole subject might return to the Security Council. International opinion had not been assisted by our sinking of the *Belgrano* with her large loss of life. Tony Parsons and Nicholas Henderson were asked to return here from the United States and join the meeting, which was also attended by Francis Pym, Tony Acland and Michael Palliser. A clutch of five men from the Foreign Office.

I have to say that Margaret Thatcher was pretty aggressive at this meeting. As Nicholas Henderson reported very accurately, Margaret accused them 'of being wet, ready to sell out, unsupportive of British interests, etc., etc.' And: 'Did the Foreign Office have no principles? She said that while we [i.e. the Foreign Office] were content to be dishonest and consult with dishonest people, she was honest.' At one stage I thought that this was all getting a bit much and I intervened in some exasperation. She then rounded on me and accused me of being rude to her! It is true, I had been. 'Those who live by the sword, die by the sword.' I am afraid these polite, civilised, intelligent mandarins as good civil servants were hardly able to retaliate, so it rightly fell to me.

In his entertaining account of this extended meeting, Henderson then goes on:

> Right at the end of the meeting Nott protested about the American attitude. Did they realise the bitterness in the UK about them?
>
> I asked him in what way the Americans had fallen short of expectations since they had declared their support for us on 30 April. Surely they had met all our demands for intelligence and equipment? With less than enthusiasm the PM referred to Reagan's recent telephone call to her urging us not to undertake military operations against the mainland. She exclaimed once again against 'ingratitude'...
>
> Nott came up to me after the meeting was over to say that perhaps he had given the wrong impression. It was simply a feeling he had that some of the speeches were bad (which is true) and that there were people, e.g. Jeanne Kirkpatrick, who were against us (also true).

The call from Reagan about avoiding military operations on the mainland reminds me of my last disagreement with Margaret Thatcher, and in this case I was also opposed by Terry Lewin.

Towards the end of the conflict, when the outcome was not in much doubt, one of our nuclear submarines found the Argentine aircraft carrier lurking within Argentinian territorial waters. We had agreed rules of engagement which allowed our submarines to sink the aircraft carrier fairly early in the conflict, as she posed a very real threat, with her A4 aircraft, to the safety of our ships. I had fully endorsed this necessary action, but we never found her right up until this late moment – and the rules of engagement did not permit an attack within Argentinian territorial waters. The Navy sought a change in the rules, although the shallow water would have posed a hazard to our submarine. Margaret Thatcher was keen to agree the change, on the basis that the aircraft carrier would present a continuing threat to our ships and to the Falklands even after we had recaptured them. I opposed the change, arguing against her and Terry Lewin on the grounds that action in South American territorial waters could bring in other countries on the Argentinian side, just as we were about to achieve a victory. We did not agree the change. Another 'What if?' of history.

***

It was while the Task Force was still sailing south that I heard that my mother had died in the night after several years of serious disability following a stroke. I wish she had lived to see the conclusion of the Falklands, though I have no way of knowing whether she understood it all; I imagine she did because she sat in front of the television day by day, but she could not communicate. Her funeral was in Northam Church, north Devon, where she had been baptised, confirmed and married. Frank Cooper had kindly arranged for an RAF HS135 to be put at my disposal. On Wednesday 21 April I woke up my daughter, Saša, who was living with me in Admiralty House, and we were in the air from Northolt by eight o'clock.

We flew down to Chivenor, near Barnstaple in north Devon, and as we came in the beautiful Taw/Torridge estuary lay before us. Drawn up on the apron were a large number of Hawk Jet trainers, a most impressive sight. Chivenor is where we train our RAF pilots for their advanced jet and weapons training. I was met by the captain of the station, who walked with me over to the buildings nearby where I chatted to quite a large group of ground crew – young men in their early twenties and even younger than that. They all seemed very cheerful and were highly curious about my arrival and what I would have to say. I told them that the RAF was putting up a splendid job, particularly on the air bridge to Ascension. The Royal Navy was getting more of the publicity, but behind the scenes a tremendous amount of valuable work had already been undertaken. I thought it wise to let them know, although the information was very restricted, that we had placed air-flight refuelling on the Vulcans and Victors, and I said that the Victors had been performing a valuable role on reconnaissance in the South Atlantic. When I said that the Royal Navy was getting more publicity, one of them said there was nothing new in that and there was laughter and agreement all round.

After the funeral we returned to my father's home for lunch, and I had only just completed it when Wendy, my social secretary, was on the line. Francis Pym was making a statement in the Commons that afternoon and if I left immediately I could be back there in time. I gathered up my three children. William, the youngest, was due back at Eton that evening so I had to take him with me. Saša also was starting at Chelsea Art College the next day and Julian was due to return to Oxford University. My wife and I had a quick discussion as to whether all the children should travel with me on the same aeroplane and, in the end, we agreed to take the risk.

We were back in London fifty minutes after leaving Chivenor and my second Private Secretary, Nick Evans, met me with the latest papers, including notes of the War Cabinet meeting which had taken place that morning in my absence. Terry Lewin's notes gave me a good feel for what had been discussed and I was, therefore, able to join Francis Pym in the House with the knowledge of what had taken place in the previous few hours.

Francis made a good statement, but the impression left on me that afternoon was an unhappy one. The House of Commons seemed to me a million miles from understanding the gap that remained between the Argentinians and ourselves. By emphasising our desire for a peaceful settlement with almost every other word, Francis, I fear, gave the impression we could see one in sight – it was only a question of one final heave and we would be home and dry. This feeling of optimism had translated itself into the House, particularly on our side, and Healey, of course, went on about the United Nations. He cannot really believe that the United Nations will provide anything other than a catastrophic defeat for us, but he goes on saying it; presumably it's the only way of holding his own Party together. I came away from that session in the House feeling depressed.

We then had to take a decision whether we should recapture South Georgia. Terry Lewin and I had discussed it several times. The Naval Staff and Northwood were anxious not to be distracted by a diversion into South Georgia and, looked at from a strictly military point of view, they were right. But Lewin had a well-known dictum that 'there is no such thing as a purely military operation, all operations are politico-military', and he was right. As a member of the War Cabinet he could see that, as politicians, we were under enormous pressure in the House of Commons and internationally to get the campaign finished; but he and I knew that the amphibious force was going to take longer to arrive in the Falklands than anyone anticipated. So we agreed that we had to go for this diversion to fill the vacuum. It was pure politics.

That evening we had another meeting. From my memory, there was the PM, Francis Pym and me and a few of our officials. It was a discussion about Francis' journey next day to the United States but, in particular, we had a major disagreement surrounding our decision to carry on with the attack on South Georgia. This had been a difficult decision earlier in the day because the mood of Parliament and, indeed, the country, had been that no shot should be fired in anger whilst the negotiating process was still going on.

Such a position would have placed us in an intolerable situation because there was no reason to believe that the Argentinians were seriously intending to negotiate. We could not detach the *Antrim* group [a naval detachment] to South Georgia and then leave it hanging around there without our orders. In every way it seemed essential to confirm our earlier decision that the reoccupation of South Georgia should proceed. Francis resisted but by this time we'd been joined by Willie Whitelaw. He supported the decision to continue with the South Georgia operation, which involved landing a team of SAS and the Special Boat Squadron on the island in order to attempt at least a partially bloodless reoccupation. The FO put up some resistance, but in the end the decision was taken: we went ahead.

Just as we were breaking up, Michael Palliser said that he thought it was necessary to inform Nicholas Henderson of what we were doing. I disagreed with this rather strongly. It did not seem to me a matter for the British Ambassador in Washington. The PM clearly agreed with me, but Tony Acland, Michael Palliser and Francis Pym all pressed the point and, in the end, we seemed unable to resist it. It was agreed, therefore, to send a message to Nicholas Henderson telling him that the South Georgia occupation had already begun and pointing out that Francis Pym would be in Washington negotiating, possibly when the news began to break.

Later that evening we had a message back from Nicholas saying that he quite understood our decision, but he felt that it would be very wrong for us not to inform Alexander Haig. He did not intend to put it other than as firm information to Haig – a decision had been taken, it was going ahead, but we wanted him to know. This was the position when we broke up that evening. It was a tense meeting but a friendly one and we resolved the difference satisfactorily.

I had dinner in the House with a group of colleagues. I remember John Stokes and two others were sitting at my table. I said how depressed I had been with the mood of the House of Commons, its belief that a settlement was near and its seeming unwillingness to face the consequences of what was likely to happen. They did not agree with me. They agreed that there was a difference of view in the Party but, on the whole, there was an acceptance that if force became necessary it would have to follow. I voted at ten o'clock and got back to Admiralty House feeling very tired. It was, after all, the day of my mother's funeral and I had just got to sleep around about 11.30 when the telephone rang. My Private Secretary asked to come round and see me; he had some messages.

The first message indicated that the SAS had already landed on South Georgia some ten miles from one of the Argentinian bases. This was a factual statement and said nothing more. But the other message was a long rambling telex from Nicholas Henderson about his talk with Haig. Haig expressed his shock that we would go ahead and re-occupy South Georgia at the present time. The peace process was still going on – it would certainly damage him in the eyes of the Argentinians. He was deeply concerned about how he would be seen, and it would certainly be thought that he had connived, if not agreed, to this military action. He said that he had no course but to inform the Argentinians of our forthcoming military action. Nicholas Henderson replied that this was quite impossible – this would be giving up our military secret and could damage lives. Haig continued to protest but in the end agreed that he would not tell the Argentinians. Was it not possible, he asked, for him to tell the Argentinians that American intelligence had discovered that we had a group of ships in the area, and that the Argentinians could be warned in this way? Henderson again protested that this would be intolerable and so their meeting broke up; but it also became apparent that Costa Mendes [the Argentine Foreign Minister] had tried to telephone Haig that evening on an urgent matter, and I believe that other members of the State Department informed the Argentinians of what we were about. It is a frightening thing that our greatest ally is not wholly on our side. I only hoped that if information had been passed by the Americans to the Argentinians about our impending assault that this did not lead to loss of life.

The week before it had been agreed that we [the War Cabinet] should have a military briefing. It was difficult fixing the time and it was necessary that it should be done before Francis Pym departed. I had had a difference of view with Terry Lewin about how the briefing should be presented to my colleagues. Normally I would have had a dress rehearsal with the Chiefs, but in the end I left them to it and they prepared it in my absence, so that the next morning they could present a set of military options.

The briefing took place in the Ministry of Defence at about nine o'clock. There were about fifteen officials present and the Chiefs of Staff. It was very well done. We went over the list of military options. The difficulty with it was – and I should certainly have warned against packing so much into such a short time – that there was such a mass of information, the decisions were so difficult and so far-reaching, that the PM protested that she could not carry on the discussion at that time.

This is how Margaret Thatcher herself describes the meeting:

It was clear that we had a period of some two to three weeks in May during which we might land without terrible casualties. And then there were decisions to be made about how much more equipment, aircraft and troops to send, how to deal with the resulting prisoners of war, what to do about South Georgia and when. There was to be no respite at all. And these decisions must be made quickly. I looked from the Chiefs of Staff to my colleagues. It was a lot for them to take in. With the exception of John Nott, who of course was already briefed on the difficulties, they seemed somewhat taken aback. By this stage the press had learnt that we were at the MoD and I asked that everyone look confident as we left.

We went into a smaller group with just Margaret, Willie, Francis and myself. There were really three decisions that needed to be taken that day. First of all, we had to decide whether to deploy the Vulcans to Ascension. They had already been fitted with air-flight refuelling, and from Ascension it would be possible for them to bomb the runway at

Port Stanley. However, that morning we had received information that the American Air Force station commander, who up to then had been extremely helpful, would deny us aviation fuel for the Vulcans and that we were not to bring them there. This was an intolerable and disgraceful episode, indicating that the State Department had got in touch with Ascension to block the Vulcans going there. This can only have come from Haig himself. I said to Francis that the Americans had no right to take such measures, they were our allies, and the first thing he should do on arriving in Washington that morning (he was going on Concorde) was to protest loudly that the Americans, under the agreement, had to make the airfield available to us in an emergency.

The second issue was whether we should sail the advanced amphibious group from Ascension on Saturday and Sunday. I had been against doing this because I did not want the amphibious group to set sail and, having set sail, for it to turn back as a result of the negotiations. I was therefore in favour of holding it for a few days until Francis had returned to London. In the end it was decided not to sail on the Saturday. I recommended that we had a meeting at Chequers at which we could spend four or five hours knocking the whole thing around and so, just before Francis's departure, it was agreed that this should happen.

Richard Hill's biography of Lewin (*Lewis of Greenwich*) covers this disagreement as follows:

> There was one occasion when he was overruled. John Nott intervened to delay by two days the sailing of the force south from Ascension when it appeared that there might be some chance of Haig's latest initiative (one more spin of the 'Haig Shuttle') succeeding. This, he knew, would irritate all the naval authorities because they were working to a desperately narrow window of opportunity ... But he reasoned that if the task force sailed south and it then turned round because there had been a settlement, it would look as though it had turned tail in defeat.

The most important thing of all, however, was to get Francis back from Washington in time. If Francis was to remain there negotiating for ever without getting anywhere then we were in a hopeless state. The negotiating process overlapped and conflicted with the necessary military measures. The amphibious group could not remain for ever on Ascension without our credibility being at stake. So I pleaded with Francis – you must be back by Sunday. We had to get a clear decision as to whether it was really worthwhile Haig going back to Buenos Aires or not, because the military timetable and the diplomatic negotiations were beginning to get in conflict with one another. The meeting broke up, Francis went off to catch Concorde to Washington and, after a short pause, Cabinet began.

Whereas at Cabinet on the previous Tuesday there had been a full briefing by Francis on the diplomatic situation, on this occasion I gave a very full briefing to the whole Cabinet on where the Argentinian forces were; where our troops were deployed. I announced for the first time that Special Forces were already embarked on South Georgia and I listed some of the military options. I think this came as a shock to the Cabinet but, on the whole, it went down well. I had preceded my remarks by pointing out the difficulties of the diplomatic process. I read out another cable, which had come from Nico Henderson the previous night, indicating that there were fifty or so people to negotiate with in Buenos Aires, but that they were always changing their view and that Galtieri was drunk.

The Cabinet was quite contrary to Tuesday, where it had been drifting off in high-flown views about international law, with Geoffrey Howe mumbling on as usual and Leon Brittan trying to display his legal pyrotechnics. Tuesday's Cabinet had been depressing but Thursday helped to concentrate people's minds and Willie, as usual, came in as an enormous help. The only dissenting voices were Jim Prior and Peter Walker. Jim Prior was clearly upset about the whole thing. The previous night I had been on my way home to bed and had drifted in to pick up a piece of paper out of the Chief Whip's office from Michael Jopling, I found Willie there. He'd been out to dinner and was in his normal after-dinner state. He, Jopling and Jim Prior were all together. I joined them. Willie and I tried to persuade Jim that we just had to go forward with military preparations; we could not hold them up. Jim, in fact, was okay at Cabinet but he was obviously deeply concerned that we were going to fire a shot and the whole peace process was going to break down. Peter Walker too expressed his great concern about the South Georgia operation. He, like Jim Prior, was concerned that we should be actually embarking on an operation in South Georgia at the same time as we were negotiating in Washington. Neither of them seemed to see that, on the whole, we'd got as far as we had already purely because we had kept up our military pressure. I pointed out that exactly the same arguments had been used against the declaration of the exclusion zone at that very critical meeting on the night of the Wednesday debate. The Cabinet agreed the way forward with only some dissent from these two colleagues. Perfectly reasonably, they were more cautious than the others.

I had told Margaret that I'd had three weeks without any rest at all and that I intended to fly back home to Cornwall for a day or so. All I wanted to do was to go home to see my wife and our farm! She said she was happy with that, so I went back to the office to sign off some papers with the idea of picking up my bags and flying down to Cornwall. At that moment I was paged and I went to the telephone. I was needed urgently in the Ministry. I went back there. My Private Secretary, David Omand, clearly had had a terrible shock and Terry Lewin came in to see me – they had bad news. In fact, it could not have been worse. We'd had a telephone message from Northwood which indicated that two Wessex helicopters had had a white-out in a Force 11 blizzard and had crashed in South Georgia, probably in the mountains, with their crews aboard. Evidently the SAS, as we subsequently found out, had been caught in a terrible blizzard and the men were beginning to get frostbite and needed lifting off. Clearly the captain had decided the danger of leaving them there was too great, and so in these appalling conditions he despatched two Wessex helicopters. They evidently managed to pick up the crew, but coming off they were hit by this white-out and the helicopters crashed. We knew no more about it.

I said that I thought we should not await a further signal but should immediately inform the PM. Terry Lewin and I went across to No. 10. They had been warned that we had unhappy news. When we got there, Margaret was sitting in the Cabinet Room with her two Private Secretaries and Robert Armstrong. I said I feared that we had some unhappy news to tell her and Terry Lewin then told her what had happened. It was a great shock to all of us. However, just as we were going in to see her, we heard slightly better news, namely that four of the SAS and one aircrew had been picked up by another helicopter. This did at least give us hope. When we got back to the Ministry the news was even better. It seemed that the helicopter had found the other SAS and their crew and, although the helicopters were broken down and smashed up against the mountain, maybe everybody was all right. We then waited to see the latest news. I decided not to hang back and I went to Northolt. I telephoned David Omand from there and he said he had no more news. Evidently ten of them were still on the mountain.

When I arrived at St Mawgan I asked to use the secure line. I got on it to David and we were able to talk. The men were still on South Georgia, but they'd got a helicopter to them and there seemed to be no casualties. In the evening I found out that they had managed to lift them off and abandoned the helicopters on the mountain. When they returned to the ship it was found that they had bad frostbite and were in a poor condition; but nevertheless, that same day members of the Special Boat Squadron had been landed further down the coast, so it was too soon to say that the operation had been aborted. Subsequently I heard that, although we were minus two helicopters which we hoped to pick up later, the force commander had decided not to abandon the assault. The relief was great

– it would have been an appalling situation had our very first operation resulted in loss of life as a result of the crash of a helicopter. One could imagine the sense of dismay at home that some accident of this nature had occurred before we had made contact with the Argentinians.

'Still, it worked out not too badly,' I wrote next morning sitting in the sun in my garden at Trewinnard. 'We have no helicopters and I am worried about how we can get ashore but, basically, the position is infinitely better than it was a few hours ago.' On a more personal note, I added that 'the cattle look fit' and that 'already after three hours at home and one short night I feel better and ready to go again'.

It was around this time that we heard of one of the most tragic accidents of the whole campaign. A helicopter transporting a whole team of the SAS crashed into the sea, and all were lost. It was devastating to lose so many of our most valuable, brave and effective soldiers in such an accident.

After this short break, I returned to London to await the news from South Georgia. It was recaptured without loss of life. Quite late on Sunday evening, the 25th, I went across to No. 10 with a draft statement, as I felt that this first victory should be announced by Margaret, but she was insistent that the task should fall to me. We went out into Downing Street and I read out the agreed statement. I remember the occasion for two reasons.

I had returned from Cornwall on my RAF plane wearing an appalling spiv's suit, which had been made for me by the only tailor in my constituency. It never occurred to me that it would see the light of day; but as soon as I had completed my statement, the large number of assorted hacks and newshounds, accompanied by a huge congregation of cameramen, started shouting questions at me.' What happens next, Mr. Nott? Are we going to declare war on Argentina, Mrs. Thatcher?' To which Margaret replied in a high-pitched voice,' Just rejoice at that news and congratulate our forces and the marines … Rejoice.' Somehow it was highly embarrassing, although she was only trying to get the wretched media to acknowledge our success. We retreated hastily into No. 10.

Second only to my interview – or non-interview – with Robin Day, this incident known as 'Rejoice, Rejoice' was to dog me on the television for the next twenty years. Every time I see it, I cringe at that awful suit and the millions of people around the world who have now been able to judge the quality of Cornish tailoring.

***

In the early stages of the campaign, it had been very much a naval operation, which was sensible. The Chiefs of Staff of the Army and the Air Force were intimately involved through the Defence Operations Executive, but the contributions of the Army and the Air Force, apart from their gallant efforts in helping to get the Fleet to sea and operating the air bridge to Ascension, were limited. The RAF, in particular, was anxious to get involved and sought my political view as to whether a bombing raid on the runway at Port Stanley would be acceptable. I was wholeheartedly in favour. With amazing despatch the RAF equipped all the Hercules, the Victors and the last remaining Vulcan bomber with air-flight refuelling. In retrospect it is amazing what was achieved in a few weeks; it would have taken years of dithering bureaucracy to get anything similar decided and accomplished in times of peace. Another example was to equip the helicopters on the carriers with Searchwater radar, which had been used for years successfully for anti-submarine warfare on Nimrod maritime patrol aircraft; but no one had pressed forward to adapt the same radar for the airborne early warning of approaching aircraft.

The Vulcan practised bombing runs in the Highlands of Scotland and, just three weeks after the Argentine invasion, it set out to bomb the runway at Port Stanley and needed seven tanker aircraft to get it there and back. The impact of the raid was more psychological than real – only one bomb actually hit the runway – but it was an early indication that we meant business. More important was the equipping of the RAF Harriers with air-flight refuelling and, in an utterly remarkable feat of skill and endurance, the RAF pilots flew them down to join the carriers – stopping off only at Dakar and Ascension on the way. I met some of the young RAF pilots before they left, and it was remarkable to see their confidence and courage.

Mitterrand and the French proved useful allies. In earlier years we had equipped the Argentine Navy with our former destroyers, while the French had supplied them with the Mirage and Super-Etendard aircraft. The ships, especially the *Belgrano*, and the aircraft were equipped with modern Exocet missiles. As soon as the conflict began, Hernou, acting on the instructions of Mitterrand, got in touch with me to make available to us a Super-Etendard and Mirage aircraft, so that our Harrier pilots could train against them before setting off to the South Atlantic. The French supplied us with detailed technical information on the Exocet, showing us how to tamper with the missiles.

A remarkable worldwide operation then ensued to prevent further Exocets being bought by Argentina. I authorised our agents to pose as bona fide purchasers of equipment on the international market, ensuring that we outbid the Argentinians, and other agents identified Exocet missiles in various markets and covertly rendered them inoperable, based on information provided by the French. It was a remarkably successful operation. In spite of strenuous efforts by several countries, particularly the Israelis and the South Africans, to help Argentina, we succeeded in intercepting and preventing the supply of further equipment to the Argentinians who were desperately seeking resupply.

I had spoken to Henry Leach at the beginning of the campaign to ask him why he was so determined that the Royal Navy could do the job with so few men. He assured me that this was an amphibious operation suited to the Royal Navy's experience and that the Royal Marine Commando, supplemented by battalions of the Parachute Regiment, was sufficient to meet the objectives of the Task Force.

I did not believe him, although I understood that he wished to make it the Royal Navy's show. It was not my job to interfere. I consulted Dwin Bramall and senior civil servants, and their attitude was that plans would change and that the Navy itself would decide in favour of a back-up force. As I expected, General Bramall came to see me a week or two later to say that the Chiefs of Staff had decided to embark another brigade and wished to requisition the *QE2* to take it there. There ensued an amusing conversation:

Nott:	Who are you intending to send, Dwin?
Bramall:	We will send the 5th Brigade at Aldershot, but as it has lost two parachute battalions which are already part of the Commando Brigade's landing force, I will supplement it by two Guards battalions.
Nott:	Where are the Guards battalions now?
Bramall:	I am taking the Scots Guards and the Welsh Guards off ceremonial duties in London.
Nott:	But how can you do that? They will be hopelessly unfit. Haven't you got other infantry battalions available which are already fit and well trained?
Bramall:	I am sending them this weekend to the Welsh mountains for a period of concentrated battlefield training – they will be fine at the end of it.
Nott:	Oh! Which is the third battalion making up the Brigade strength?
Bramall:	The 7th Gurkhas who are already part of 5th Brigade.
Nott:	Dwin, you can't send the Gurkhas. We are having frightful trouble holding things together in the United

Nations and it is more than likely that the Indians will kick up a frightful fuss. It is just too risky politically to send the Gurkhas in my view.

Bramall: The 7th Gurkhas are part of 5th Brigade, the designated strategic reserve, and if we recoil from sending them now there will always be some reason for not sending the Gurkhas on future operations.

Nott: I agree that point and, as an ex-Gurkha, I would, of course, be mortified if we spoilt their chances.

Bramall: Look, Secretary of State, I am the Colonel of your Regiment [the 2nd Gurkhas], and I am telling you that they must go and I am requiring your support to fight our corner with the Foreign Office.

Nott: If you are instructing me in your capacity as Colonel of the 2nd Gurkhas, then of course, Dwin, I have no option but to obey!

So the matter was settled without more ado. My devil's advocacy had been heard and rightly rejected out of hand. Dwin Bramall was correct to call rank and, since he was the Colonel of my Regiment, I obeyed his instructions. It was nice for me to feel like a junior officer once again.

This anecdote reminds me of my mood in the middle of the crisis whilst the Task Force was still proceeding south. Immediately after the conclusion of the war, Dwin Bramall wrote me a delightful letter, which I quote towards the end of this chapter. In my reply, dated 20 June 1982, I expressed my feelings:

Of all the letters that I have received yours was the most generous and welcome. This is partly because you were just close enough to the centre of the stage [i.e. the War Cabinet] to understand what was happening, but also because you will have understood some of the personality problems and tensions which will always play a key role in such great events. Having had a good 'start' (not a good speech!)

and having helped in the government's initial recovery, I confess that I found the 'middle' weeks very difficult. This was partly because the diplomatic phase saw the PM at her most belligerent and inflexible – and partly because there was so little information coming from the Navy with which to conduct the political and PR campaign. In spite of distance – and the overriding need for commanders to be free of interference – there will always be other (equally) important battles being waged consecutively with the soldiers'/sailors' battle on the ground. I think we need a Staff College session on this subject. Once your magnificent soldiers were ashore – and we had the simple task of winning the war – everything became easier again.

On 30 April the 200-mile maritime exclusion zone, which had first been announced by me in the House of Commons on the 7th, was extended into a total exclusion zone. This made it clear that any ship or aircraft was liable to be attacked if it was carrying supplies or reinforcements for the Argentine forces. There was an additional clause, which was subsequently to become an item of contention, that these measures were 'without prejudice to the right of the UK to take whatever additional measures may be needed in its exercise of the right of self-defence, under Article 51 of the UN Charter'. A week earlier, on the 23rd, a message had been sent to the Argentine government and published internationally. It stated:

> That in this connection (with Article 51) Her Majesty's Government now wishes to make clear that any approach on the part of Argentine warships, including submarines, naval auxiliaries or military aircraft which could amount to a threat to interfere with the mission of British forces in the South Atlantic, will encounter the appropriate response.

This was the very least that we could do – and it is often forgotten that the only reason why *we* had not suffered serious loss of life to the Royal

Marines in the initial assault by Argentinian forces was that, following our receipt of the intercepted Argentine signal to invade, we had instructed the Royal Marines to abandon their barracks at Moody Brook and disperse themselves around the island.

When preparations were made by the Argentine forces on 2 May to make a strike with their carrier-based aircraft against the Task Force, we were aware that a pincer movement was also being organised for the *General Belgrano* and her escorting destroyers to exploit the air strike on the Fleet. We had already given Admiral Woodward rules of engagement, enabling him to attack the Argentine carrier *Veinticinco de Mayo* wherever he found her, inside or outside any exclusion zones; the extension of this right to attack the *Belgrano*, given the clear warnings given, was really not more than a formality. The two nuclear submarines given the task of shadowing the *Veinticinco de Mayo* seemed to have lost her temporarily, but *Conqueror*, the third submarine, was following the *Belgrano*. Terry Lewin asked me whether there would be any political problems in extending the rules of engagement to cover an attack on the *Belgrano*, knowing the grave danger she posed with her Exocet and other armaments to our ships. I agreed that we should attempt to neutralise her.

As it happened, we were due to meet at Chequers on Sunday, 2 May to discuss a range of matters, and Terry Lewin, Margaret Thatcher and I agreed there that we had no option but to agree to an attack on the *Belgrano*. It was one of the easiest decisions of the whole war and was subsequently endorsed by the War Cabinet at its meeting later in the morning.

Next day I received a terse, one-line signal from the Fleet just before I was due to make a statement to the House of Commons. I hardly had time to compose my statement, so I knocked the final version together in the car. My final statement was not seen – and vetted – by officials, as there was no time for this to happen. I remain astonished to this day, although knowing the House of Commons I should not have been, that anyone should consider the momentary compass bearing of the *Belgrano*'s passage to be of any consequence whatever. Any ship can turn about in an instant. She was sunk in international waters in strict conformity with the warnings that we had given – and for us to have taken any other decision, given her threat to the Fleet, would have been a serious dereliction of duty on our part.

I was shocked when I heard of the terrible loss of life that followed, and I regret it deeply, but I fear this was the consequence of a war that we did not initiate. I do not know why the Argentine destroyers did not stay in the area to pick up the survivors – I believe that our ships would have done so. I have no doubt that, although this incident turned international opinion against us, particularly in neutralist-minded Germany and in Argentina's cousin countries Spain and Italy, it did in fact save many British lives. If we had been forced to contend with an aggressive Argentine Navy, as well as the courageous Argentine pilots, things might have been different. As it happened, Admiral Anaya, the most aggressive member of the Argentine junta and more than anyone responsible for the conflict in the first place, decided to keep the Argentine surface fleet in port following the sinking of the *Belgrano*. By neutralising the whole of the Argentine Navy, our decision proved to be correct and fully justified.

Two days after the sinking of the Belgrano, on 4 May, the Argentines attacked HMS *Sheffield* with an Exocet missile. It was the first British naval tragedy of the war. The ship sunk, with some forty casualties, and it was my job to announce this loss to the House of Commons – an unhappy task. The sinking of the *Sheffield* at last brought home to the British public that we really were at war. Because I knew of the hazardous nature of the whole enterprise, I may have been anticipating a disaster more than most.

As the Task Force moved south, plans were being made at Northwood in consultation with Admiral Woodward about the timing and place of the amphibious landing.

I quote from my account soon afterwards of the relevant discussions in Whitehall:

> It was on Tuesday 18 May that one of the most important meetings of the war took place. An informal gathering with the members of the War Cabinet was called, partly at my prompting, to give the Chiefs of Staff collectively an opportunity of setting out to the PM and her colleagues the risks attached to the landing at San Carlos, following the briefing which I had received at Northwood about the place of the landing on 14 May.
>
> I had been anxious throughout the conflict to get the Chiefs of Staff collectively together as often as was reasonably possible without interfering with the day-to-day decision-making process, so that my political colleagues were fully aware of all the problems and risks attached to the decisions that they were taking. We all knew that the actual amphibious landing was the most critical and difficult of all the operations, so the day before the meeting with the War Cabinet we had a rehearsal in my room in the MoD at a long three-hour lunch.
>
> At the meeting, as might have been expected, the Chiefs of Staff could not restrain their enthusiasm for making political comments. Henry Leach implied that our national honour was at stake. Dwin Bramall said the same. Terry Lewin, as usual, kept more or less to the military implications and Michael Beetham concentrated on the air side. The meeting went very well indeed.
>
> Terry Lewin spoke first. He said that it was the unanimous view of the Chiefs of Staff that a long blockade was not feasible. This was supported later by Henry Leach, who said that the rate of attrition from accidents to aircraft, ships and men, if the whole operation were to be extended further, would probably lead to greater loss of life and greater

loss of equipment than if we went forward and conducted the landing at the earliest possible time.

In a way the most striking of all the four presentations by each of the individual Chiefs was that by the Chief of the Air Staff, Sir Michael Beetham. He made the point very graphically that we had not succeeded, as we had hoped, in neutralising the Argentinian Air Force. This point was also confirmed by Bramall, who said that it was an established principle of modern war that a hazardous amphibious landing should not normally take place without air superiority. Both of them agreed that this had not yet been achieved. The Argentinians, said Michael Beetham, had already succeeded in locating our ships; they had clearly solved the problem of how to find out where they were; and, as the task force approached in one group to perform the amphibious landing, they would be even more exposed than up to now and, of course, would bring themselves within easy range of Argentinian land-based aircraft. He pointed out that the Argentinians still had a substantial force of Skyhawks, Mirage and Super-Etendard and that the threat was significant. Some aircraft would be likely to get through our defensive shield. He thought that ships might well be lost, and it was very important in his judgement that the approaching task force should come in at night and limit their exposure-time to the absolute minimum essential. Beetham took the view, as did all the other Chiefs, that the risks were substantial, that a blockade made no sense because of attrition in the appalling weather and conditions of the South Atlantic, that delay was possible but only at the expense of even greater risks; given all the worries that we undoubtedly possessed, he thought we had no political or military option but to move forward as soon as possible to establish a bridgehead and then go ahead to reconquer the islands.

We also discussed at that meeting the threat that existed from the Argentine forces on the land; the lesser threat was from the naval forces, but we believed they had been more or less successfully neutralised since the sinking of the *Belgrano*. There had also been considerable discussion internally in the MoD and at my earlier briefing on 14 May about the danger which still existed from the Argentinian submarines. But the whole tenor of the meeting with the members of the War Cabinet was concern about the dangers from Argentinian aircraft, and there was no doubt that we went into this amphibious landing at San Carlos with our eyes wide open, knowing very well that we were likely to lose ships and men. My own private view at this stage was that we were likely to lose up to five or six ships; and it was vitally important that we spread the troops around as many ships as possible, so that if we lost a ship with all its crew and all its equipment and all its men, at least we would limit the number of casualties and deaths to the absolute minimum. The meeting agreed that we should go ahead with the landing as proposed, leaving the actual timing to the force commanders on the spot.

We were also aware of the pressure that was bound to mount internationally as soon as our troops were ashore. We, as politicians, expressed our collective view to the Chiefs of Staff that the length of time between establishing a landing and total repossession of the islands was a matter of concern to all of us. We thought that international pressures were bound to mount and mount and, therefore, speed was of the essence to this whole operation.

In discussion in the MoD afterwards it was felt that the air threat was probably higher than the Cabinet realised, and there was a general view, which I supported, that colleagues should be told and should realise that we were about to embark on a highly hazardous operation and we needed all the luck that we could get. It was, however, decided because of the vital security aspect of the whole affair not to inform Cabinet colleagues about the date of the landing, although of course all of them were conscious of the fact that this had to be within the foreseeable future.

We did have luck on our side – and with the heroism and skill of the Royal Navy and the Royal Marines, the initial landing took place in darkness on 21 May without a single life lost. The place of landing, San Carlos Water, had been the subject of some concern as the Army, in particular, was worried at its distance (some sixty miles) from the main defensive positions of the Argentines around Port Stanley. There was considerable worry that, if the Argentines counter-attacked our forces, we could get bogged down halfway across the island in winter weather, with international opinion building up against us. This danger was enhanced when the *Atlantic Conveyor*, carrying a huge amount of stores and the crucial troop-carrying Chinook helicopters, was sunk. But the choice of San Carlos proved correct: it had space, some protection from submarine activity, depth of water, accessibility for ships and landing craft and, crucially, a hilly terrain which made it difficult for sea-skimming Exocet attack and low-level bombing. We did lose HMS *Ardent* and *Antelope* in the Sound, and *Coventry* outside it; had not so many of the Argentine bombs failed to explode, our casualties and ship losses could have been much worse. Many ships were hit, but the fuse setting on the bombs was not in conformity with the low-level attacks forced on the Argentine pilots by the hilly terrain and air-defence missiles on ships and shore.

After the conflict was over, I flew down to the Falklands in a Hercules, with the aid of several air-flight refuellings, and I had the privilege of inaugurating the cemetery overlooking San Carlos Water. Whenever I travelled around the world on duty, as Chairman of the Commonwealth War Graves Commission, I visited our war cemeteries and they were always sad and contemplative occasions. But the immediacy of the Falklands conflict – and a beautiful, clear sunny day shining on the beautiful San Carlos Water – made this one of the most moving occasions of my life.

The loss of the *Coventry* created a very unfortunate but not untypical dilemma in the Ministry of Defence. The timing for the announcement of casualties always generated problems, because often we knew that a particular ship had been hit but, understandably in the confusion surrounding such an incident, it was some time before we were aware of casualties. We had an overriding obligation to inform the next of kin before a public announcement, but the Argentinian media with their propaganda broadcasts often forced our hand prematurely.

The day of the *Coventry* disaster (25 May) was one of the worst at sea. It was also the day that we lost the *Atlantic Conveyor*; the Exocet attack by the Argentine Air Force failed to target a carrier, but hit this large and vital converted roll-on roll-off ship instead. Fortunately her Harriers had been flown off just in time before she sunk, with loss of life, including her Captain North.

That evening I was due to make a broadcast on ITN just after the 10 o'clock news, so we gathered in Terry Lewin's room at 9.30 to decide what I should say. There were three admirals – Lewin, Leach and Fieldhouse – and one politician, me. I wanted to announce that *Coventry* had been hit, but the admirals did not want to give specific information away to the Argentinians at that stage. They had a justified operational point. I argued that, in spite of their operational view, it was unwise to talk about the loss of an unnamed ship. However, in the end, I had to defer to their judgement.

I was much criticised for my announcement – as the telephone exchanges were jammed all night by calls from families of the entire Task Force worried about their sons and daughters. My judgement was often wrong, so I could hardly criticise others for taking a different view, and anyway it was my function to take the media flak whether the blame was mine or not.

Another occasion of a similar kind took place soon afterwards in connection with the attack on Goose Green, when we lost Lieutenant Colonel Jones, VC, and a number of his gallant men of the 2nd Battalion, the Parachute Regiment. Colonel Julian Thompson, a Royal Marine who had been in charge of the amphibious landing and had handled it brilliantly, was understandably concerned to consolidate and build his bridgehead at San Carlos. But in London we were in severe trouble both with domestic and international opinion, and it was urgently necessary for our troops to establish early contact with the Argentine forces – it was just as possible for us to lose the war in London as it was to do so on the battlefield of the Falklands. It was a classic case of the military priorities on the ground conflicting with the wider political requirements thousands of miles away. As politicians, we were determined not to interfere with military decisions. Fortunately, Lewin and Fieldhouse understood the dilemma, and Julian Thompson was pressured by them to break out of the bridgehead, perhaps before he would have chosen to do so.

Although it was obvious to the world that British forces were about to move forward, we were shocked in the MoD to read in the newspapers that our troops were about to attack Goose Green. It was a classic case of why we had tried to keep the No. 10 briefing machine as much in the dark as possible. The obsession with unattributable background briefing – what today goes by the name of spin – remains the curse of politics.

Following the ghastly tragedy to the Welsh Guards when *Sir Galahad* was attacked at Bluff Cove, the Argentines believed that our casualties were even worse than those we had sustained. We got in touch with the next of kin but did not release the full casualty list, as the final assault on Port Stanley was about to begin with an attack on Mount Longdon, Two Sisters and Wireless Ridge.

On Saturday 12 June, HMS *Glamorgan* was hit by a missile. The signal from the Fleet simply said, 'HMS *Glamorgan* struck by suspected Exocet missile. Large fire in vicinity of hangar and in gas turbine and gear room. Power still available. Ship making 10 knots to the south.' There were no details of casualties. It was the morning of trooping the colour on Horseguards Parade, so it was not an auspicious start to the day. Meanwhile, back in the Falklands, John Witherow of *The Times* reported:

As the sun climbed into the sky next day the Welsh Guards attempted to get what sleep they could in the open. Colonel Reckitt, lying in his sleeping bag, said that at the moment the Guards should have been at the Queen's Birthday Parade in Horseguards. 'We are celebrating the Queen's Birthday by lying here in the cold. We tuned into the World Service and heard them marching down the Mall.'

I joined Margaret Thatcher on the stand with my young son, William, to watch the parade, and afterwards we adjourned to No. 10 for lunch. Margaret had asked Rex Hunt and his wife, but really made it an occasion to entertain the children of her staff in the large dining room upstairs. I remember David Wolfson and his wife and their children, together with several other youngsters. I asked Margaret who had prepared the lunch. 'Oh, I did,' she said, 'Mary and I stayed up late last night to put a meal together.' I recall it so well because here was the Prime Minister in the middle of a war, provided with no staff whatsoever, and yet she had found time personally to prepare a meal late at night for the children. Her image as a ruthless, uncaring harridan was misplaced; no one took more care of her staff and she was always scrupulous in showing her concern for the health and wellbeing of her friends. It was strange how she could be so cruel and unreasonable to her ministers, but so kind and thoughtful to her immediate circle. Margaret had a warm and generous heart – and yet she presided over an unhappy Cabinet, continuously undermined by gossip and malicious unattributable briefing.

By the end of lunch, Margaret and I had heard that after fierce battles Two Sisters, Mount Longdon and Mount Harriet had been secured. Again, I leave it to John Witherow, who filed this pooled despatch (appearing in the press on 15 June), to describe these battles:

Red tracer bullets lit the night sky and hillsides were engulfed in explosions and sheets of flame as British forces on the Falkland Islands launched their offensive on Port Stanley early on Saturday morning. The attack was made on three fronts at key strategic points, defending access to the capital, and by daylight all the positions had been secured, pushing British troops to within five miles of Port Stanley. The first raid was made by 3 Paratroop battalion on Mount Longdon to the north. They approached Argentine positions stealthily soon after midnight GMT, observing radio silence. As soon as the first clash took place field artillery opened fire, blasting enemy trenches and dugouts.

To the south Royal Marines of 42 Commando seized Mount Harriet after a five-hour battle and then 45 Commando attacked and captured the mist-enshrouded Two Sisters.

It had been the intention to push straight on that night to strike at the well-defended positions on Mount Tumbledown and Mount William; but the troops were tired and more time was needed to bring up ammunition, so it was decided to wait.

In London we knew that everything now rested with our soldiers and sailors. So we all kept strictly to our self-imposed rule not to pester Northwood for news about operations in progress.

On my trip to the Falklands, just after the war, I tramped around the battlefield and spent some time on Tumbledown, which had been taken at night by the Scots Guards in one of the fiercest battles; they were one of the battalions previously on public duties in London. Tumbledown was defended by some of the best Argentine regular troops and on the ground it looked well-nigh impregnable. Nevertheless, with great bravery and skill, the guards managed to get in amongst the trenches at night and fought a hand-to-hand battle with the defending troops. I met some of the wounded guardsmen in Woolwich Military Hospital on my return.

Next door to Mount Tumbledown was Mount William, which saw the final episode of the war just before white flags began to fly over Port Stanley on 14 June. The 7th Gurkhas, to their immense frustration, had been held back by General Moore until this final moment. When the Argentine troops saw the Gurkhas approaching, kukris drawn, they abandoned their positions and fled down the hill into the town.

The war was over.

***

My feelings at this moment of victory were surprising. I just felt an intense sense of relief that it was over. Although I recognised the tremendous achievement of our forces and their leaders – and the courage and determination shown by Margaret Thatcher – personally I felt no sense of triumph. I wanted to sneak away and hide. I knew what the Duke of Wellington had meant when he said that 'nothing except a battle lost can be half so melancholy as a battle won'. Just over a thousand had died on both sides and it all seemed so unnecessary.

Casting around to find something that I might have written at the time which could express my private thoughts, I have come across the copy of a private, handwritten letter that I wrote to Peter Carrington on 28 May, in the middle of the crisis:

I feel very bad about my failure to drop you a line about the tragedy of your resignation. Over the past few (hectic) weeks I have several times sat down to do so, but a series of interruptions has driven it out of my mind ...

I shall always remember that Thursday evening when you returned exhausted from Israel but where you showed immense determination to get the Fleet to sea.

I suppose you must long to be part of it all still – I wish that I could exchange my place for yours. The crisis brings me no pleasure at all. I am hating every minute of it! But we are all trapped by events as is so often the case in politics ...

Yes, I felt a sense of sadness about the waste of it all. Of course I am proud that I played a small part in our victory, but I would rather have been elsewhere. Fame is the spur but fame is an empty chalice. Each generation has to discover that for itself: I had drained the chalice dry.

Victory on the battlefield had been won, but there were a hundred problems still to solve: how to handle the 11,000 Argentinian prisoners; how to accommodate large numbers of our soldiers and airmen in the coming Falklands winter and how to get the majority of them home; how to defend the Falkland Islands in the future when we still faced a major threat to NATO; how to go through a tedious argument with the Treasury about replacing all the ships and equipment that we had lost.

And then there were the victory parades and dinners, the self-congratulatory speeches about our will to resist aggression, and the strengthening of the deterrent posture of the alliance. All true. Great Britain emerged from the Falklands a more self-confident nation. It had taken a quarter of a century to recover our pride after the shambles of Suez. But I did not enjoy the celebrations.

I least of all enjoyed the stupidity of the bishops of the Church of England when arranging the thanksgiving service at St Paul's at the end of July. No one was more in favour of reconciliation with Argentina than I; we could all say prayers privately, if we wished, for the dead and maimed of both sides; but this was a service for the veterans of the war and, in particular, for the families of the British dead. It almost seemed as if our disagreements on the form of worship were more about the Church of England's own war against Margaret Thatcher and her policies than about comforting the families of our dead. Archbishop Runcie had been a brave soldier, but he got drawn into a purposeless argument about the appropriateness of the hymns and prayers. Enough said – the modern Anglican Church is beyond my comprehension. It should be laid to rest alongside the BBC.

As soon as I could decently do so, I went back to Margaret Thatcher in late August and reminded her of my intention to retire from politics. She said she was very surprised that, after the Falklands victory, I did not want to change my mind. My immediate colleagues in the Ministry of Defence were equally surprised when I told them that I had informed her as far back as the previous December of my intention to retire from politics. I was keen to step down straight away, because I thought that my successor should have a reasonable period to acclimatise himself before the general election – and I knew that as the deployment of US Cruise missiles in Europe was imminent, nuclear policy would be a major source of controversy during the campaign.

My preference was for joint control of these weapons. 'John Nott before he left his post as Defence Secretary had been attracted by the dual-key option', Margaret Thatcher correctly notes in her memoirs. 'But neither Michael Heseltine, his successor, nor I shared his view.' It was another reason to make the change in time. Our policy had to be decided. However, Margaret insisted that I stay on to conduct a review of the lessons arising from the Falklands campaign, which we published (as Cmnd. 8758) a few weeks before I eventually stepped down from the MoD four months later at the end of December.

I have often wondered since whether it could have ever happened thus if the Prime Minister had been a man. In her relationships with a male-dominated Cabinet – and one that had traditional attitudes to the place of women in society – she often behaved in ways that would have been unacceptable for any man. Above all, she had a woman's courage. A different kind of courage from a man's.

She really did believe that men were 'wet', and particularly the species called 'gentlemen'. Of all the men that I knew in my time in politics, I cannot think of any who would not have sought an honourable settlement. I am sure that Margaret never meant to do so, but she went along with the diplomatic game because to 'win' she had to do so. In my letter I said that her approach was instinctive, 'so very unmasculine'. She was confronted with a crisis for her government and she shut her mind to the risks of conducting such an adventure 8000 miles away. Of course, it is always easier to be in charge; to be leader if you have it in you, rather than to be the staff officers who make it happen. But, in the last resort, it was a woman's war – and the woman in her won.

†††

I said in this extract from my memoir that I did not enjoy the celebrations of our victory. Sometimes they felt a little too triumphant. It was a little like Margaret Thatcher's exclamation on the steps of Downing Street, with me standing slightly embarrassed next to her, when she ordered the assembled press to 'Rejoice, Rejoice' following our capture of South Georgia. Well, she deserved a little bit of rejoicing, it had been something of a cliff-hanger on the way.

But now, according to the newspapers, I shall be asked to go through the celebrations again in June this year. Oh dear! But of course, I wouldn't have produced this chapter were I not proud of what was achieved.

I shall enjoy observing the comradeship of the participants; it will be great to get the veterans together. Most of them had a very nasty time. War is ugly. Although I began life as a regular soldier and participated in a sort of war myself, I have no martial qualities or inclinations. I admire seeing it in others, but it is not for me.

Assuming that I am invited, I shall do my duty and attend the Thanksgiving Services, dinners and the marches. But I shall have to steel myself against the feeling, quite unjustified I'm sure, that I was in part responsible for so many dead and wounded and disabled. Chance dictated that I happened to be where I was, when all this happened.

And if the reader has the stamina to read this book to the bitter end, he or she will find that I do not agree with a strategy which equips our forces to fight this kind of war again. I think what is now called 'expeditionary warfare' is a nonsense – that is not to say that I would abandon the Falkland Islanders to their fate. I would not. We must defend them as best we can.

But our first duty is to defend our own countrymen here at home against the terrorist and we are ill-equipped to do so. Major changes in attitude and strategy are needed for the future. Will they happen? I rather doubt it. Institutional prejudices are very strong.

HMS Hermes – Sunday 4 April 1983

Dawn, 21 May 1983 – first men ashore on the Falkland Islands

Admiral Fieldhouse in London during the campaign

Return of the QE2

Above and below
Inauguration of the cemetery, San Carlos Water – a sad occasion

The Falklands Memorial Dinner – No 10 Downing Street – front row, from left

Parsons, Woodward, Fieldhouse, Bramall, Parkinson, Whitelaw, Lewin, Prime Minister, Lord Mayor, Nott, Havers, Leach, Beetham, Moore, Henderson

"TIME IS GETTING SHORT — AND "WE ARE DOING EVERYTHING TO SEEK A NEGOTIATED SOLUTION""

The Daily Telegraph, March 1982

The Sun, April 1982

AFGHANISTAN
1839–42

'Mark my words, there will be a signal catastrophe in Afghanistan'

(General Keane on his departure for England, 1839)

TROOPSHIP TO INDIA

Charles Nott was born in 1753 on the family farm at Shobdon in Herefordshire. He was the second son and left home to seek his fortune. As a young boy, he travelled to London where a richer branch of the family lived. The *Dictionary of National Biography* says of Roger, the father of Sir Thomas Nott, a Royalist, that he 'was a wealthy citizen of London who suffered much for his loyalty in the Civil War'. Charles Nott met a young lady from Norfolk, Miss Bailey, and married her in the church of St Andrew's, Holborn. He stayed in London for a time, but he was a farmer's son and enjoyed a reputation as an agriculturist. So he left London, probably in the 1770s, and farmed in several places in Wales, including Neath and Cowbridge, where his sons went to the local grammar school. He finally arrived in Carmarthen and rented a series of farms from Lord Cawdor, then the greatest landowner in South Wales.

Charles Nott was something of an entrepreneur and towards the end of the eighteenth century he bought the Ivy Bush Inn. As the first coaching inn on the road to London from the Irish ferry at Fishguard, the Ivy Bush was an astute purchase. (It is now the leading hotel in Carmarthen.) Moreover, not only was Charles a prosperous farmer and innkeeper, but he was also a mail contractor – one of the most profitable occupations before the coming of the Penny Post. To post a letter from Carmarthen to London in those days cost 12d, equivalent to about £10 in today's money, and the charge for a pair of horses to travel from five to twenty miles was between 20d and 30d. A traveller, 'Mr. M.', recorded in his diary a visit to Carmarthen with his wife and son. It was at the time of the French Wars:

Monday, 7 September 1801

We drove to the Ivy-bush Inn, a very ancient built house, with oak stairs and floors to the rooms rubbed brown, but good accommodations and civil people; indeed Mr.. Nott, the master, appears to be far above the common rank of Inn-holders in Wales. He possesses a very large farm about a mile from the town, and undoubtedly has the best Chaises and Horses in the country.

While dinner was preparing we surveyed the town, which is considered as the principal one of South Wales. It is well supplied with everything, the shops are good and well furnished, and plenty seems to abound.

The streets were full of soldiers, the Cardigan Militia were quartered here and the Carmarthen Fencibles. The 'Bush' alone had 35 privates and 5 Officers quartered there.

After agreeing with Mr.. Nott for a chaise for a few days to be ready in the morning, we retired to rest. Our berths were not of the first-rate, but we slept well, having long since got the better of being over nice…

Monday, 14 September 1801

A fine grey morning, we were ready to set off at 7 o'clock. Mr.. Nott was already risen, and had prepared tea with us, which he refused to charge for, indeed the attention and polite behaviour of this gentleman and his family, the superiority of his horses and carriages, the skilfulness and civility of his drivers entitle him to that preference which he so eminently receives.

In a stout, well-built chaise, and four fine horses, we set off for Aberystwyth, a journey of 50 miles, to be performed in one day, and with the same poor animals – we dreaded the very idea, but Mr.. Nott assured us the horses would go through it with ease …

Charles Nott of Carmarthen had several sons. His youngest son William, my great-great-great-grandfather, was born in January 1783. 'I frequently fancy that if it had been my fortune to have received a proper education', he would write many years later of his childhood, 'I should have been exalted and conspicuous among the John Bulls. I never received any schooling, but what my own fist knocked into my own dull head after I left our fatherland.'

William helped his father in his farming operations and inherited the paternal attachment to agriculture, which he retained to the day of his death. He used to boast, when he had reached high military rank, that he had often guided the plough. By the time that William approached his fourteenth birthday, the French were planning an invasion of England. His devoted Victorian biographer, J. H. Stocqueler, memorably describes the atmosphere:

> The whole country was inspired with military fervour; every boy girded on a sword, and longed to confront the enemy; even mercantile London forgot the vulgar selfishness of commerce in the chivalry of the moment, and not only gave her money but formed her citizens into urban soldiery to oppose the French regicides. But it was in Wales that the fire of patriotism burnt with the most intense brilliancy. The hardy Cambrians could not forget, in the ruins of castles scattered over the principality, how the land had once groaned under Norman tyranny and feudalism, and they dreaded a repetition of scenes which had prostrated their daring ancestors

Well over a thousand Frenchmen landed at Fishguard on 22 February 1797 and for several days held possession of the town, while the remaining invasion force stayed offshore waiting to land. The Pembroke Fencibles, the Cardiganshire Militia, the Fishguard and Newport Principals, and the Cawdor Yeomanry headed for Fishguard. 'Lord Cawdor, commander of the Pembroke Yeomanry, was summoned from dinner to be told that the French had landed,' was how one later account put it:

He hastened across the county with a makeshift militia armed largely with scythes and pitchforks to meet some 1500 equally makeshift Frenchmen, half of them released from Paris jails for the occasion and almost all of them completely drunk on brandy looted from a wreck. The heroic yeomanry had no trouble rounding up the sozzled invaders, who according to legend had been reduced to a state of abject terror by Welsh women in scarlet cloaks dodging among the rocks to look like redcoats. To this day the yeomanry bear on their cap badges the proud legend 'Fishguard' – the only domestic battle honour earned by any British regiment.

Foremost of the counties in arming to resist invasion was Carmarthenshire, where a volunteer corps was formed. William Nott, 'sharing to a great degree in the general enthusiasm', enrolled as a member in 1798, 'tho he was but a boy of 15'. And often in later years he 'laughably told the tale of this his first and bloodless campaign; what heroes he and several of his companions thought themselves as they marched back from the scene of their first military essay into their head-quarters in Carmarthen'. Indeed, these brief days of military glory determined his destiny. 'Having once imbibed a military atmosphere, nothing could or would content his soul but a commission in the army.'

Happily, commissions at this time were much more easily obtained than in the nineteenth century, and William's elder brothers were granted commissions in the Royal Army; William, by contrast, secured a Bengal cadetship of the East India Company. Subsequently, throughout his military service he would display much fury at the patronage granted to the officers of the Royal Army over the more experienced officers of the East India Company. His attitude might have been different if he had taken a commission in the Royal Army himself.

***

We cannot really conceive today when we fly around the world in comfort – or visit exotic places in a luxury cruise ship – that travelling at the end of the eighteenth century was hazardous in the extreme. The voyage to India was dangerous and a significant number of the 'Indiamen' foundered in storms or on the rocks. William Nott was ordered to join the *Kent*, which sailed from Torquay in March 1800. The *Kent* was accompanied by the *Queen*. Indiamen in those days were convoyed or accompanied by an armed escort in case they met French privateers in the Indian Ocean. It was the time of the Napoleonic Wars.

This same ship, the *Kent*, met with disaster some twenty-five years later on 1 March 1825 when carrying Her Majesty's 31st Foot. She caught fire in the Bay of Biscay and exploded. The captain and 139 of the crew perished. However, some three hundred men of the 31st Regiment were saved, together with forty-six of the Regiment's wives and forty-two children. 'The soldiers behaved with their customary bravery, put the children on their backs and swam with them to the boats.'

As a twenty-year-old Gurkha subaltern I sailed from Portsmouth to Singapore on one of the few remaining troopships in 1953. Nothing much had changed in the intervening two hundred years when it came to keeping order, discipline and cleanliness on board, except that we were not accompanied by live animals for food.

In the eighteenth century most Indiamen stopped off for a period at the Cape where officers and cadets were allowed ashore but the soldiers were normally confined to the ship as there was a strong possibility that they would get drunk and desert. After the squalor of life in England and the horrors of the voyage, the Cape offered a life of abundant food and pleasure. Why go on to India with its intolerable heat, forced marches, endless tedium and vicious battles, with only fame as compensation?

Sometimes when the weather was favourable, to much distress among the passengers, the captain passed the Cape into the Indian Ocean seeking anchorage in the Islands. There the ships were approached by swarms of local boatmen selling fruit, fresh meat and eggs, saying 'Englishman man very good man, drinkee de punch, fire de gun, beatee de French, very good fun'. And they were right; at the time of William Nott's voyage, the passengers lived in considerable terror of the approach of French privateers.

It is time to return to William Nott's voyage on the Kent in 1800.

After crossing the Equator, tempestuous weather drove the *Kent* and the *Queen* on to the coast of South America where they were detained to make repairs at St Jago. Whilst there, the *Queen* 'took fire' and burned to the water's edge. Her passengers were transferred to the *Kent*. Hugely overcrowded, stinking below decks with soldiery, live animals and luggage, the *Kent* eventually entered the Bay of Bengal.

The war with France was raging fiercely and the French fleets congregated in Mauritius where they carried on predatory warfare against English commerce on the Eastern seas, capturing from first to last not less than £2 millions worth of the property of the British and Indian merchants living under our flag.

The *Kent*, overcrowded with the passengers of the *Queen*, 'did not escape the buccaneers'. Sourcoff, who commanded the French privateer, attacked the Indiaman and although the *Kent* put up a stout resistance she was boarded by the Frenchman. 'Young Nott did his part gallantly, but received a severe wound from a boarding pike. Sourcoff then completing his capture transferred all the prisoners to an Arab vessel.'

The French had nowhere to send their captives; their ports were often in the hands of the English and their allies were unreliable. One privateer captain sent hundreds of prisoners to safe custody with Tippoo Sultan who, in spite of his promises to the French, treated them with great cruelty; among his strange ways was to wake up suddenly in the morning and issue orders for the forcible circumcision of all his male English prisoners! William Nott was first transferred to disreputable pirates in Sumatra where he and the other English passengers were then re-embarked on the Arab vessel for Calcutta.

The miseries endured on the Arab vessel, William Nott often described as the most fearful that it had ever been his lot to witness. The vessel was crowded to suffocation after the loss of the *Queen* and to this was added the crew of the Arab. Among the prisoners of the French privateer were many wounded and several ladies: 'the latter divested themselves of all the linen which they wore to bind up the wounds of the sufferers'. The ration of water was but half a wine glass each and this misery lasted for weeks. William Nott landed in utter destitution, sick and suffering. But his passage to India, although eventful, was not untypical of the hazards of this voyage. The journey from England had taken nearly six months.

After long months on board, it was a delight to reach Calcutta, if the ship avoided the hazards of the mudflats in the Hoogly River. By 1800 Calcutta had developed into the rich, thriving capital of the East India Company. But in one respect it had not much changed since Clive's day. He described it as 'one of the most wicked Places in the Universe. Corruption, licentiousness and a want of Principle seems to have possessed the minds of the Civil Servants.'

A little later a Mrs. Sherwood described 'the splendid sloth and the languid debauchery of European society in those days – English gentlemen overwhelmed with the consequences of extravagance, hampered by Hindoo women and by crowds of olive-coloured children' in utter destitution. Lord Macaulay described a character in a play called *The Nabob* as: 'An Anglo-Indian chief, dissolute, ugly and tyrannical, ashamed of the humble friends of his youth, hating the aristocracy yet childishly eager to be numbered among them, squandering his wealth on pandars and flatterers, and astounding the ignorant with jargon about rupees, lacs and jaghires.'

Fortunes were made in a few years and lost in a night at cards. An Army chaplain who had looked forward to a pleasant evening at cards was irritated when he had to postpone his game 'because he had a damned soldier to bury'.

Immediately on William Nott's arrival in Calcutta, sick and penniless, he was appointed an Ensign on 28 August 1800 and was at once posted to the Bengal European Regiment stationed outside Calcutta. He became an enthusiastic and happy officer.

THE MARCH TO KANDAHAR AND KABUL

In the next thirty-six years William Nott led the life of an Indian Army officer, marrying and fathering fourteen children; only four survived him. The boys were sent back to England for their education. He was a great letter writer; in particular, one of his many letters back home to his sons William and Charles is worth recording. It is a classic of its kind:

I hope I shall find that you have made great progress in learning. I should be sadly disappointed indeed were I to find it otherwise, as my best and fondest hopes of happiness depend upon the knowledge of my boys.

I have requested your uncle to send you immediately to some public school, which will probably be Eton, where I fully trust your conduct will be such as I could wish and that you will be conspicuous for your attention to the precepts of your learned teachers, and for your honourable and gentlemanly behaviour.

I am depriving myself of many comforts to enable me to see you well educated; but I shall feel myself amply, nobly repaid, if your conduct equals my fond expectation.

I trust you will be particularly careful in forming acquaintances while at Eton. Always bear in mind that virtuous poverty is far preferable to titled vice and indolence. Not that you may meet with those among the rich and great, who are possessed of every good and desirable quality; however, never lose sight of the old proverb – *noscitur a sociis* [the people you associate with]. It is not easy to get rid of evil companions where an intimacy has once subsisted with gay and dissolute young men. I would therefore have you be cautious in forming friendships.

Never allow the supercilious smile of the idle and superficial, or the loud laugh of the ignorant, to lead you, even for a moment, from the path of learning, honour, truth, and virtue; the pride of the supercilious is even beneath contempt, and the loud laugh of the presumptuously ignorant will meet with self-punishment. But though you will meet with many such characters, you will also find every good principle and disposition combined in others, whose acquaintance will confer honour, and whose friendship I would have you cultivate …

You must be great tall fellows by this time; your mother and myself anxiously look forward to the period of meeting. Farewell my much loved boys. Your mother joins in love to all. Write to me frequently, and tell me all you see and think.

He was still in India when in 1836 the new Governor-General, Lord Auckland, arrived to take up his post. One of Auckland's earliest moves was to seek to establish commercial relations with Afghanistan. The background was briefly this: the time had arrived when it was clear that the East India Company must sooner or later establish closer commercial and political relations with Afghanistan and the surrounding states in Central Asia and, to this end, create an understanding with these neighbouring powers. These considerations led to the employment of Captain Burnes upon a long-contemplated commercial mission to Afghanistan in 1836. Burnes had not been long at Kabul before he discovered that the Russians were at work to persuade Dost Mohammed, the Emir, to form an alliance with Persia.

Subsequently, from November 1837 to September 1838, a powerful Persian army laid siege to Herat – traditionally regarded as the key to India, because it stands on the high road between Afghanistan and Persia. Moreover, the Shah of Persia made it clear that it was not his intention to let his Eastern conquests stop short at the possession of the city of Herat. He claimed also the principalities of Kabul and Kandahar.

These developments aroused great alarm in both India and England, with Russia being seen as the instigator and as likely to reap the benefit of any gains made by the Persians. Palmerston, then Foreign Secretary, took the robust view that urgent measures were needed to nip in the bud such dangerous schemes. The British press likewise advocated prompt intervention, as innumerable pamphlets revealed Russia's planned encroachment and declared that the invasion of India was the eventual objective.

Palmerston decided that the best way to resist Russian designs was to counter a pro-Russian ruler in Persia with a pro-British ruler in Afghanistan. Burnes' report had cast great doubt on the motives and interests of Dost Mohammed. Even before Auckland's departure for India the Court of Directors of the East India Company had met and given instructions to him that 'he was to judge as to what steps it may be proper and desirable for you to take to ... counteract the progress of Russian influence in a quarter from which its proximity to our Indian possessions could not fail, if it were once established, to act injuriously to the system of our Indian alliances and possibly even to interfere with the tranquillity of our own territory.'

Auckland met in Simla, the summer residence of the Governor-General, to consider his course of action. It was proposed to form a close alliance with Ranjit Singh, 'the Lion of the Punjab' and a good friend of the British in India, and march with him and his troops through the Kyber Pass to Kabul, placing Shah Suja, the previous ruler of Afghanistan, back on the throne in the place of Dost Mohammed. It seemed a good scheme not least because Ranjit Singh had been at war already with the brother of Dost Mohammed and had taken the fertile province of Peshawar from the Afghans. In fact, Ranjit Singh later decided against participation with the British, which meant that an invading army would have to take a far longer route to Kabul, north via the Bolan Pass and then, passing through

Kandahar, march past the Afghan stronghold of Ghuznee, thought to be an almost impregnable fortress on the route.

Although the plan had the strong support of Sir William Macnaghten, the influential Secretary to the Political Department in Calcutta, it was strongly resisted by the Commander-in-Chief, General Sir Henry Fane. Back in London, the Duke of Wellington also strongly opposed military intervention in Afghanistan. Fane warned against 'such a wild and unmeasured expedition'. Even if an initial invasion were successful, argued Fane, it would be next to impossible to maintain large bodies of troops in countries so distant, and which hardly produced sufficient food for a very 'scanty population'. In the event, that the Governor-General was determined on his plan, Fane advised on 'as large a force as possible' to be drawn from both the Bengal and Bombay Presidencies. It was to consist of six regiments of cavalry, eighteen of infantry, two brigades of artillery and supporting units.

Have we not heard of all this since!

The numbers were subsequently reduced but the so-called 'Army of the Indus' was to comprise 10,000 fighting men, with a huge baggage train on 30,000 camels and as always with the movement of Indian troops, some 40,000 camp followers. A logistic nightmare. Nott would not have disagreed with the views of his biographer: 'The movements and establishments of the Persians under Xerxes and Darius were here repeated upon at least the same scale.'

In the Falklands campaign the logistics of getting 100,000 men and women across 8000 miles of ocean and into an environment as unpredictable as the mountains of Afghanistan caused me some initial concern. In retrospect, however, the journey of the Task Force was more predictable than the march across India to Kabul.

Whereas the Task Force was embarked with sufficient rations, weapons and ammunition at least to see the troops ashore, the Army of the Indus was dependent on local forage for the cavalry and for the

30,000 camels of the baggage train. At least 45,000 of the infantry and the vast contingent of camp followers marched on foot – and for hundreds of miles through deserts and mountains where water and local supplies were scarce. In London, during the passage of the Task Force we were concerned with the presence of Argentinian submarines, the ability of aircraft from the Argentine carrier to strike at our ships, and the danger from Exocets on the *Belgrano*; the Army of the Indus was equally threatened by armed robbers who mercilessly attached themselves to the camp followers and baggage train.

Armed robbery was a profession carried on throughout the width and breadth of India. Only a proportion of the letters and dispatches ever reached their destination, as the letter carriers, the 'dawks', frequently came to a nasty end. Sitting in London, I cursed at the scarcity of information coming from the Task Force with which to feed the ravenous appetite of the world's press but at least information eventually arrived back home, and often via Argentinian propaganda so well disseminated by the BBC!

'It is difficult to convey a notion of the enthusiasm which pervaded the Indian Army when it became known [in August 1838] that a force was to be assembled in the northwest', Nott's biographer would write. The Army had been long inactive – indeed, the officers had almost degenerated into 'mere pleasure seekers, or carping critics at the measures of the government'. However, he went on:

> The faintest sound of the war-trumpet produced a magical change in their feelings. To fight with any power which had braved the British flag was agreeable, but to contend at the head of sepoys against the European cohorts of the Czar in regions beyond the Indus, was an honour so rare and unexpected, and was fraught with so much promise of distinction and advancement, that not a soldier in the whole length and breadth of India could for a moment tolerate the idea of being left behind.

It was decided that a considerable force should ascend the Indus from Bombay under the command of Lieutenant-General Sir John Keane; and that this force would form a junction with the Bengal detachment on the River Indus. Until then the command of the Bengal Army devolved upon Major-General Sir Willoughby Cotton, and that of the First Division of the Army of Indus upon Major-General Nott.

The officers regarded the expedition as little other than an extensive pleasure promenade – an enormous picnic. One officer even boasted that his mess had 'two camel loads of the best manillas', and in general scant attention was paid to the instruction to commanding officers to 'move disencumbered of every article of baggage which could, without compromising the efficiency of the corps, be dispensed with'. In Stocqueler's scornful words again:

> Jams, pickles, cheroots, potted fish, hermetically-sealed meats, plate, glass, crockery, wax-candles, table linen, &c., were all deemed indispensable to the 'efficiency of a corps'. Many young officers would as soon have thought of leaving behind them their swords and double-barrelled pistols as march without their dressing-cases, their perfumes, Windsor soap, and eau-de-cologne.

Letters from William Nott to his daughters back in Calcutta are interesting to show his mood at the outset of this great adventure. At this juncture, he did not bother himself with politics like his superior General Fane – that was to come later.

On 25 October 1838 he wrote:

> Marched to Barota, ten miles. The road covered with troops, guns, gun-carriages, ammunition and treasure. It required patience in man and horse to wend their way between these hackeries and implements

of war. When will man cease to destroy his fellow-man? Passed a miserable day in thinking of times gone by, and those I dearly love…

And on 25 November 1838:

I shall march my column into Ferozepore the day after to-morrow. We have a thousand reports in camp, but it would be useless my repeating them to you, and my time is so fully employed that I have no time to spare. I have been very lucky in bringing this large column thus far without a single casualty, either European or native, since we left Kurnaul, and without a complaint. Men and officers are in high spirits. I understand this has not been the case with the first brigade, and that disputes between Brigadier Sale and commanders of corps have been so high as to cause references to superior authority. It is now, I believe, certain that the Commander-in-Chief goes home immediately, and that only *part* of the force is to go to Caubul. I hear that great intriguing and manoeuvring, and disputes between the Government and Commander-in-Chief are going on, as to what officers and what corps are to go, and who to remain behind. As I have not a particle of interest, I suppose I shall be thrown overboard as mere lumber. Well, perhaps they will do right, and I care not … The Commander-in-Chief is fighting to give his friend S____ a higher command, at least this is the report.

I like the Buffs, both officers and men, very much. I was six hours on horseback yesterday. I have had so many people in my tent, that it is too late to write more, or send my letter to-day.

Notwithstanding all this superfluous baggage, few problems were experienced in the early stages of the march across India. By the end of February 1839, however, the original enthusiasm had waned: provisions were beginning to get scarce in camp, camels had dropped on the road, and their loads were necessarily left prey to marauders and followers who hung about the line of march.

As time wore on, things got worse and worse. Nott's biographer gave the situation the full treatment:

> The annals of the British campaigns in India, or indeed in any other part of the world, do not furnish a parallel to the miseries and losses experienced by the unopposed 'Army of the Indus'. The marches lay through extensive sandy deserts and dry jungles; the water was everywhere extremely scarce, and such as was obtained was muddy, brackish, stagnant, poisonous; forage was obtained with great difficulty; the camels died by fifties and hundreds; the Baluchi mountaineers plundered at every opportunity, assassinating stragglers and bearing off their burthens; the sun was powerful, the glare distressing; communication with the rear was seriously interrupted, for the marauding propensities of the Scinde robbers extended to the dawks, and not one letter in a dozen ever reached its destination.

Nott himself reported at one stage that 'the 4th Brigade alone has lost during the last four days 244 camels by death – namely starved', and that 'my horses have not had a blade of grass or any forage for four days'. Finally, on 6 April, General Sir John Keane with the Bombay column joined up at Quetta with the Bengal column, and new arrangements were made for command

At this point, it is worth recording a passage in a book, *The Choice of a Profession*, published in 1857. The author had this to say of the Army of the East India Company:

> This splendid army, great in emoluments, and eminent in services, though looked down upon by the Queen's officers, can afford to hold its own, both on the ground of the magnificent empire it has won and keeps for Britain, and the high character and military talents of its officers ... The supercilious Queen's officer, whilst affecting to despise the servants of the Company, is forgetting his early training in London drawing rooms, and has few opportunities of showing his superiority

to his fighting brother of the Company, except in blackballing him at his club. At the same time the Company's officer is winning empires in the East, and enjoying a hearty grumble that an ancient professional jealousy excludes him from general command.

Now, in spring 1839, General Nott saw once again the Queen's officers being placed above those of the Company Army, and he resolved to seek an interview with Sir John Keane, the Commander of the Army and well known for his rough tongue. 'Your Excellency is aware,' began Nott, 'that the column about to advance is composed almost entirely of Bengal troops; that in this column there will be no less than four of Her Majesty's General Officers, but not one Company's, unless I am to go.' There ensued a fierce argument on this score, prompting Keane to say to Nott: 'Your conduct, for an officer of your rank, is very extraordinary – the most extraordinary I have ever heard of.' The encounter (described by Nott to his son Charles) ended without any meeting of minds:

> 'General Nott, I see clearly that nothing that I can say will convince you.' 'No, your Excellency, nothing that you have said on this subject can convince me.' 'You insult my authority.' 'I am not aware that I have; what I have said is my deliberate judgment, which nothing can change.' After much more debate, warm on his part, cool on mine, I said, rising to retire: 'Well, your Excellency, I trust that I have left no ill impression upon your mind. I see the whole affair; I am to be sacrificed because I happen to be senior to the Queen's officers.' 'Ill impression, Sir! I will never forget your conduct as long as I live!' 'Oh! your Excellency, since that is the case, I have only to wish you a very good evening.'

With all these black marks against his name, it was hardly surprising that General Nott's protests were of no avail. He was left behind in Quetta in charge of a brigade, and General Keane marched towards Kandahar and onwards to Kabul with the bulk of the army. It arrived outside the walls of Kabul on 6 August 1839. There, Shah Sujah – the British choice – was put on the throne by force in the place of Dost Mohammed. It was to prove, as it does today, that outsiders cannot impose their choice of government upon the Afghan people.

There were no signs of welcome for the invading army and the inhabitants of Kabul looked on with 'the most complete indifference'. As Shah Sujah rode in, Macnaghten (the appointed Envoy to Kabul) and Burnes (the appointed Resident) rode alongside him in the full fig of the diplomatic service. Their resplendent uniform comprised 'a cocked hat fringed with ostrich feathers, a blue frock coat with raised buttons, richly embroidered on the collar and cuffs, epaulettes not yielding in splendour to those of a field marshal, and trowsers edged with very broad gold lace'. Such are still the pretensions of our envoys living in fine palaces around the world, in spite of the reduced circumstances of our country. On this occasion the British in their finery quite outshone the Shah, and only a prophet could have known that it would not be long before both Macnaghten and Burnes would be hacked to death and hung in pieces around the walls of Kabul.

General Keane's arrival in Kabul was greeted as a triumph back in England. Keane was made a baron and, with a neat sense of timing, retired to England. He handed over command to General Cotton, who was subsequently succeeded by General Elphinstone. As Keane departed for India and England, he famously said: 'Mark my words, there will be a signal catastrophe in Afghanistan.' Was he, by any chance, prophesying events in 2007–8?

***

The appointment of General Elphinstone proved to be a disaster – and led to one of the most shameful episodes in the annals of the British

Empire, namely the slaughter by the Afghans of the entire retreating, 17,000-strong British Army. Elphinstone's qualifications for the post were slender; he was a sick man and did not want the job. But according to a contemporary, he was of 'good repute, gentlemanly manners and aristocratic connexions', and certainly he was loved by his men. He had last seen service on the field of Waterloo, a quarter of a century before. Emily Eden (the sister of Lord Auckland, the Governor-General) said of 'Elphy Bey', as she called him, that he was 'in a shocking state of gout, poor man. One arm in a sling and very lame. He cannot, of course, speak a word of Hindoostanee.' General Nott, always prone to cause the greatest offence, simply said of him that he was 'the most incompetent soldier that was to be found among the officers of the requisite rank'.

The British Army of 'Occupation' in Kabul, having placed the hated Shah Sujah on the throne, settled down to turn Kabul into yet another little England. The wives arrived, always a fatal turn of events in India, and 'gave themselves great airs', with 'snobbery and catty behaviour much in evidence'. It was, after all, the earlier arrival of the British memsahib in India that had divided the conquering British men from their Indian wives and mistresses, setting up the racial distinctions and barriers which survived right through until the departure of the British at Indian independence in 1947.

Slowly the English began to find the place endurable. The fine climate braced and exhilarated them. They rode races, they played cricket, they got up dramatic entertainments, they went out fishing, they went out shooting. When the winter fell upon them, to the infinite astonishment of the Afghans they skimmed over the smooth surfaces on their skates. But all was not well. 'There are truths which must be spoken,' one account soon afterwards frankly conceded. 'The temptations which are most difficult to withstand, were not withstood by our English officers. The attractions of the women of Kabul they did not know how to resist – and the Afghans were very jealous of the honour of their women.'

The fire of rebellion rose amongst the Afghans and the flames spread with amazing rapidity: 'The sword of numerous tribes was unsheathed, and every European and all who served with them – every spot they occupied – was threatened.'

By November 1841 Kabul was in turmoil. Burnes, eagerly waiting to inherit the post of Envoy from Macnaghten, was murdered. The British retreated to the military cantonments outside the walls, where Elphinstone's physical condition was rapidly deteriorating. He dithered, and under the urging of the appeasing diplomat, Macnaghten, refused to take firm action against the insurgent rebels.

Writing to his daughter at the start of November, General Nott had already given his opinion of the cause of the incipient disaster at Kabul:

> This country is in a sad state. Sir William Macnaghten's mistakes and weak system begin to tell most woefully; it must be changed, or we must walk out of this world. Lord Auckland should long ago have placed all power here, civil and military, in the hands of a General Officer, who would have used it humanely, honourably, but when needed, roughly, and even sternly. Half measures will not do here, among an indignant, half-civilized race, who have had a hated King forced upon them … Macnaghten and General Elphinstone have made a pretty mess of it; and what is worse, the moral influence of their doings is fast extending over the whole country from Persia to the Attoch.

The disaster that duly befell Elphinstone in Kabul was recorded with due solemnity by Nott's biographer:

> Capitulating to the Afghans, the troops commanded by General Elphinstone evacuated Kabul under a pledge of *sauf conduit* … The snow covered the ground, the officers and soldiers were depressed, half-starved, ill-clothed and badly supplied with ammunition; the Afghans, the Ghazees, the Morrunds, the Ghilzies, accompanied them into the passes; here the treachery of the tribes disclosed itself

in fearful colours. From the heights, where thousands of Afghans were assembled, a deadly fusillade was poured upon the columns, and bodies of furious horsemen charged them in the defiles, and blocked up their passage. Bravely and desperately they fought in spite of bad leadership; but numbers, the snow, and their disorganized condition, were against them ... The savage hordes were unremitting in their attacks, nothing could slake their thirst for the blood of the infidels. For three or four days the contest continued, and only terminated with the massacre of some 17,000 officers, soldiers and followers; 150 were made prisoners, including several ladies and children, and only one man, a Dr Bryden, escaped during the conflict to tell the piteous tale ...

This account almost understates the horrors of the retreat from Kabul in the days after 6 January 1842, and the treachery of the Afghan chief, Akbar Khan (the son of Dost Mohammed), who had promised them safe conduct.

When the news from Afghanistan reached India, each instalment was more calamitous than the last. Auckland was appalled. As his period of office drew to a close and he prepared to hand over to Lord Ellenborough, his successor, his whole policy of resisting the incursion of the Persians and Russians into India, through Afghanistan, lay in tatters. Back in London, the dismay and panic was even worse. The 'I told you so' brigade, led by the most famous Englishman of all, the Duke of Wellington, was in full flow. Queen Victoria was horrified – and Parliament, as so often in a crisis helping to make the worst of it, was in turmoil. The hysterical behaviour of the House of Commons after the invasion of the Falkland Islands, as related earlier, is a perfect illustration.

A reluctant Ellenborough was persuaded that, in order to uphold the honour of the Empire, a relief force would have to be sent. He was also induced to put in command General George Pollock, a 'Company officer'. Pollock was a veteran of the Company's Army, and it was clear that neither snobbery nor nepotism had played any part in his choice.

Indeed, he and Nott were from the same mould. They respected and liked one another.

Pollock was still in Jalalabad and Nott in Kandahar – some 300 miles apart – when the surprising order reached both of them to withdraw speedily back to India from Afghanistan. Pollock and Nott were aghast, and the two generals adopted delaying tactics, explaining why military retirement was at that moment out of the question. The argument between the generals and the high command in India continued throughout May, June and July, until at last Ellenborough, the new Governor-General, solved the problem by throwing the whole burden of decision on the generals. If Nott chose, he might 'withdraw by way of Kabul', which was in the opposite direction to India, while Pollock 'might advance to the capital and co-operate with that General'. Ellenborough, in a despatch to Nott, stated:

> It [i.e. retreat via Kabul] is an object of just ambition, which no one more than myself would rejoice to see effected: but I see that failure in the attempt is certain and irretrievable ruin, and I would endeavour to inspire you with the necessary caution, and make you feel that, great as are the objects to be obtained by success, the risk is great also.

Nott could hardly complain about having the whole responsibility placed on the generals. After all, throughout his service he had tried to insist on 'a becoming jealousy of the independence of a commanding officer'

KANDAHAR

Going backwards for three years we left General Nott in Quetta in charge of a brigade. There seems to be general agreement amongst historians – and certainly there was a strong feeling in the Company Army that had Nott received command of the Army in succession to General Keane instead of Elphinstone, the disaster in Kabul would never have happened. He had said of Elphinstone on several occasions: 'The truth is, he is a Queen's officer and I am a Company's. I am decidedly of the opinion that a Queen's officer, be he ever so talented, is totally unfit to command the Company's Army.'

Such statements made Nott unpopular and his abrasive manner did not make him a favourite of Macnaghten and the civil servants in Calcutta. Be that as it may, William Nott had his own battles to fight in Kandahar, Helmund province, Sind and Baluchistan. And this chapter is about that other Afghan war between 1838 and 1842, which understandably has received less notice than the infamous disaster in Kabul. On his arrival in Kandahar in 1839 the tribes in lower Afghanistan were about to rise up and they comprised not fewer than 20,000 fighting men in the immediate vicinity.

Nott was promoted and given command of all the troops in Lower Afghanistan and Sind but at no time did he have more than 9000 British and Sepoy soldiers to maintain order in this huge area stretching to Persia in the north down through the Bolan Pass into India proper. And, worst of all, his supply train from India totally collapsed.

The Afghans were hardy hill men like the Gurkhas in the Himalayas; they were familiar with arms from boyhood. The Afghans were, and are, natural fighters who know instinctively how to make the best use of cover; they can move from rock to rock with the nimbleness of a mountain goat. These are the men who beat the armies of the Soviet Union. Their long-barrelled matchlock muskets, known as jezails, had an important advantage over the British muskets, which had a much shorter range. And they were considered better shots. One British officer described them as 'the best marksmen in the world'. They were also skilled horsemen and presented a formidable foe with their mobility, field craft and marksmanship. How come that General Nott's force never lost a single one of the sixteen or so battles against such admirable soldiers? The answer solely lay in discipline and the ordered way in which the Company's Army – and the outstanding British regiments within it – fought their battles. The British and Sepoy soldiers were also men of outstanding courage, and usually they were well led by their junior officers.

It is as well to respect your enemies and William Nott in one of his frequent letters to his daughters gave his view of the Afghan tribesmen:

> I like the people in spite of all that has been said of them. True the poorest man you can meet places himself perfectly on a par with you; but though free and bold in their remarks there is no want of respect; so different from the mean cringing people of Bengal. I go into their villages and their gardens for 10 miles around and I always find the people very civil – they are a warm and passionate people, but then they are so thoroughly good-tempered and always cheerful. I must say that I like them.

Nott had the good fortune to have an outstanding political officer, although he was highly critical of the process, later abolished, of placing young 'politicals' or diplomats in each district; they ran a sort of diplomatic network in parallel to the army commanders. However, Sir Henry Macnaghten in Kabul posted young Henry Rawlinson to Kandahar to join the general and the two of them established a strong rapport in total agreement about the follies of the government and the goings-on in Kabul.

Rawlinson was to become famous – and he was a very great scholar – as the man who deciphered cuneiform, probably the earliest writing in the world, first invented by accountants to keep track of produce entering and leaving the palaces of Mesopotamia. Before being appointed to Afghanistan he had been sent to Persia; in a place called Bisitum, the Persian king Darius the Great had ordered a huge inscription to be carved on an almost unassailable rock face in three different languages – cuneiform, Babylonian and Elanite. Rawlinson had scaled the rock face and reported back his findings to the British Museum. In later life he became a Member of Parliament, a Trustee of the British Museum and a Director of the East India Company.

But what is so remarkable about this phase in Rawlinson's life is the high quality of his despatches, too numerous to quote, and the bravery that he showed in heavy fights with the Afghans. Whenever there was a crisis around Kandahar – and there were many – he leapt on his horse and led a charge against the enemy. I can only include one of his exploits.

In January 1842 a force of several thousand Afghans were camped outside Kandahar and a battle became inevitable. It was described by Nott in an official despatch commenting that 'Major Rawlinson, political agent, with his accustomed zeal, was in the field and gallantly led a small body of Persian and Afghan horse in the charge'.

Many years later Rawlinson gave a vivid description of the battle to his two young children in a style very different from his formal writing:

Though I was there [in Kandahar] really in a political capacity, I had plenty to do in the way of fighting, for the Afghans were constantly trying to kill us, and we were obliged to keep always on the watch, our horses ready for use, pistols under our pillows and everything in order, so that in a few minutes we could be under arms. One day, we rather suspected they were thinking of attacking us, so I went up early in the morning to the top of a high tower which adjoined my house ... There was a long range of hills about 4 or 5 miles off, and on these I could see the Afghans swarming like bees – there they were coming down the hills towards us, with spears, horses and guns evidently going to attack us. So, say I, Mr. Afghans! two can play at *that* game – away I went to General Nott – and told him the Afghans are coming down upon us – let us all go out and drive them away. And thus came to pass the battle of Candahar. The general gives the orders – the bugle sounds the Alarm ... and in one hour or less we are all mounted and out of the gates of the town, a Regt. of European Infantry Native Cavalry, 2 or 3 Regt. of Native Infantry and 6 guns. 'Now' says Genl. Nott, 'Rawlinson you like a skirmish. Take the Cavalry and do as you think best.' Well we attacked the Afghans, knocked them about, with the guns, killed some, wounded others, and sent them flying here and there in disorder. But there still remained 2,000 horsemen on the heights. So says Genl. Nott – 'Rawlinson, go after them and I will support you with the Horse Artillery'. Now, I say to my men. Don't move till I hold up my sword, and when I point it so, Charge. I held up my sword, they fired. 6 guns. 12 Shots. This knocked over a good many horsemen and threw them into confusion. Then. I said. Charge, and away I went on my black Arab Shaitan and they followed at a tremendous pace – one poor fellow was killed by my side.

After the battle of Kandahar where 9000 British and Sepoy soldiers routed around 20,000 Afghan rebels, Rawlinson's story being part of the wider battle, supplies became desperate.

The army's cattle were starving through lack of fodder; medicines and ammunition were running low – and the only flour obtainable for making bread 'was at least one-third honest desert sand to two-thirds of flour'.The Kandahar Army had not been paid for four months and the Treasury was completely empty.

Much of this period was taken up with an extended row between General Nott and Brigadier England in Quetta because each time England attempted to force the Kojuk Pass with supplies he was beaten back by the Afghans.

There were so many violent encounters throughout the region that only the odd one can be reported. In the appendix to Stocqueler's memoirs, however, there is one rather typical incident which I include. Unfortunately the author is not named but I believe it was from a Captain Craigie, who was sent by General Nott to defend the garrison of Kelat-i-Ghilzie. There was a great deal of correspondence between the generals about whether the detachment at Kelat was adequate and the following will, maybe, answer that:

We marched into quarters at Khelat-i-Ghilzie in November 1841. Our barracks were excellent, but the fortifications of the place were little more than commenced on, and along some hundred yards of the works there was neither wall nor ditch. Directly we got news of the insurrection at Cabul the sepoys were set to work to strengthen the defences of the post – scarps, palisades, parapets, and a ditch at the most accessible parts of the works were commenced on, and both officers and men continued to work at them until the winter set well in, and the frost rendered the ground so hard, that there was no longer any working it. On the 9th December about fifteen hundred Ghilzies made their appearance, with the intention, as they said, of besieging us ….

A fall of snow compelled them to decamp after nine days, and the only damage they did us was to make all the Chiefs in our neighbourhood 'yagee'… [mutinous]. The winter now set in with severity, and the cold soon became excessive. We had no doors for the barracks, and neither doors nor glass for the windows of our quarters … and our supply of firewood we were obliged to husband, so that we never could keep our rooms warm … Snow lay for two months on the ground, and the thermometer fell as low as forty degrees below the freezing point. With no doors to the barracks, and only such rough purdahs as grain bags, which were all we could get, you may conceive how much our men suffered ... I have never experienced a winter so continuously cold ... We had occasional communication with Candahar by means of highly paid cossids, and we thus learned the disastrous fate of our Cabul comrades. The tedium of the winter was excessive, but it passed at last. With the spring our labours on the defences recommenced, and as soon as the weather became mild, the hostile Chiefs of the two great Ghilzie tribes in our neighbourhood made their appearance ... The hostile Ghilzie Chiefs at first brought only a few hundred men with them ... As they approached, our range necessarily became more limited, and we had neither cavalry nor the means of moving a gun, and the country round Khelat is full of ravines, and exceedingly favourable to the skulking mode of fighting which these gentry most approve of ... Towards the middle of May the enemy commenced to dig trenches round the place, working at them all night. By the 26th they had completely surrounded us with them, the nearest being within to hundred and fifty yards of our defences. These were all loop-holed, and afforded the enemy perfect cover ... From these trenches the hottest fire any of us had ever seen Affghans keep up was poured upon any one who exposed himself; obviously picked marksmen were selected for the duty, for they fired exceedingly well for Affghans, and at ranges of from 600 to 700 yards, their long jezails threw balls with great accuracy ... On the evening of the 20th of May the enemy were unusually quiet, and so few of them visible...

Officers and men had, for several nights previously, kept at their posts; there was bright moonlight, and the night passed with unusual quietness, until towards morning the moon went down. The attention of the officer on duty was then suddenly arrested by the clatter of horses' feet, indicating the close presence of a large body of horse, and the word was passed round to get ready. Shortly afterwards the whole face of the works was assaulted by dense bodies of the enemy. The morning was so dark, that they were within a hundred yards before they were observed, though we were on the look out for them, and they came on with great boldness, shouting 'Allah! Allah!'. They were received with discharges of grape, and a hot fire of musketry, which must have done heavy execution among their dense masses; still they pressed on, pushing their attack with the greatest vehemence … During the height of the assault, the enemy fired little; they had apparently slung their matchlocks and came on sword in hand, but they were met by a fire so deadly and well sustained that they had no chance of success. The officers of the garrison were all surprised at the boldness and determination of the attack, but we understood afterwards that, trusting to their numbers, and emboldened no doubt by their previous successes at Cabul and Ghuznee, they reckoned so confidently on taking the place, that many of their women were waiting in the ravines close at hand to share in the plunder of the garrison ….

Had we possessed a few good cavalry we should have inflicted a heavier loss on them, but they were strong in horse, having about 800 in the field, while we had not a mounted man, and so it was judged prudent, as the ground afforded excellent cover for their mode of fighting, to rest satisfied with the thrashing we had given them, and to permit them to carry off their wounded without incurring the loss of our own men in moving on to attack them. They left 104 dead bodies at the foot of the defences, and within a few days after the assault, the Political Agent ascertained that the number of killed, and of wounded men, who died within a few days after the action, considerably exceeded 400 … Computed by themselves the lowest number of assailants was stated at 5,500 men, the highest at 7,000 …

The garrison consisted of about 900 men, about 500 of whom were actually engaged …

Two days after the defeat of the enemy, we heard of the advance of Colonel Wymer's brigade to relieve us, which arrived on the 26th of May. We moved into camp, the barracks and defences of Khelat were destroyed, and the 7th of June saw us safe at Candahar.

***

I came across an excellent story in my Regimental Magazine about a similar incident in July 2006. It has just been written by Rifleman Yam Roka Pun of D Company of the 2nd Royal Gurkha Rifles deployed behind enemy lines at Now'zad, Helmund Province on 2 July 2006.

"We were ordered to 'maintain the defensive position' located in the District Compound which was centred in the main bazaar, with civilian buildings all around. Now 'zad is a Taliban stronghold and we realised that the enemy were all around us.

The social problems faced by the local communities are illiteracy, polygamy, poverty, a high infancy death rate and blind faith. War is a tradition in Afghanistan where the peace died long ago – and after the Russian occupation the country was in a wretched condition.

The evening of 13 July 2006 was lit by a full moon as the dogs continued their customary chorus of howling. Suddenly the insurgents launched a terrific attack on the compound and the sangars came under a massive amount of fire. One of the sangars suffered a direct assault from close quarters and the situation seemed hopeless, but we made a courageous fight-back.

On 16 July there was another brutal fire-fight where every sangar was engaged by enemy firing points that seemed to surround the compound. The enemy used an extensive tunnel system to get within twenty metres of the compound, but they were soon despatched with grenades and the awesome fire-power of the Apache attack helicopters.

The Taliban insurgents are a competent and capable fighting unit, whose knowledge of the ground and tenacity made them a formidable foe. However, our discipline, confidence and superior training made it a fight that they could never win.

The Platoon complete, after a period of one month, returned safely to Camp Bastion near Kandahar despite the deprivation of the living conditions, having to survive on rations, suffering from trench foot, not to mention the deafening noise of the guns. Over the period 11 Platoon had a total of 28 fights with the enemy. The devotion of duty and the inspired acts of bravery has written another page in the history of the Gurkhas. We certainly have a story to tell. Now'zad – we were there!"

Haven't we been here before?

It was in 1839 disaffected Afghans recovered a document which was being sent around the Afghan chiefs and they reported it to General Nott. I think it is very interesting, because it is indicative of the attitudes and religious fanaticism of the Muslim tribes, maybe not just in Afghanistan.

To the high and exalted Nobles, Leaders and Moslem Followers of the Chief of all Prophets (on whom be peace) among the Belooch and Brahoe tribes.

Be it not concealed, that when the Christians of England took Shah Soojah by the hand, and invade, with a large force, Moslem countries, it was evident to the followers of Islam, that as His Majesty Shah Soojah had for thirty years enjoyed the protection of the English Government, and was fully assured of the good faith and sincerity of this Christian nation, it was not unreasonable that they should put forth their strength and assist His Majesty, the hereditary King of Moslem countries; but, after establishing him in his dominions, return to their own countries.

In confirmation of which, His Majesty often remarked in public Durbar, that the English advanced no claims of their own, but would retire.

The followers of Islam believing His Majesty in full possession of uncontrolled power, joined him with all their strength.

But few understood the real truth; so the English threw aside the veil, and day by day employed themselves in uprooting the religion and causing separation among the followers of Islam, and by the force of their power carried into execution whatever they pleased, from the day of their arrival up to the present moment.

The Moslem nation, viewing all this, and considering it opposed to its interests, plainly see that the King was entirely without authority.

Hence the warriors and champions of Islam from among the Doranees, Ghilzies, Persians, Kohistanees and Lohuzurees, with men of other districts, girded up the loins of valour for the restoration and strengthening of the Moslem religion, and spared neither their lives, their honour, nor their wealth in their holy cause; but according to the Sacred Book, placing not regard on the smallness of their worldly means, have drawn forth the sword of honour and commenced performance.

Although by the wise ordering of the Almighty, the association of the Faithful and the unity of their hearts is perfect, still it is necessary and proper that, for all affairs of importance, there should be a leader; therefore, the exalted in dignity, the Nuwab Mahomed Zuman Khan, Barukzye, Ghazee, in kindness the flower of the times, and in religious sentiments the wonder of the age, has been selected by the Moslems of all tribes, under the title of Ameer of the Faithful and Imam of the Holy Warriors, and as such recognized by all.

By the favour of God, the numbers of the Faithful will daily increase, and become countless.

To the True Followers it is therefore addressed, that all brothers in the religion of the Sacred Prophet, rejoiced in heart at these glad tidings, may continue firm and faithful to the Holy Cause.

(True translation.)
WM. ANDERSON.

Surely there never was a better description of what intervention in the affairs of Afghanistan is all about?

We now come to the final part of this sad story as the Afghan war drew to a conclusion. General Nott was stuck in Kandahar without cavalry, without ammunition, medicines and enough camels to carry the baggage train towards Ghuznee and Kabul.

Nott had a high opinion of General Pollock, a fellow Company officer, and he was anxious to press on to Ghuznee and Kabul, with Pollock approaching it from Jalalabad towards the Kyber Pass. In a dispatch to Pollock he said: 'I ought to have been on my way to Ghuznee to extend my hand to you, instead of which I am obliged to make a movement on the Kojuck. As far as cattle are concerned we are nearly helpless. God knows why such a delay has occurred in sending me money and stores. This is dreadful.'

He always found time to write to his daughters in Calcutta. On 22 April 1842:

> The people in power are all mad, or Providence hath blinded them for some wise purpose. I am very tired, tired of working, tired of this country, and quite tired of the folly of my countrymen, and I long more than ever for my clay-built cottage. My soldiers are four months in arrear; there is not one rupee in the Kandahar Treasury. I have no medicine for the sick and wounded. I have no camels for the troops, nor money to buy or hire and therefore cannot move. I have no good cavalry, and but little ammunition. I have been calling for all these for 6 months but not the least aid has been given me. I might now have been on my way to Cabul.

On 21 June 1842 a despatch came to William Nott from Ellenborough, who had succeeded Auckland as Governor-General:

> I have heard with great pleasure of the constant success of your troops in the several actions in which they were engaged towards the end of last month.
>
> The resolution exhibited at the defence of Kelat was very gratifying.
>
> From the decided course which has been taken by the Russian Minister at Tehran, in conjunction with the British Minister there, I am disposed to think that you will not be troubled with a demonstration of a hostile character from the side of Herat [Persia].

Ellenborough then went on to commiserate about the disaster which had occurred in Ghuznee when a Colonel Palmer had surrendered under a promise of good conduct only to find half his soldiers killed as they marched out of the fortress, the rest being taken into slavery. He went on:

> There is no account, on which any reliance can be placed of the circumstances under which at Ghuznee, six officers remain alive, and all the solders have been destroyed, or carried away as slaves.
>
> I feel great commiseration for the soldiers, if any such there be, and I should be grateful for any information you may be able to procure with respect to them.

These were later to be found and released by General Nott when he successfully assaulted the fortress at Ghuznee.

Another letter to his daughters one month later:

> They have behaved most shamefully to me in not publishing any of my dispatches especially that of the 12th January wherein I told them that my noble regiments had defeated 20,000 men. Mark me, the Army at Kandahar has defeated the enemy in some 16 actions, tranquilised the whole country, made every Afghan bend the knee, never met with reverse however outnumbered by the enemy – and no notice has been taken of it.

Then on 5 August everything changes. Supplies had arrived. Action at last:

> At last they have untied my hands and mark me, the grass shall not grow under my feet. I wish they had done so two months ago. I have a march before me truly. Whatever may happen I shall still be with my little army. They shall be victorious wherever they go or I will perish.

If I can I will send you a message during my adventurous march [to Ghuznee and Kabul].

His biographer records, '… though successes in the field and great honours and rewards awaited him; it may be doubted if any time in the course of his career, Nott experienced more pleasurable feeling that now reigned in his bosom'.

On 7 August 1842, 'from a camp near Candahar', he wrote to the Governor-General:

My Lord

I have been honoured with your Lordship's letter of the 16th July, 1842. It is not necessary for me to trouble your Lordship with a detail of the difficulties I have encountered during the last ten days in arranging for the march of my own and General England's columns. All is now prepared.

I dare say I shall meet with difficulties but our march through the centre of Afghanistan via Ghuznee, and Cabool [about 300 miles) will have a great influence throughout Asia even if I should not have an opportunity of striking a blow for the reputation of our army, and I think I shall accomplish it to your Lordship's satisfaction.

The only fear I have is the want of forage in the valley of Cabool, and thence to Jellalabad in the event of General Pollock's army advancing to the former City. I can only say that I deem my little Army fully able to carry into effect your Lordship's views, and I think a larger force would perhaps cause the loss of so many animals as to render our retirement difficult.

The reason why the general had reduced the size of his force and sent part of it back to Quetta under General England was the inability to find enough forage for his animals and baggage train. The whole story of the Afghan campaign is one of poor logistics over great distances, insufficient troops, too large an area to master, too many small detachments hazarding their security against the mobile Afghan rebels, not enough transport (is it helicopters or camels?) and a shortage of cavalry (tracked personnel carriers!).

The road was smooth until 28 August when the Afghans appeared to the general's rear. On 30 August as he approached Ghuznee, Shumsoodeen, the Afghan governor, brought nearly the whole of his army, 12,000 strong, into the vicinity of the general's camp at a place called Goine.

> I marched out with one half of my force; the enemy advanced in the most bold and gallant manner, each division cheering as they came into position; their left being upon a hill of some elevation, their centre and right along a low ridge, until their flank rested on a fort full of men. They opened a fire of small arms, supported by two six-pounder horse artillery guns which were admirably served.
>
> Our columns advanced upon the different points with great regularity and steadiness, and after a short and spirited contest, completely defeated the enemy, captured their guns and dispersing them in every direction.
>
> One more hour of daylight would have enabled me to destroy the whole of their infantry. Shamsoodeen fled in the direction of Ghuznee accompanied by about thirty horsemen. The behaviour of our troops, both European and Native, was much as I anticipated, and afforded me complete satisfaction.

My family coat of arms, as well as showing the Campaign Medal of Kandahar, Ghuznee and Kabul is also surmounted by a banner bearing the word Goine.

General Nott was expecting a major battle for the capture of Ghuznee and laid his plans accordingly. Every man in the Army 'burned for the opportunity of inflicting chastisement on the treacherous captors of Colonel Palmer and his men', who had been tortured, confined in appalling conditions and sold into slavery. 'But the craven hearts of the Ghuznees failed them at the critical moment. The battle of the 30th August at Goine had opened their eyes to the power of a well-organised force in the hands of such men as Nott, Wymer [a brigadier] and McLaren. They fled from Ghuznee before the guns opened on them.'

The general had the great satisfaction of recovering about 320 of the Sepoys of the 27th Regiment of Bengal Native Infantry who had been sold into slavery but the European officers had been marched north, and placed with those who had been captured in the Kabul passes. They were later rescued. Scrawled on the walls of a dungeon was a list of the incarcerated British officers reading:

Prisoners in Ghuznee through the treachery of Surdar Shooms and Dean Khan in having broken every article of two treaties solemnly sworn to. If on the arrival of any British force, the prisoners are not forthcoming, avenge them on ... ...They had charge of the prisoners, and treated them most infamously, having tortured the Colonel, and taken every opportunity of being insolent and oppressive.

Signed C. Harris

On 1 October he received a letter from Ellenborough in Simla:

I had the satisfaction of receiving yesterday your despatches of the 8th saying that you were in possession of Ghuznee. I congratulate you on your having achieved a conquest, of all others the most gratifying, even if it had not been attended by the recovery of so many sepoys whom the Afghans had placed in slavery.

Believe me, General

With the greatest respect

Your very faithful friend and servant

Ellenborough

The Army of Retribution, as it came to be called, continued its march towards Kabul, not, however, without interruption, for on the road he found Shumsoodeen, Sultan Jan and other Afghan chiefs with an army of 12,000 men occupying a succession of strong mountain positions directly in his path. The troops 'dislodged them in gallant style'.

Meanwhile, Major-General Pollock in the north had made good progress through the passes which had been the scene of the bloody massacres of the previous January, having defeated an Afghan army on the way. General Nott reached Kabul on 17 September, two days after Pollock.

***

Nott and Pollock became Victorian heroes and returned to India laden with honours – Nott being given 'the new title of "Envoy to the King of Oude", in substitution of the lesser title of Resident at the Court of Lucknow', then the most profitable of all appointments in British India. But by now he was a sick man, and he did not last long in Lucknow – to the distress of Ellenborough, with whom he had developed a strong mutual affection, in contrast to his contempt for Auckland. Late in 1843 or early in 1844 he set sail for England.

Great were the celebrations there at the recovery of British honour. The Prime Minister, Sir Robert Peel, moved a motion of grateful thanks to General Nott in the House of Commons; he was given the Freedom of the City of London; and he was invited to Apsley House by the Duke of Wellington. The young Queen Victoria asked him to stay at Windsor. But it was all too much. He wanted nothing more than to return home to Carmarthen and to take up residence at his estate, Job's Well. How right he was – 'And what have kings that privates have not too, save ceremony

…?' His entry into Carmarthen on 9 September 1844 touched him more than all the honours and feting in the capital. All activity in the town ceased for the day, and the whole population came out to welcome him.

He lived for only a few more months and died on 1 January 1845. His statue stands to this day in Nott Square, Carmarthen, although he is today a forgotten general of the Empire from a forgotten war. So many episodes in his story encapsulate what command is all about in time of war. So much depends on the twists and turns of fortune.' Is he lucky?' asked Napoleon about one of his generals.

Emphatically Elphinstone was not a lucky general; he died whilst in captivity with the Afghans.

***

I hope that President Hamid Karzai does not go the way of Shah Sujah. By all reports he is a good man, struggling against overwhelming odds. He rules in Kabul, but the countryside has reverted to its traditional condition, run by tribal chiefs and warlords. Deals, double deals and gold sovereigns have always been the currency of Afghanistan, today replaced by the opium poppy.

Karzai was elected President but he cannot shuffle off the fact that he was promoted by the Americans, just as the British promoted Shah Sujah and placed him on the throne. He cannot avoid being seen as the creature of the Feringhee. When the economic condition of the people does not improve, he will be discarded. The Afghan despatch, which was circulated around the tribes in 1839, says it all. It is as true today as it was then.

The British are in Afghanistan today to stop the Taliban returning and the country reverting to a haven for Al Qa'eda and their like. But, Al

Qa'eda has havens all over the tribal areas of northern Pakistan, Waziristan and Baluchistan. President Pervez Musharraf can no more police these areas than the British can police the provinces around Kandahar. There are vast tracts of desert and mountains, alien to good order and stability. The lessons of history are clear: you can do deals, bribe corrupt officials, enjoy hearty friendships but, in the end, the Afghan tribes unite to expel the foreigner.

I noticed a comment in the press last autumn (*The Times*, 30 October 2006) by one Nafaz Khan, the former militia commander in the northern Helmund province town of Musa Qala. It was there that he fought alongside the British. 'I loved those British soldiers, he said, 'they were great fighters and knew each of my men by name. Together we killed many many Taliban.' Then we were ordered to leave. 'The British soldiers were cursing with us when we were all told to leave. They said that they had fought and lost friends to keep the town. And now these tribal elders, who are in charge of Musa Qala, are the same who gave the Taliban support when they fought against us. The deal was just a clever trick to get the foreign soldiers to go.'

One of the elders in Musa Qala said, 'Most of the fighters weren't real Taliban. There were some outsiders, but most were local men who were angry with the government, its robbery and corruption, who were persuaded to fight against the foreigners by our preachers in the mosques. We'll see how long the deal lasts.'

The British cannot avoid becoming embroiled in defending criminalized district officials engaged in the drug trade. Referring to another of Helmund's battle zones in which the British saw heavy action, one British official said, 'We should never have gone near it, it was straight-up face-off between two drug lords and we were used to tip the balance.'

As in Iraq, our presence is getting us nowhere. Similar to Iraq, we will be the cause of further instability as the tribes unite against us. And winter gives way to spring. The Afghans are a warrior people and they will fight as soon as spring returns. The NATO presence in Afghanistan will inevitably end in humiliation, as it did for the Soviet Union. It is often wise to know when to retreat. The Duke Of Wellington gave some good advice to Generals and Politicians alike, "The real test of a general is to know when to retreat and to dare to do it."

***

I own a remarkable book called *The Costumes and Scenery of Afghanistan* by James Rattray, published in 1848 which is dedicated to 'the officers of the British and Indian armies who served in Afganistan under the command of the late Major-General Sir William Nott GCB'. I include it here as an addendum to the chapter because it is a fascinating historical record of the many officers who fought in the Campaign of Kandahar, Ghuznee and Kabul.

LIST OF SUBSCRIBERS.

Herring, Major E., Invalid Establishment · 1
Heysham, Lieut. R. T., 2nd Bengal Grenadiers · 1
Hodgson, W., Esq., Madras C.S. · 1
Hoggan, Lieut.-Col., Com. 53rd B.N.I. · 1
Holroyd, Lieut. G., 43rd Bengal Light Infantry · 1
*Hoppe, Captain, 16th Bengal Grenadiers · 1
*Hopkins, Captain, 27th B.N.I. · 1
Holmes, Lieut. J. G., Adj. 6th Irreg. Cav. · 1
Hood, Lieutenant, 49th B.N.I. · 1
Horsfield, Captain, Bengal Artillery · 1
Hughes, Lieutenant E. J., 57th B.N.I. · 2
Hunt, Captain, 22nd B.N.I. · 1
Hurford, R., Esq., V.S., 16th Queen's Lancers · 1
Hutton, Captain J., Mussooree · 1
Impey, Lieutenant, Bengal Engineers · 1
*Jacob, Dr, 38th Bengal Light Infantry · 1
*Jackson, Lieutenant, Pol. Asst., Kandahar · 1
Johnson, Captain H., Pay-Master, Kusowlee · 1
Kay, Captain R. D., Depy. Asst. Adjt-Gen. · 1
Kaye, Lieutenant E., Horse Artillery, Meerut · 1
Kennedy, Captain W., 5th B.N.I. · 1
Kirke, Captain H., Supt. Doon Canals · 1
Knowles, Captain, H.M. 50th · 1
Laing, Captain, 36th B.N.I · 1
Lane, Lieut.-Col., C.B. · 1
Larkins, Captain W. H., Dep. Com. Saugor · 1
Layard, Lieutenant, 19th B.N.I. · 1
*Le Geyt, Lieut., 1st Bombay Light Cavalry · 1
*Leech, Major, C.B. · 1
*Leeson, Captain J., Commg. 2nd Irreg. Cavalry · 1
Leadbeater, Major W. E. B., 53rd N.I. · 1
Liptrott, Captain J., 3rd Irregular Cavalry · 1
Login, Dr J., Res. Surgeon, Lucknow · 1
*Lumsden, Lieutenant H. B., 27th B.N.I. · 1
Lumsden, Lieutenant, 59th B.N.I. · 1
Luard, Lieutenant P. L., 55th B.N.I. · 1
Luard, Lieutenant-Colonel · 1
Macan, Major, 16th Bengal Grenadiers · 1
Macgregor, Major G. H., C.B., Bengal Artillery · 1
Macgregor, A., Esq. · 1
*Maclaren, Lieut.-Col., C.B., Com. 16th Gren. · 5
*Maclean, Captain, A.D.C. Governor-General · 1
Macdonnell, Captain, 5th Shah's Infantry · 1
*Mackay, Lieutenant · 1
MacKean, Captain R., Regt. Kelat-i-Gilzie · 1
Mackenzie, Capt. C., late Political Assistant, Peshawur · 1
MacDuff, Captain J., H.M. 40th Foot · 1
Macgowan, Captain J. A., H.M. 40th Foot · 1
Mackenzie, Major, 64th B.N.I. · 1
Maconochie, Lieutenant, 11th B.L.C. · 1
Mackintosh, G. G., Esq., B.C.S. · 1
Mackay, Captain A., 16th Bengal Grenadiers · 1
Macnaghten, Lady W. H. · 1
M'Andrew, Dr, H.M. 40th Foot · 1
M'Curdy, Dr, 19th B.N.I · 1
M'Clure and Son, Messrs · 2
Mainwaring, Bt.-Major E. H., 16th Bengal Gren. · 1
*Mainwaring, Lieutenant, 2nd Bengal Grenadiers · 1
Maling, Captain C. S., 68th B.N.I · 1
*Manning, Captain, 16th Bengal Grenadiers · 1
Mannington, Captain J., 24th B.N.I. · 1
*Marshall, Captain, 6th Shah's Inf., 61st N.I. · 1
Martin, Captain T., 20th B.N.I. · 1
Master, Captain G., 4th Bengal Light Cavalry · 1
Matthews, A. H., Esq. · 2
May, Miss, Bath · 1
Mayne, Major W., 37th B.N.I · 1
Melville, Captain H. B., 54th B.N.I. · 1
Metcalf, Lieutenant J., 3rd B.N.I. · 1
73rd Mess · 1

Mills, Lieutenant, 2nd Bengal Grenadiers · 1
Mills, Lieutenant, Bengal Horse Artillery · 1
Milne, Captain H., Dep. Asst. Comy.-Gen. · 1
Moorcroft, Lieutenant, 1st Shah's Infantry · 1
Moorhouse, Captain, 35th Bengal Light Infantry · 1
Morris, Captain A. B., 20th B.N.I. · 1
Morrison, Captain J., 50th B.N.I. · 1
*Morrieson, Lieutenant, 54th B.N.I. · 1
Morgan, Lieutenant-Col., C.B., Madras Cavalry · 1
Morgan, R. B., Esq., B.C.S. · 1
Morton, Lieutenant, H.M. 9th Foot · 1
Moseley, Lieutenant-Colonel, C.B., 64th B.N.I. · 1
Nelson, Captain, H.M. 40th Foot · 1
Nepean, Captain, 38th Bengal Light Infantry · 1
*Newton, Lieutenant, 16th Bengal Grenadiers · 1
Nicholson, Lieutenant J., 27th B.N.I. · 1
Nicholas, Lieutenant B., 64th B.N.I. · 1
Norgate, Captain, 18th B.N.I. · 1
Norton, Lieutenant, 35th Bengal Light Infantry · 1
Oldfield, Major C. E. T., C.B., 4th Irrg. Cavalry · 1
Oliver, Lieut.-Col., 57th B.N.I. · 2
Olpherts, Capt., 1st W.I. Reg, Sierra Leone · 1
Ommanney, M. C., Esq., B.C.S. · 1
O'Connor, Lieutenant E. N. T. B., 61st B.N.I · 1
Orr, Lieutenant C. A., Madras Sappers and Miners · 1
Ouseley, Major, Haileybury · 1
Ouseley, Captain R., 50th B.N.I. · 1
Owen, H. T., Esq., Bengal Civil Service, Meerut · 1
Palmer, Lieut.-Colonel, Commanding 27th B.N.I. · 1
Parsons, Lieutenant-Col. J., Comy.-Gen. Bengal · 1
Pattinson, Captain, H.M. 16th Lancers · 1
Pennington, Lieutenant R. C., 11th B.N.I. · 1
*Pereira, Colonel, Bengal Artillery · 1
Petrie, Mr J., Overseer Doaba Canal, Bengal · 1
Peyton, Mr J., Survey. Dep., Bengal · 1
Phillipson, Dr, Asst.-Surgeon, Garrison, Buxar · 1
Place, F. W., Esq., Editor of 'Delhi Gazette' · 1
Plowden, Lieutenant E. W., C.B., 8th Irreg. Cav. · 1
Plowden, T. C., Esq., Civil Service, Meerut · 1
*Pocklington, Lieutenant, 38th B.L.I. · 1
Pogson, Lieutenant W. Q., 43rd B.L.I. · 1
Ponsonby, Major A.A.G., 11th Light Cavalry · 1
13th, or Prince Albert's Light Infantry · 1
Pratt, Captain E. J., H.M. 16th Lancers · 1
Radcliffe, Lieut. C. W., 7th Bengal Light Cavalry · 1
Raper, Lieutenant M., 64th B.N.I. · 1
Rattray, Captain, R.N. · 1
Rattray, Capt. T., Prince Albert's Light Infantry · 1
Rattray, Lieutenant T., 64th B.N.I. · 1
Rattray, Mrs, Daventry · 1
Reid, Lieutenant C., Adjutant Sirmoor Battalion · 1
*Reid, Lieutenant, 53rd B.N.I. · 1
Reynolds, Lieutenant J. H., 53rd B.N.I. · 1
Richards, C. T., Esq., Calcutta · 2
Richardson, Mr · 1
*Rind, Captain, 37th B.N.I. · 2
Robb, Major F. C., Southsea · 1
Roberts, Lieutenant-Colonel A., C.B. · 1
Robertson, Lieutenant, Bengal Artillery · 1
Ross, Captain, 42nd Bengal Light Infantry · 1
Scrivenor, Lieutenant, 63rd B.N.I. · 1
Shakspear, A., Esq., B.C.S. · 1
Sheridan, Capt., Prince Albert's Light Infantry · 1
Shute, Lieutenant E. C., 19th B.N.I. · 1
Sneyd, Lieutenant C. M., Adjutant Kelat-i-Gilzie Regiment · 1
Smith, Lieutenant, 63rd B.N.I. · 1
Spankie, Captain T., B.A., 48th B.N.I. · 1
Squire, Colonel, Prince Albert's Light Infantry · 1
Stapylton, Captain G. C., Prince Albert's Light Infantry · 1

Stanton, C. H., Esq., Stroud, Gloucester · 1
Stedman, Lieut.-Col. R. A., 7th Bengal Light Cavalry · 1
Stevenson, Dr, 29th B.N.I. · 1
Stopford, Major, H.M. 40th · 1
*St George, Lieutenant, 37th B.N.I. · 1
*Sturt, Captain, Engineers, Shah Soojah's Service · 1
Sullivan, Captain J., H.M. 3rd Dragoons · 1
Swale, Lieutenant-Colonel, Royal Marines · 1
*Swayne, Major, 5th N.I. · 1
Swetenham, Major E., Invalids · 1
*Swetenham, Lieutenant, 16th Lancers · 1
*Swinton, Lieutenant J. M., 53rd N.I., Adjt. Conv. Depot, Landour · 1
Swinton, ---, Esq., H.M. 44th Foot · 1
Syers, Major, 19th B.N.I. · 1
Taylor, Lieutenant J. H. G., 20th B.N.I. · 1
Tebbs, Captain G., 33rd B.N.I. · 1
Thomas, H., Esq., B.C.S. · 1
Thomas, Captain, H.M. 40th Foot · 1
Thompson, Lieutenant J., 19th B.N.I. · 1
Todd, Captain J., H.M. 40th · 1
Torrent, Robt., Esq., Bengal C.S. · 1
Tottenham, Captain, 3rd B.L.C. · 1
Timbrell, Lieutenant, Bengal Horse Artillery · 1
Travers, Captain, Adj. Bhopal Contingent · 3
Travers, Captain, H.M. 3rd Dragoons · 1
Trench, Lieutenant H. Le P., 35th Bengal Light Infantry · 1
Trollope, Lieutenant F., Adjutant, 62nd B.N.I. · 2
Tronson, ---, Esq., "Great Liverpool" steam-ship · 1
Troup, Major C., 48th B.N.I. · 1
Turner, Abraham, Esq., Kidderminster · 1
Turner, Captain G., 38th Bengal Light Infantry · 1
Turner, T. J., Esq., B.C.S. · 2
Turnbull, Lieutenant M. J., Adjutant 7th Light Cavalry · 1
Turnbull, M. H., Esq., Surrey · 1
Tytler, Lieutenant, Asst. Qr.-Mr.-Gen., Bengal · 1
*Van Homrigh, Captain, 48th B.N.I. · 1
Vigors, Colonel, Prince Albert's Light Infantry · 1
*Wade, Lieutenant H. M., 44th Foot · 1
Wale, Lieutenant F., 48th B.N.I. · 1
*Walker, Captain, 4th Irreg. Horse, Shah's Force · 1
Walshe, Captain T. P., 52nd Madras N.I. · 1
Watkins, Mrs, Bodby House · 1
Watson, Major-Gen. A., 11th Bengal Light Cavalry · 1
Webster, Captain, H.M. 16th Queen's Lancers · 1
Wheeler, Colonel H. M., C.B., Comdt. 48th B.N.I. · 1
White, Major-General M., Bath · 1
White, Doctor A., 63rd B.N.I. · 1
White, Doctor, H.M. 44th Foot · 1
White, Doctor, H.M. 16th Lancers · 1
White, Major, C.B., H.M. 8th Foot · 1
Whitelocke, Captain G. F., 13th B.N.I. · 1
Williams, Rev. E., Turberville, Chepstow · 1
Williams, Lieutenant Willis, H.M. 9th Foot · 1
*Williams, Lieutenant W., Prince Albert's Light Infantry · 2
Williams, Lieutenant, 27th B.N.I. · 1
*Willis, Dr, Veterinary Surgeon · 1
Wilmer, Captain W., 14th Dragoons · 1
Winter, Captain F., 59th B.N.I. · 1
Wittal, Dr R., 26th Bengal Light Infantry · 1
Wood, Captain H., H.M. 3rd Dragoons · 1
Woodcock, T. P., Esq., C.S. · 1
Young, Major T., 2nd Bengal Grenadiers · 1
Young, Brigadier G. · 1
Young, Lieutenant, Adjt. Sap. and Min., Delhi · 1
Young, Lieutenant W., 7th Bengal Light Cavalry · 1
Young, Lieutenant H. E., 64th B.N.I. · 1

Major General Sir William Nott, GCB

'Encampment of the Kandahar Army under General Nott outside the walls of Kabul on the evacuation of Afghanistan by the British.'

(Published by Hering and Remington, 137 Regent Street, 1848)

Gurkha rifleman in the Malayan jungle – 1950's

PALESTINE
1917–26

'The Middle East is a delicious meat, but it poisons those who eat it'

Joseph-Arthur, Comte de Gobineau (1816–82)

Lloyd George and Clemenceau met in London in December 1918, following the end of the First World War, to agree the division of the Ottoman Empire. The Ottoman lands stretched from Mesopotamia, now most of Iraq, to the Mediterranean, including all of what is now Palestine, Lebanon, Syria, Iraq, Jordan and the deserts of Arabia.

Clemenceau was buoyed up by his visit to London, and the warm friendship expressed between the two victorious nations. Vast crowds cheered him in the streets as a great hero. His aide commented, 'really among such a phlegmatic and cold people, it speaks volumes'.

'Well,' said Clemenceau, 'what are we to discuss?' Lloyd George replied, 'Mesopotamia and Palestine.' Clemenceau said, 'What do you want?' Lloyd George replied, 'Mosul' (it was about to become a major oil producer). 'You shall have it,' responded Clemenceau; 'anything else?' Lloyd George: 'Yes, I want Jerusalem too.' Clemenceau: 'You shall have it, but Pichou, my Foreign Secretary, will make difficulties over Mosul.'

In return Lloyd George offered to support France against the Americans in its ambition to take control of the Lebanese coast and most of Syria. France could share somehow in whatever oil was discovered in Mosul.

Arnold Toynbee, who was an adviser to the British Delegation at the Peace Conference, remembered that he once found himself alone with Lloyd George who was muttering to himself, 'Mesopotamia – yes – oil – irrigation; Palestine – yes – the Holy Land – Zionism – we must have Palestine. Syria – hmmm – what is there in Syria? Let the French have that.'

Woodrow Wilson, Lloyd George and Clemenceau had met in 1917 to divide up the world at the Paris Peace Conference, a meeting wonderfully described in a brilliant book, *Peacemakers*, by Margaret MacMillan. All world leaders of consequence, accompanied by vast delegations, billeted themselves in Paris for one whole year, making vulture-like claims on the rotting remnants of the Ottoman and Austrian Empires. Progress was delayed, not just by the competing claims of the Allies, by the greedy behaviour of the Italians who had entered the war in its final years; by centuries of religious differences and jealousies, particularly in the Balkans; and most of all by the 'experts'. Every diplomat and adviser had his opinion on what to do and where to go. Diplomats are good at analysis, but they only have one solution – appeasement. So, in growing exasperation at the lack of progress Lloyd George and Clemenceau laid out maps on the hotel floor, dismissed the advisers and settled down to make all the decisions for themselves. The decisions that they made, particularly in Palestine, Iraq and the Balkans, still haunt us today.

The deal over the Middle East had been complicated by the Sykes–Picot Agreement of 1916 made during the middle of the war when promises were cheap and the prospect of defeat quite real. The Gallipoli landings of 1915–16 had failed and an Indian force had surrendered to the Ottomans in Mesopotamia. Basically Sykes–Picot agreed that the Syrian coast, today's Lebanon, would go to France whilst Britain would take control around Baghdad, and the southern area around Basra. Sykes was a wealthy English dilettante who fluttered around the fringes of diplomacy; such intellectual butterflies exist today. He had a good relationship with the Frenchman Picot, but he apparently had an aristocratic disdain for Picot's countrymen. 'The French,' he once said, 'are incapable of commanding respect, they are not sahibs, they have no gentlemen, the officers have no horses, or guns, or dogs.'

Palestine was a more difficult problem, but the British were smugly content as the Sykes– Picot Agreement had placed France in Syria and Lebanon, between themselves and Russia – shortly to become Bolshevik Russia. As the chapter on Afghanistan makes clear, the British had been obsessed for at least a century before at the steady advance of imperialist Russia towards their Indian dominions. It had been the cause of the First Afghan War.

Balfour was the British Foreign Secretary at this time – the author, or perhaps more accurately the principal instigator, of the famous declaration that bears his name. It proposed a 'national home for the Jews' in Palestine.

Curzon, who succeeded him as Foreign Secretary, said of Balfour:

His charm of manner, his extraordinary intellectual distinction, his seeming indifference to petty matters, his power of dialectic, his long career of public service, blinded all but those who knew him from the inside to the lamentable ignorance, indifference and levity of his regime.

He never studied his papers, he never knew the facts and he never looked ahead. He trusted to his unequalled powers of improvisation to take him through any trouble and enable him to leap lightly from one crisis to another.

For vituperation amongst colleagues this seems familiar! Balfour became Prime Minister, Curzon did not. Someone said of Balfour that his smile was 'like moonlight on a tombstone'. Lloyd George, when asked about

Balfour's contribution to history, said that 'it would be just like scent on a pocket handkerchief'. However, Lloyd George and Balfour were joined together by the idea of 'a national home for the Jews'. Both had been seduced by the charm, magnetism and determination of Chaim Weizmann.

Weizmann's family came from Russia and he was brought up in one of the 'darkest and most remote corners' of the Pale of Settlement where millions of Jews in Russia were 'piled on top of one another', suffering frequent anti-Jewish riots and pogroms. The Jews may have been rich in tradition, intellect and faith, but they were desperately poor. Quite a number of the Russian Jews, like Trotsky, became revolutionaries, as did some of the nastiest specimens of history like Beria; others managed to migrate to North America, Germany and England.

Weizmann took up the cause of Zionism when the struggle for a Jewish homeland appealed to only a small number of 'cranks and visionaries', but during the First World War Zionism grew. And Weizmann and his supporters eventually captured the imagination of the languid, intellectual Balfour and the little Welsh wizard Lloyd George. Both had grown up with the Bible: 'I was taught far more about the history of the Jews than about the history of my own land,' wrote Lloyd George. 'I could tell you all the Kings of Israel, but I doubt whether I could name half a dozen of the Kings of England.'

Lloyd George was thrilled when General Allenby, accompanied by his junior staff officer, Major Lewis Nott, captured Jerusalem, 'something which generations of the chivalry of Europe failed to attain'. He told Harold Nicolson that 'Jews were the most gifted race that mankind has seen since the Greeks of the fifth century'.

The French regarded all this enthusiasm for the Jews with distaste; anti-Semitism was rife amongst the French elite at the time; they claimed that Lloyd George had a mistress who was the wife of a prominent Jewish businessman!

Lloyd George's concern about the desperate plight of the Russian Jews and his quasi-Napoleonic ambitions to dominate the Middle East, acquire its oil and protect the Suez Canal as the road to India all combined to gain his support for Zionism. I doubt whether the livelihood and future of the Palestinian Arabs much crossed his mind.

The concept of a homeland for the Jews was far from capturing other parts of the British political establishment or the overwhelming number of assimilated Jews. Curzon thought the concept absurd. 'What is to become of the people of the country?' he asked. It then numbered about 700,000 mostly Palestinian Arabs, Christians and some Jews. Edwin Montagu, the Jewish Secretary of State for India, described Zionism as a 'mischievous political creed, untenable by any patriotic citizen of the United Kingdom'. Was he now to be told that his true loyalty lay in Palestine, and not in England, his adopted country?

At one stage in the endless battle for a Jewish home, Weizmann wrote to Albert Einstein, 'All the shady characters of the world are against us. Rich servile Jews, dark fanatic Jewish obscurantists, in combination with the Vatican, with Arab assassins, English imperialist anti-Semitic reactionaries etc.'

However, the Balfour Declaration went ahead, mumbling about protection for the 'existing non-Jewish communities in Palestine'. It represented a widely held view that Palestine was somehow empty: 'A land without people – for the people without land.' The Jewish settlers who had arrived before 1914 thought the place and its inhabitants to be primitive beyond belief. The early recruits to Zionism believed that with the liberal and progressive attitudes of the Jewish immigrants the Arabs would be assisted to grow more prosperous, helped out of their tradition-dominated lives. But even before 1914 Arab nationalism was stirring.

In a later chapter I refer to a contemporary diary by Colonel Richard Meinertzhagen. A Zionist, he was right in the centre of social/political affairs, as the following diary entries illustrate:

February 1918, War Office

Lunched with Lady Crewe, both Asquith and Balfour were there. Walther Rothschild showed me a copy of the Balfour Declaration. It is an ambiguous document – and can be interpreted in many ways. I cannot see how a Jewish State can ever be established which would not prejudice the civil and religious rights of the Arabs. I put a straight question to Balfour, 'Is this a reward or bribe to the Jews for past services and was given in the hope of full support during the war?' Balfour at once said, 'Certainly not, both the Prime Minister and myself have been influenced by a desire to give Jews their rightful place in the world, a great nation without a home is not right

.'

24 March 1919

I lunched with Lloyd George and Philip Kerr. I wrote the following to Lloyd George on the 25th March:

My Dear Prime Minister

You asked me yesterday to send you an unofficial letter ...
We are very wise in allowing the Jews to establish their National Home in Palestine. We have also freed the Arabs from the Turkish yoke and we cannot forever remain in Egypt. This Peace Conference has laid two eggs – Jewish Nationalism and Arab Nationalism: they are going to grow up into two troublesome chickens ...

The British position in the Middle East today is paramount; the force of nationalism will challenge our position. We cannot befriend both Jew and Arab. My proposal is based on befriending the people who are more likely to be our loyal friends, the Jews.

The cost of British rule in Palestine was more than 13,000 British and Commonwealth soldiers' lives. The Turks under their German generals fought valiantly but brutally; they were better armed and supplied than the British. One regiment, the Royal Scots, with whom I served in 1954, found that the Turks had mutilated the dead at a place called El Arish and in retribution few captured Turks remained alive. The Royal Scots had already lost two-thirds of their number in Gallipoli. Twice the British assaults on Gaza were repulsed by the Turks with huge casualties. Allenby replaced General Murray and, learning from the mistakes in the trenches on the European front, he moved his headquarters forward to the battlefield (as Montgomery did years later) and devised an encircling strategy which ended the suicidal onslaught over open ground in broad daylight.

The Allied air offensive against the retreating Turks, flying the planes very low and emptying their machine guns into the retreating columns, was combined with flexible cavalry assaults, mainly by the Australians. 'The newest and oldest arms met and mingled, and the result was a victory that will live in history', wrote the correspondent of the *Nation*.

The British, Indian and white Commonwealth soldiers had a dreadful time. They were weighed down with haversacks and the other impedimenta of the infantryman. Wearing their desert tunics they were sent into the Judean hills in mid-winter in rain and sleet with only one thin blanket to keep them warm in the cold nights. Greatcoats had been left behind at the Suez Canal, with all heavy equipment, for greater mobility.

Lloyd George had ordered Allenby to meet the deadline of 'Jerusalem by Christmas – the symbolic prize to raise Allied morale. The swarms of the anopheles mosquito tormented the troops and huge numbers were prostrated with malaria.

To raise the morale of the soldiers the Crusader image was involved in field briefings and religious gatherings. The Rev. Spence quoted the 20th Psalm and said, 'In the Middle Ages, you remember how the arrival of Christendom came to this land to fight against the infidels for the possession of the holy places. And we too are Crusaders, soldiers of the Christian faith, fighting so that the spirit and teaching of Jesus Christ may prevail throughout the world.'

In 1917 the whole of Palestine had been devastated by the war and nowhere more so than the town of Gaza. Turkish-forced conscription had denuded the villages of men who then filtered back home to find that all their livestock and crops had been taken to feed the Turkish troops. All the trees had been cut down within a ten-mile radius of the railway line to provide fuel for the Turkish locomotives. A locust invasion had ravaged the crops in 1915. Many were starving in the towns and typhus raged. The British had employed 120,000 Egyptian fellahin as labourers, porters and servants and many of them absconded in Palestine, adding to the numbers without jobs or sustenance.

My grandfather, Lewis Nott, had been recruited by General Allenby to join his staff whilst he was serving in Alexandria as Chief Censor in Egypt. It seems an odd post to have held, but he was probably given the job by the War Office because he was a fluent Arabic speaker and something of an army rarity in that regard. It was possibly the same reason that led to his posting to Allenby's staff for the invasion of Palestine. His life and career, although he was never a major player in this story of twentieth-century British imperialism, beautifully illustrates the genesis of the chaos in the Middle East which continues to this day.

After the conquest of Palestine he was appointed by Allenby as Military Governor of Gaza, which had seen the worst fighting of the whole campaign and then, when the Colonial Office took over from the military government in 1921, he became Civil Administrator of that city. Later he was moved to be Governor in Nablus and Tulkaram.

My family records only contain one letter from General Allenby to my grandfather, dated 9 August 1921, written from 9 Upper Cheyne Row, Chelsea, SW, apparently after Allenby was given his peerage and returned to England:

My Dear Nott

I am glad to hear that the people of that sorely stricken town [Gaza] are bravely facing the task of reconstruction; and I know that a new Gaza may arise, happy and prosperous as the Gaza of old. I wish you every success in your efforts to help in reviving the arts and crafts of that town.

All best wishes to you
Yours sincerely

Allenby

We also have a letter, dated 29 June 1920, from Major-General Sir Louis Bols, Chief Administrator in Palestine, written from 'Headquarters, Occupied Enemy Administration (South) Jerusalem', which reads:

My dear Nott

I thank you deeply for all you have done for me during the last seven months, and I want to tell you how much I appreciate your hard work & your loyalty to this Administration and to me

We have had some delicate and difficult periods, athough I have been supported by the certainty that all possible has been done by you and your officers for the good of the country and for the honour of our Empire. Will you please convey this message to all officers and officials under your command.

I wish every one of you all success in the future.
Sincerely Yours

L J Bols

There is a further letter from Sir Wyndham Deedes, Civil Secretary of the Palestine Government - written on 28 Februrary 1920 - which reads:

Secretariat

Government House

Jerusalem

My Dear Nott,

A line to thank you most warmly for the most enjoyable and interesting
time spent with you
Although the physical aspect of Gaza town is depressing the spirit of
the people, is most encouraging and is easy to see where they derive
their inspriation.I have given HE a glowing account of it. I will do all I
can to help in the various matters you brought to my notice and enclose
£5 for the school (girls).

Sincerely

Wyndham Deedes

and please convey message to both your nice notables and the Mayor

My grandfather was born in India in 1869 whilst his father William was
serving there as an officer of the Hampshire Regiment. His mother came
from a prosperous Jewish family called Woolf. Her brother was the
Liberal MP for Pontefract in 1880 and the family, who had been china
merchants in London, bought and ran a substantial ceramics business
in Knottingley. I do not know where the Woolf family came from,
but I suspect that they were originally immigrants, via Germany, from
Tsarist Russia, the home of some seven million Jews, half of the world's
population of Jewry at the time.

William Nott of the Hampshire Regiment, my great grandfather, was
the son of a snobbish Victorian parson, also William, who had married
into the aristocracy. My great-grandfather's parents deeply disapproved
of his marriage, and so did his regiment. It was considered entirely

inappropriate for a colonel in the Hampshire Regiment to marry a Jewish lady, however respectable; he left the regiment under a cloud.

My grandfather was brought up as a Christian and the fact that he had a Jewish mother seems not to have clouded his judgement. Indeed, as far as one can judge, he, like the majority of serving officers in the Mandate administration, had strong sympathy for the Palestinian Arabs, not least I suspect because as an Arabic speaker he could actually communicate with them, unlike the vast majority of his colleagues. His friendship with King Abdullah of Transjordan lasted all his life.

As a young man, he had joined the Army and was commissioned in 1879 into the York and Lancaster Regiment. His religious beliefs became the foundation of all his motives, his career and outlook. He found the boisterous nature of mess life, the gambling, drinking and womanising of the officer class, distressing. He resigned his commission and went out to Nigeria as a missionary with the Church Missionary Society.

Northern Nigeria was a Moslem country. My grandfather was a good linguist and he learnt Arabic and Hausa. When he contracted blackwater fever he returned to England and joined the London School of Oriental Languages, where he helped to compile the first English Hausa dictionary. He also translated the New Testament into Hausa and wrote children's stories for the schools; they were still in use when I visited Nigeria as Trade Secretary in 1979.

When the First World War began he rejoined his regiment, the York and Lancasters, and was posted to Egypt, which is where this story of his life begins.

Several of the original sources of the Mandate administration are held in the Israel State Archives in Jerusalem, but they represent perhaps one-fifth of the whole. Much of the documentation was destroyed when Jewish terrorists destroyed the administrative wing of the King David Hotel in 1946. Other files were destroyed when the British evacuated Palestine, including much of the personal material on the Mandate's employees.

The papers of Lord Samuel, the first British High Commissioner in Palestine, do exist, as do the papers of Sir John Chancellor, the third High Commissioner, which are in St Anthony's College, Oxford. But of the actual documents of my grandfather's time as Military Governor in Gaza, and as a Governor in Tulkaram and Nablus, few seem to exist. I therefore have had to rely primarily on the vivid memory of my grandfather and grandmother who died with their brains very active at the respective ages of ninety-six and ninety-seven; and also of my uncle, now approaching one hundred years of age, who spent his school holidays in Palestine between 1918 and 1925.

An American historian, William Roger Louis, has written, 'One of the fascinations of the candid British documentation of the era which does exist is the sense of men struggling against overwhelming odds with an acute awareness of moral purpose.'

Meinertzhagen's diary records:

2 July, Port Said
The position of many officials in Palestine is desperate – conflicting loyalties, rival claimants, the intelligence of the Jews and the senseless fanaticism of the Arabs, the varying interpretations of justice etc.

The author Naomi Shepherd, an academic historian of this story from whom I have drawn much of the material for this chapter, wrote a book entitled Ploughing Sand. Indeed, my grandfather and nearly all the administrators of the Mandate were 'ploughing sand'. Ronald Storrs, the Governor of Jerusalem, once said, 'Two hours of Arab grievances drive me into the synagogue, while after an intense course of Zionist propaganda I am prepared to embrace Islam.'

Whether it could all have been different without the Balfour Declaration and, instead of the Mandate, the British had retreated from the region, it is impossible to say. The structure of Arab society, ossified by 400 years of Ottoman rule, with deep suspicion between Shia and Sunni, and with tribal rivalry throughout the region, perhaps suggests that we might have inherited a different kind of chaos. Would the Middle East have been more stable, less militant and less of a threat to Western values had the British stayed away? It seems unlikely.

And where would seven million Russian and Polish Jews have gone? It seems inconceivable after generations of anti-Semitic discrimination they would have remained settled and peaceful in Bolshevik Russia. The pressures were everywhere reaching bursting point and, having served as a senior politician, I can see the intractability of so many human problems around the world.

The first High Commissioner to Palestine, Sir Herbert Samuel, who replaced General Allenby in 1920, stepped ashore in Jaffa wearing the full kit of a Colonial Governor. He had been appointed to the post by Lloyd George who had offered him the Home Secretaryship, a post that he had held under Asquith; but he had declined in dissatisfaction at the manner in which Asquith had been supplanted by Lloyd George.

Meinertzhagen's diary records:

> Herbert Samuel was one of the best administrators which mandated Palestine had. Being a Jew he naturally sympathized with the National Home, but on every occasion observed strict fairness, often slightly leaning against his own people.
>
> Samuel was fortunate in having at his side Chief Secretary Wyndham Deedes, a man of complete integrity and one of the purest Christians I have ever met. His essential character was saintliness and he had a genius for making those he met the better for it.

Samuel had been a fervent supporter of Zionism in England, so he was under the deepest suspicion and distrusted by the Arabs. The Jews were delighted at his appointment, only to be disillusioned as he grappled with the problems of the Jewish Home. Samuel came from an assimilated

Anglo-Jewish family and he found that Zionism provided an outlet for his Jewish allegiances. In a rather famous memorandum, which he had circulated around the British Cabinet during the First World War, he had written that Zionism promises that 'the sordid associations which have attached to the Jewish race which had "produced great men in Palestine", would do so again'.

My grandfather met Herbert Samuel many times, liked him and had great respect for his endeavours. Samuel did everything that he could to reconcile Jews and Arabs and tried, from his earliest days, to help Arab agriculture and education. His first concern was to bring Arabs and Jews together in some kind of representative assembly as a first step towards the creation of some self-governing institution. But the Arabs would have none of it.

Samuel genuinely believed that if he could attract skilled Jewish engineers to develop the country for the benefit of Jews and Arabs alike, it might be financed by world Jewry. The British Treasury provided nothing, insisting that Palestine must be financially self-supporting, but neither the right Jewish immigrants nor the investment funds were forthcoming.

In spite of Weizmann's ambitions, the Zionists were only able to recruit a few thousand immigrants in the early years, but this was sufficient to create Arab hostility and devastate Samuel's genuine and sincere ambitions for the country.

The tension exploded in the first anti-Jewish riots in May 1921. There is an interesting letter to my grandfather in our family records, dated 12 May 1921, from a Jewish Committee 'Rehobot' near Jaffa, stamped with the Star of David, which reads:

> To the District Governor, Gaza
> Dear Sir
>   With great joy we received your invitation to come to Ber-tonya tomorrow, and we are thanking you infinitely for your kindness

But, dear Sir, although there is a complete peace and a full mutual understanding between us and our neighbours north of Gaza, the road is not as secure yet as to venture travelling on it.

If you could come over to us, dear Sir, we believe that the success of your undertaking to favour peace, would have been sure – Believe us, dear Sir,

Your obedient servants

A Eisenberg

Two Jewish groups, Socialists and Communists, quarrelled and the street fighting spread. Arabs set upon the Jewish demonstrators and in the resultant chaos many Jews were killed and their homes looted. The Jews fought back and more than a hundred Jews and Arabs were killed. After two days of rioting Samuel declared martial law and suspended Jewish immigration. Later he made a speech which qualified his earlier support of Zionism and redefined the Jewish National House as something which had to be balanced with the British obligation to the Palestinian Arabs.

The Mandate officers, including my grandfather, were supportive of Arab grievances and saw amongst the small Jewish Communist Party the vanguard of a sinister Russian, anti-British and anti-Christian conspiracy. Most concluded that Zionist provocation and contempt for local Arab customs were the cause of the rioting – and there was widespread dislike for the arrogance of the new Jewish immigrants who walked around 'scantily clad' with their secular attitudes that offended Muslim and Christians alike.

Samuel continued to try and compensate the Arabs for the disadvantages which they were seen to be suffering under the Mandate, but it was impossible to find representatives for the Arab cause in post-Ottoman Palestine Arab society. As today, the Arabs were divided amongst themselves and seemingly unable to organise their own interests or leadership.

The first Civil Secretary, Wyndham Deedes, knew my grandfather well, had been Chief Intelligence Officer with the British Army in Sinai and Palestine, Military Attaché in Constantinople and Director of Public Security in Egypt. A personal and confidential letter from Wyndham Deedes, dated 9 May 1921, to my grandfather reads:

> My Dear Nott
>
> I am directed by His Excellency the High Commissioner to convey to you his great satisfaction and appreciation of the fact that during the recent troubles in the country you were able to maintain law and order in your District without having recourse to the active intervention of His Majesty's Forces.
>
> That you succeeded in so doing bears eloquent testimony to the influence which you exercise over the population in your District, and to the confidence which the latter repose in you.
>
> Wyndham Deedes

Deedes was amongst the many outstanding servants of the Mandate who were, in part, and slowly in the 1920s, to be replaced by career colonial civil servants who moved from post to post – Sudan to Egypt to Africa as part of their career path. It was frustration at Colonial Office-control from London and an influx of colonial officers that eventually led to my grandfather's resignation in 1930.

It is worth setting out in full, in memory of my grandfather, the speech of the Mayor of Gaza, made of course in Arabic, when my grandfather left Gaza for Tulkarm:

> My Respected Sir; Ladies and Gentlemen
>
> We are gathered here in this reception by one noble motive: bidding farewell to our beloved Governor and sincere friend, Mr. L H Nott. The mere presence of us all notables, olamas, officials, lawyers, doctors,

farmers and merchants, is a clear proof of our love and loyalty to our Governor, and of our firm connection with him.

Sir, we have come to bid you good-bye after you had spent among us two years of good service and strong exertion. Your connections with the natives in general and with the municipality in special, had been personal more than official. No problem had risen between you and the Beladiya, either from the natives or from the Government, but was solved with mutual understanding which was due to your wisdom and excellent management. So it is not strange to see us gathered to-day to explain our utmost regret for your departure. Gaza will never forget your efforts and hard struggles to uplift the district in every way.

You had worked and toiled day and night for the welfare and happiness of the town.

Good-bye, our good Governor, good-bye, supplied with our best wishes for you and your honourable wife, and we wish you would always be the source of goodness and virtue to all.

I like also to seize the opportunity of the presence of Mr. Cartwright among us, who is said to be the sub-governor of Gaza proper, a District, to welcome him. The days of your absence on leave had shown the strong desire he has for uplifting the district. So it is a comfort for us all to see that our beloved Governor has left us a good successor; and we hope that his days would be the same as yours, days of work and energy.

In conclusion, I again bid you farewell and ask the Almighty to protect you day and night and guard you wherever you go or live.

N Nakhla - for the Mayor of Gaza Municipality

The Governors, as they were called, or District Commissioners in today's parlance, had an enviable if frustrating task. Their authority over their districts was similar to the officers of the Indian Civil Service, who ruled over vast tracts of the populated Punjab or Uttar Pradesh. Similar authority was held by colonial officers in Africa; surely these appointments were amongst the most satisfying and constructive careers ever held by

Englishmen. Unfortunately there was a significant difference between the officers of the Indian Civil Service, the Sudanese Colonial Service and their colleagues in Palestine.

Whilst the Civil Administrator in Palestine District combined the function of Lord Lieutenant, County Sheriff, town planner, police superintendent, county councillor, poor law guardian, justice of the peace and coroner, he was never able to act without endorsement from the Central Government in Jerusalem. The great Victorian builders and adventurers in India were hardly subject to the control of the East India Company in Calcutta; they expanded the British Empire on their own initiative; with a healthy contempt for the centre.

The British regional authorities in Palestine attended evenings of vice-regal formality at Government House, their names called out in turn for an official handshake with the High Commissioner. Guests were chosen carefully from the religious professional and administrative elite of each community, though the Muslims seldom attended. Mandate officials went straight from Sunday Service at St George's Cathedral to cricket matches at the Jerusalem Sports Club. Samuel lectured on the poetry of Keats. Storrs, the Governor of Jerusalem, much disliked by my grandfather, played Shylock in The Merchant of Venice. The wives competed at flower shows, held tea parties, set up charitable institutions for the needy, but seldom, partly because of language barriers, invited the locals to their homes.

When the Colonial Office in London expanded its influence in Palestine as the 1920s drew to a close and the nightmare of Arab-Jewish conflict intensified, my grandfather's frustration increased, particularly with the Arabist regime in Jerusalem. His father had served in India and the Sudan and somehow Palestine did not measure up to the authority held by District Commissioners in these countries.

Herbert Samuel, unable to find a genuine Arab representative organisation until the later formation of an Arab Executive, had to rely on his Political Secretary, Ernest Richmond, who in the early days became a sort of mediator between the Arab community and the High Commission. In the late 1920s, after elections according to Ottoman precedent and a great deal of manoeuvring amongst the leading Arab families, the man appointed Mufti, or leader, was Haj Amin al-Husseini, a young nationalist who had been condemned to ten years' imprisonment for his part in the 1920s riots. He was amnestied by Samuel, but still blacklisted by the police as an agitator.

Samuel had proposed elections, but they were boycotted by most Arab electors; he then proposed an Arab agency to balance the Jewish Agency, but this too was rejected. Eventually a new body called the Supreme Muslim Council was created and Husseini became its President. It was in total opposition to the Balfour Declaration, but the Colonial Office in London was satisfied that Samuel had reconciled the Palestine Muslims to the Mandatory regime. It was to become a third parallel government in Palestine, the Jewish Agency and the British High Commission being the others.

The differences amongst the British authorities exploded when Richmond, in spite of Samuel's efforts to create a balance between Jewish and Arab interests, resigned in 1924. In his resignation letter he claimed that his objections were not merely political but moral and even religious. He had tried 'to alter the machine', ending support for the Jewish National Home. He argued that the Zionist Commission, the Middle East Department of the Colonial Office and Samuel's administration were 'dominated and inspired by a spirit which I can only regard as evil'. Richmond was an ardent Catholic, much disliked by my grandfather, who was an equally ardent evangelical. My grandfather was a strong supporter of Samuel and a believer that many of the authorities in Jerusalem, together with the Colonial Office in London, had been captured by the Arabists. It still is an oft-repeated charge against the Foreign Office today.

With all these troubles beginning to build during Herbert Samuel's time as High Commissioner, the most contentious issue became the whole subject of Jewish immigration, my grandfather's memories are worth recounting primarily because of the lessons which it teaches us about uncontrolled immigration into the United Kingdom.

British Palestine did not correspond to anything in Palestine's past. The borders, as Margaret MacMillan explains in Peacemakers, had been delineated at the Paris Peace Conference to divide up the region between the French and the British. There was no corresponding Ottoman frontier and a substantial section of the population, particularly the Bedouin tribes, were nomadic. There were a number of official entry points in Haifa and Jaffa, at Beersheba and Gaza, on the Lebanese border and on the River Jordan, but the rest of the country was porous. There was a steady demand by illegal immigrants for the services of local people who knew the tracks over the hills, and guides or smugglers established themselves in Lebanon and Syria.

Commencing in Samuel's time a continual struggle was undertaken to control illegal Jewish immigration, but without success. District officers and the police were authorised in 1925 to order summary deportation, and there was no Human Rights Act to obstruct their efforts. The worst problem came with what were known as 'travellers', people who came on three-month tourist visas and then remained. Sir John Chancellor, the third High Commissioner, wrote to the Secretary of State for the Colonies in 1930, 'It is extremely difficult to find a man once he has entered Palestine, if he does not wish to be found, and even if he is found, the difficulties in the way of deportation are often insuperable'! As anti-Semitism and economic need grew in Eastern Europe the pressures became intolerable. Albert Hyamson, the Jewish Director of Immigration, fought a continuous battle for more restrictions and laws. He was particularly concerned at growing Bolshevik influence in Palestine as a result of illegal Jewish immigrants from Russia.

However, the truth was that most of the Mandatory authorities thought that the demands for greater documentation and authorisation were absurd. As new rules became more complicated so new stratagems to evade them multiplied.

In the summer of 1922 Winston Churchill, then Colonial Secretary, produced a White Paper incorporating many of Samuel's second thoughts on the National Home and laid down a principle that immigration should be limited to 'the economic capacity of the country ... to absorb new arrivals'. Categories of 'desirable' immigrants were concocted – those of independent means, those with prospects for employment and those who were dependants of those already resident in Palestine. It all sounds familiar, but the truth was that the whole system, in spite of efforts by governments in London and Jerusalem, had broken down – and, of course, with the rise of Nazism after my grandfather left, it collapsed altogether.

Are there lessons to be learnt from the Palestine experience? Nothing, I fear, that will satisfy British public opinion and the press in Britain today. The United Kingdom may be an island but as a large, prosperous, open economy it is as porous as Palestine was in the 1920s and 1930s.

Economic migration may be inhibited by rules and regulations, but it will never be satisfactorily controlled in a free society. I suspect that the senior officials grappling with this problem today know in their heart of hearts that the strident demands of ministers and the press are as absurd and as impossible to implement successfully, as was the case in Palestine in the 1920s.

According to my grandfather, the second contentious issue which dominated his life was the land issue. We do have one letter from Herbert Samuel in Jerusalem whilst High Commissioner, dated 23 March 1922, congratulating my grandfather on chairing the Tithes Commission, which concerned itself with Land Tenure in Palestine:

> My dear Nott
> I have read with great interest the admirable report presented by the Tithes Commission and desire to express to you my warm thanks for a very thorough and valuable piece of work.
>
> Yours sincerely
>
> Herbert Samuel

The Ottoman Land Registry had been so badly administered and was so riddled with fraudulent claims that its content provided insufficient evidence of ownership. The last Sultan, Abdul Hamid, had commandeered around one-seventh of all the land in Palestine – and Turkish reforms in the mid-nineteenth century had favoured the landlords over the tenants, who were impoverished with debt and exploitation. The urban class had purchased much of the best land for a pittance over earlier years. It is believed that as much as two-thirds of the land was actually held in unregistered title because ownership rendered the landlord liable to taxation and conscription into the Turkish Army. So untraceable pseudonyms were the norm.

The Commissioners had an obligation to find land for the Jewish immigrants. Until 1925 or so the Arab politicians were so active in railing against the Balfour Declaration and Jewish immigration that they did little to resist the sale of Arab land to the Jews. Indeed, most of the land sales to the Jews were by absentee Arab landlords in Syria and the Lebanon. An example was the sale of a large area of fertile land on the coastal plain between Haifa and Tel Aviv by a Palestinian Arab family, who tried to conceal their names when they sold it to the Jewish Agency.

The largest single sale was the marshy, but potential fertile, land in the Esdraelon Valley which was sold by a Palestinian family of Beirut in the mid-1920s.

My grandfather, who helped the Jews settle in the Esdraelon Valley, told me of how the early Jewish immigrants were given seed, food and subsistence shelter, together with diesel oil to counteract the swarms of marsh mosquitoes. Of course within a few years the Jewish immigrants made this neglected land fertile and productive. In the Tulkaram district at a village called Zeita no fewer than 906 families had claims over the same land.

The most effective opponent of land sales to the Jews were not religious leaders of the Arab community, the Mufti, who only got around to issuing a fatwa forbidding land sales to the Jews in 1935, but the third British High Commissioner, Sir John Chancellor. He decided to bring an end to the collusion between Arabs and Jews; he was worried about the dispossession of the fellahin on the social structure of the country. In attempting to ban all land sales to the Jews, he was really reversing the Balfour Declaration, but heavy lobbying by the Jewish Agency in London led to disagreement between him and the Colonial Office, so the land sales went ahead. In public the Arab executive demanded an end of land transfers, whilst in private its own members were busily profiting from the high land prices pushed up by the Jewish purchasers. There is much talk today of Jewish settlements on Arab land, but much of the good land in Palestine was sold in the 1920s by greedy and unscrupulous Arab landlords who shifted their profits into Beirut.

***

There does come a moment with every seemingly intractable problem when a window opens up to provide some way forward. Often it is on the edge of an abyss. Tony Blair grasped such an opportunity in Northern Ireland when the IRA saw that they might make greater progress in achieving their objectives through politics rather than the gun. Blair worked for a solution with courage and persistence.

I do not believe that such a window of opportunity yet exists with the Arab-Israeli dispute. President Bush has been criticised by the Europeans for failing in his promise to open up a fresh dialogue around the so-called Two-State Solution. But neither the will nor the atmosphere exists for genuine dialogue and concession; what is the point in pursuing a course of fruitless diplomacy?

With Hamas an election victor, albeit dismayed at the chaos they have created all around them, and with a resurgent Hezbollah in Lebanon, where could a way be found? Both organisations remain committed to the destruction of the Jewish State, a course volubly supported by the President of Iran. Blair's attempts to secure his legacy in the Middle East are really rather sad. I fear that, like all prime ministers who outstay their welcome, however well they might have performed in that isolated haven called No. 10, self-delusion eventually gets them. I recall my comment in my memoir:

If I was a historian, I would place some Labour leaders higher in the history books than their Conservative counterparts. I would place Atlee, Blair and Callaghan higher in the pantheon of Prime Ministerial talent than Eden, Macmillan, Home, Heath and Major. Taking all these individuals together only Atlee and Thatcher stand out as great post-war holders of that office. Blair is an interesting phenomenon. He might have been a candidate for that hall of fame, but I suspect that hubris will lead to his premature demise.

I wrote that in early 2002.

In this chapter I have covered the many efforts made during the British Mandate to bring the two sides together, but British diplomacy was rejected every time, the Arabs claiming that all the land of Palestine was theirs. In 1946–7 British rule was attacked from both sides, in particular by the Jewish terrorist organisations led by Menachem Begin. A series of fruitless proposals were made to find a way forward by the Atlee government, but all failed, more often as a result, again, of the intransigence of the Arabs. In the end the British government simply cut and ran, contrary to the United Nations mandate. Then followed the Arab-Israeli War in 1948–9 between the new State of Israel and neighbouring Arab regimes. It ended in another disaster for the Arabs.

There is a viable aspiration in existence – and it has been around for nearly one hundred years. It was well expressed by Shimon Peres, former Israeli Prime Minister, in May 1998:

For Israel to remain a Jewish State, both morally and demographically, it needs a Palestinian State. Today 4.7 million Jews and 4 million Arabs lie between the Mediterranean and the River Jordan. Without two separate states, a bi-national state will come into being, to the great frustration of the two peoples.

Then I quote the words of a noted peace activist, Marian Kromkowski, in a paper dated 4 December 2003 – and we are back at square one because she outlines just a few of the fundamental problems for the Arab side:

The two-state solution is not just. It is no solution to the turmoil in historic Palestine because at the core it does not undo any wrongs. It is unjust because it is premised on the continued acceptance of the Zionist claim to at least th ree-quarters, if not all, of Palestine as being the exclusive land of the Jews.

It is fundamentally flawed as it denies Palestinians the right of return; it abandons the Palestinians living within Israel; it does not provide Palestinians any semblance of an independent sovereign state and it allows the US to maintain the role as the main imperialist occupier of the entire Middle East.

If any solution is impossible that does not 'undo past wrongs' then all progress is impossible. The State of Israel will survive by force or be destroyed by force. I see no other outcome in my lifetime.

IRAQ –
THE BETRAYAL OF THE ARABS
1920

In a book I wrote in 2003, *Mr Wonderful Takes A Cruise,* I described a visit that I made to the International Institute of Strategic Studies in London in December 2002, for a meeting on Iraq which was to be addressed by Paul Wolfowitz, then Deputy Secretary of Defense at the Pentagon:

> Mr Blair, on President Bush's instructions, wants to invade Iraq, but I am opposed to military intervention, as I believe it could destabilise the whole Middle East; and how can intervention by the Americans do anything other than escalate Islamic extremism all around the world?
>
> The replacement of the doctrine of deterrence with pre-emption – the doctrine of pre-emptive war – will bring about an unstable and dangerous world.
>
> We have unfinished business in Bosnia, Kosovo, Afghanistan and Palestine, and the Americans imagine that they can introduce a liberal democracy in Iraq and police the Middle East – it beggars belief. Have they never studied the British Mandate in Palestine and 150 years of our attempts to stabilise Afghanistan?

Mr Wolfowitz explained how the Americans saw themselves 'bringing about a strategic transformation of the whole region. What nonsense he talks.'

I make no great claims to prophesy, but my worst fears have been realised. The invasion of Iraq is the latest disaster to befall the Arabs. It has fractured society in the most tragic way. I do not accuse the Americans of imperialist ambitions either for oil or territory – just naivety and ignorance of history. There is no excuse for the British government and less still for the Conservative Opposition, both of which were seduced by the neo-conservative voice in Washington, urged on no doubt by the Jewish lobby. A short study of post-First World War history would surely have convinced these politicians that Western intervention in the cauldron of the Middle East is the surest way of destabilising the whole region and ultimately threatening our own security. Saddam Hussein, evil as he was, was maintaining a tenuous balance of power in the Middle East and through terror was imposing a fragile truce between Sunni and Shia; it has now broken down. The West had no option but response when Saddam invaded Kuwait in August 1990, but the argument for intervention to bring about regime change in Iraq was madness. Now the protagonists for the invasion are hiding their embarrassment by claiming that it was poor post-war planning that has caused the catastrophe. It was nothing of the sort. The invasion itself was the problem.

***

I became interested in the plight of Arabs as a result of talking to my grandfather, Lewis Nott. He was clearly a far-sighted and successful official, as the following letter from Wyndham Deedes makes clear:

Government House
Jerusalem

My dear Nott

I must write and thank you for one of the most enjoyable and instructive tours I have had here. I gave His Excellency a full account of all your work and he is watching with interest your various experiments with a view to more general adoption of them if successful – I think, if I may say so, it is wonderful what you have done and do with your people. If only you could stamp out politics!

I have urged that you be put on the Loans Committee and Col Cox will have to spare you for that and I dare say other things. Your deep knowledge of local affairs must be placed at general disposal.

Your leave letter (if answered) please re-submit for His Excellency's instructions. It may be a special case, let him decide it.

Sincerely and with renewed thanks

Wyndham Deedes

My grandfather used to talk, of course, about the Palestinian Arabs, but also with enthusiasm of King Abdullah of Transjordan, the great-grandfather of the present king, of whom more later. On the recommendation of the government in Jerusalem, Abdullah visited Nablus in Palestine with a large Arab caravan and many retainers when my grandfather was Governor there. The two of them got on famously, no doubt because they could communicate in Arabic. He came to visit the Palestinian Arabs in my grandfather's district and told him how his family had been more or less abandoned by the British in 1920. Being a great gentleman he expressed no resentment and certainly no suggestion of betrayal.

After their time in Nablus, Abdullah asked my grandfather to visit him in Jordan as his guest, but he was never able to do so. When Abdullah made an official visit to London in the 1930s, he asked to see my grandfather, who entertained him and his entourage at Brown's Hotel, off Picadilly. The dinner took a large chunk out of my grandfather's income; but my uncle insists that he paid the bill!

Many years later, as Defence Secretary, I made frequent visits to the Arab world, especially to Saudi Arabia and Oman. On one occasion my wife and I were given a family dinner by King Hussein, the grandson of Abdullah, and the only Hashemite to have survived as a ruler. After dinner at his country estate outside Amman we were invited into the garden and there, in the far distance, were the flickering lights of Jerusalem. Hussein pointed to Jerusalem and said that he couldn't go there any more but, as a young man, he had made frequent forays into the city. It was rather sad.

When the First World War began, the Ottoman leaders in Turkey gambled, and failed. In deciding to oppose Russia, which was allied to their old friend Britain, they joined the war on the side of Germany and Austria-Hungary. In historical terms it was an odd decision for them to make. At Gallipoli and in Mesopotamia the Turks had humiliated the Allies but by 1918 the Ottomans were exhausted; they had lost most of their European empire in 1908, which had previously stretched to the walls of Vienna, and all of their huge territories in the Middle East were gone. Their Arab subjects, who had lived largely in feudal poverty, had no champion to protect them. Certainly the Arab urban elite, who had grown prosperous at the expense of the rural peasants, intermarried with Syrians, Christians and Turks, were in a mood to grab what they could in the disintegrating structure of old Ottoman society. As landlords they had no compunction about exploiting the rural Arabs, selling their properties to the Jews over the head of their tenants.

There was no sympathy for the Ottomans in London. Curzon, Chairman of the Middle East Committee of the Cabinet, said, 'their record is one of misrule, oppression, intrigue and massacre almost unparalleled in the history of the Eastern world'. Lloyd George shared his views and had inherited his hostility to the Turks from Gladstone. The Turks, wrote Gladstone, 'one and all, bag and baggage, shall, I hope, clear out from the province they have desolated and profaned.' The memories of the Bulgarian and Armenian massacres were still in men's minds.

In 1915, the British were in pretty desperate straits in the Middle East. Obsessed with protecting the Suez Canal and the route to India, they cast around for help and alighted on a charismatic Arab aristocrat named Faisal. He was to lead the Arab revolt against the Turks, with the help of British weapons, advisers and lashings of gold sovereigns. Faisal, descendant of the Prophet and a member of the old Hashemite class, was clever, determined and very ambitious. Although he had been brought up in a cosmopolitan atmosphere in Constantinople he was everyone's image of what a noble desert Arab should be. The Zionist and anti-Arab diarist Colonel Richard Meinertzhagen observed: 'The Arab with his picturesque clothes and romantic surroundings, has always appealed to Englishmen: his simple mind, often a cloak for stupidity, and his dignity, usually a cloak for lack of humour, has always appealed to those who administer him.'

In 1915 Sir Henry McMahon, a senior official in Cairo, had opened discussions with Faisal's father Hussein, the Sharif of Mecca. Hussein was head of one of the Arab world's most ancient and distinguished families, guardian of Islam's holiest sites through the Hejaz. Although the correspondence was much disputed subsequently, McMahon promised Hussein that if the Arabs rose against the Turks they would have British assistance and post-war independence. To protect British and French interests some areas were specifically excluded from Arab rule, namely the coast of Syria and Lebanon as well as the Turkish provinces of Baghdad and Basra. The British pretended subsequently that Palestine had also been excluded, but it had not.

Whatever the intention of the parties may have been – and in their position of desperation the British were not overly concerned with tomorrow – Hussein and his supporters certainly believed that they had done a deal with an imperial power that they trusted. Hussein believed that even in the excluded areas the government would be Arab under European supervision, stretching from the Arabian peninsula up through Palestine to the interior of Syria and to Mosul, including Mesopotamia.

Like the Sykes–Picot Agreement, the Hussein–McMahon letters were a short-term expedient rather than a decided strategy and the most conflicting promise of all turned out to be the Balfour Declaration.

However, in June 1916 the Arab revolt began and the British were pleased with their diplomacy. Hussein declared himself King of the Arabs. Four of his sons fought the Turks, but Faisal was the leader. Riding at Faisal's side was the British liaison officer T. E. Lawrence, who was later to be known as Lawrence of Arabia, the author of The Seven Pillars of Wisdom.

Colonel Richard Meinertzhagen was General Allenby's Political Officer for Palestine and Syria, acting as a sort of commissar, reporting behind the back of his superiors to the politicians and senior mandarins in Whitehall. When his manoeuvring made his post in Egypt and Palestine impossible, he was recruited by the Colonial Secretary, Winston Churchill, to become his Military Adviser on Middle Eastern Affairs. He sat for some time at a Colonial Office desk opposite Lawrence, who was, of course, in contrast to Meinertzhagen, a passionate supporter of the Arabs.

Meinertzhagen said of Lawrence:

> though I probably knew him as well as anybody else, I am quite unable to be consistent about this very complex and interesting man. To know him well was to love him. To know the worst in a man whom one respects and likes, increases affection. It is when one suspects the worst that contempt creeps in. He was a shy show-off with little to show, a mass of contradictions and an artist in trying to hide himself in a blaze of limelight. He practised secrecy lit up by publicity; he neither denied nor confirmed many complementary myths about himself.

Meinertzhagen, who met and communicated with all the principal political and military figures of his day, left a contemporary diary which has proved to be one of the most valuable documents of the time. (His nephew, Daniel, would proceed me as Chairman of Lazard Brothers in the City in the seventies.) His diary is very similar to, and his judgements equally as suspect as, those of that modern diarist Alan Clark (see also the chapter on the Falklands). Like Alan Clark he had a great capacity for intrigue and manoeuvre, but he brings the troubles of this period alive with his pithy observations.

In 1910, on his thirty-second birthday, Meinertzhagen was dining with the British consul in Odessa when a pogrom erupted in the streets outside. He watched with impotent rage as Jewish shops were looted and Jewish men, women and children were hunted down, beaten and left dead in the gutter. 'I am deeply moved by these terrible deeds', he recorded in his diary, 'and resolved that whenever or where I can help the Jews; I shall do so to the best of my ability.'

These events helped to turn Meinertzhagen into a Zionist, though he – who was neither Jewish nor, in any conventional sense, a Christian – said that he was also much influenced by 'the Divine Promise that the Holy land will forever remain Israel's inheritance'. He worked hard and effectively for the Zionist cause, in the Middle East (where he first met Lawrence) and in Paris at the Peace Conference after the Great War.

It was Meinertzhagen's zeal for the Jewish cause that brought him to Berlin in the 1930s: he had hoped for some assurance from the Nazi leaders that the Jewish citizens of the Reich would be well treated. Naturally, he received such assurances, and naturally he soon came to understand how false they were: in Berlin one July morning in 1939, less than three months before the outbreak of war, Meinertzhagen was summoned into the presence of the Reichschancellor. It wasn't their first meeting: five years earlier, Colonel Meinertzhagen had taken the long, slow walk from the door of Hitler's office towards the small, distant figure wearing the swastika armband. When they finally met in the middle, the Führer had thrown up his hand and yelled, 'Heil Hitler!' Naturally wishing to be polite, Meinertzhagen had done the same: 'Heil Meinertzhagen!' he had shouted. Nobody laughed.

When the war ended, the difficulties began. How were the British and French to square this circle? They had agreed in the Sykes–Picot deal that France should have Syria, but the British had promised Hussein that Faisal should be ruler of an independent Syria. Lloyd George urged Clemenceau to accept Faisal as ruler of Syria and warned of the consequences if he did not do so. Allenby was summoned to Paris from Syria and warned that the Arabs would violently oppose a French occupation.

Lloyd George is reported to have said to Clemenceau:

> Except for Great Britain, no one had contributed more than a handful of black troops to the Expedition in Palestine. I was really surprised at the lack of generosity on the part of the French Government. The British had now some 500,000 men on Turkish soil. The British had captured three or four Turkish armies and had incurred hundreds of thousands of casualties. The other government (the French) had only put in a few nigger policemen to see we did not steal the Holy Sepulchre!

Clemenceau retorted that the French had far more troops than the British on the Western Front and that the war would have ended earlier if the British had not diverted so many soldiers to the Middle East. In Paris, the row between the British and French continued, culminating in a violent scene between Lloyd George and Clemenceau.

Curzon and the Foreign Office were determined to restrict the French presence in the eastern Mediterranean: 'After all the two countries had fought for centuries over Europe, North America, India, Africa and the Middle East. Their friendship by comparison was a recent affair.' He went on:

> A good deal of my public life has been spent in connection with the political ambitions of France, which I have come across in Tunis, in Siam and in almost every distant region where the French have sway. We have been brought, for reasons of national safety, into an alliance with the French, which I hope will last, but their national character is

different from ours, and their political interests collide with our own in many cases. I am seriously afraid that the great power from whom we may have most to fear in the future is France.

Faisal, accompanied by Lawrence, had gone back and forth to Paris where Woodrow Wilson, Lloyd George and Clemenceau were trying to agree amongst themselves. The French saw Lawrence as Faisal's 'evil genius', who had turned the simple Arab against them.

Meinerzthagen's diary on 7 August 1919:

> I have come up here to arrange better relations between the French and the Emir Faisal …
>
> But it is difficult ground on which to work, as the Arabs completely mistrust the French, seeing all their bad qualities and their selfish methods of colonial corruption and administration …
>
> The French mistrust the Arab, treat him and his ideals with contempt and consider we are responsible for all Arab hostilities towards them!

His diary continued:

> 4 November 1919, Cairo
> In the afternoon I had a long interview with George Picot, the French Haut Commissaire. He is the local fountainhead from which all French evil springs in the Near East. He is obsessed with a suspicion of the English and has from the start to finish made it as difficult as he can for Allenby …
>
> George Picot, in aiming to do us harm, has done us incalculable good and has ruined his country's reputation in Syria.

Several times the French tried to obstruct Faisal when he attempted to enter France and lobby the Supreme Council. Whilst Faisal was feted by the British and the Americans, the French muttered darkly about his unreasoning hatred of their country; they believed that the British were using Faisal to weaken their own case for Syria. 'British Imperialism with Arab headgear', said one French diplomat. The French press attacked Faisal as a British puppet and French intelligence opened his letters and delayed his telegrams back to the Middle East. Finally, Clemenceau had a long-delayed meeting with Faisal and found him friendlier and more reasonable than he expected.

When Faisal went to London he received a warmer welcome, but the news was depressing. The British, anxious to agree some overall settlement with France to secure their own position in Palestine and Mesopotamia, warned Faisal that he might have to accept French overlordship in Syria. They also pressed him to sign an agreement with Chaim Weizmann, recognising the Zionist presence in Palestine, and to agree that it was not part of Syria. Faisal was lonely and isolated; he needed British support in face of French hostility. He signed the document, the validity of which has been in dispute ever since.

Finally, at the San Remo conference in April 1920, after months of quarrelling, the terms of the settlement were finally agreed. The British awarded themselves the Mandate over Palestine and Mesopotamia; the French Syria. The year 1920 remains one of disaster for the Arabs. Palestine was gone; Syria and Lebanon followed and finally Mesopotamia.

In fact the French were eventually prevailed upon to agree to Faisal becoming Ruler of Syria, but only on condition that he kept order. Within Syria, however, Faisal did not have full support. Lebanese Christians proclaimed their separate independence in March 1920 and chose the French tricolour, with a Lebanese cedar in the centre, as their new flag. Arab radicals accused Faisal of being too obedient to the French. Whenever the Arabs have to keep together they can be relied upon to divide amongst themselves. The French demanded that Faisal punish the Arabs who had attacked them and, when French troops swept aside a poorly armed Arab force, Faisal and his family went into exile.

***

Mesopotamia – the former provinces of Mosul, Baghdad and Basra – was also stirring. Arnold Wilson was another servant of the Mandate. He had once mapped the border between Ottoman Turkey and Persia, joined the army in France, but was then ordered back to the Middle East to be assistant to Sir Percy Cox, the Chief Political Officer of the Mesopotamian campaign. When Cox was recalled in 1918 Arnold Wilson effectively became Governor of Mesopotamia at a critical moment in history.

Wilson had firm ideas as to how Mesopotamia should be ruled. He thought that Basra, Mosul and Baghdad should be a single unit for administrative purposes. It made no more sense then than it does now. In 1919 there was no Iraqi people, history, or religion. Geography pulled the people apart. Basra looked south towards India and the Gulf, Baghdad had strong links with Persia, and Mosul had ties with Turkey and Syria. Putting together the three Ottoman provinces and expecting to create a nation was like joining Bosnian Muslims, Croats and Serbs into a country called Yugoslavia. As in the Balkans, the clash of empires and civilisations had left deep divisions.

The population was about half Shia Muslim and a quarter Sunni, with the minorities composed of Jews and Christians. Half the inhabitants were Arabs, others Kurds, Persians and Assyrians. In the countryside hereditary tribal and religious leaders dominated. The concept of Iraqi nationality was a nonsense as Iraq did not exist, only Arab nationalism, and the Arabs' interest was in a greater Arabia, not in separate Arab nations. Arnold Wilson said, 'Our best course is to declare Mesopotamia as a British Protectorate under which all classes would be given the maximum degree of liberty and self-rule, compatible with good and safe government.'

London ruled this out; it preferred indirect rule – something that it had used in India, with the princely states, and in Egypt.

Meanwhile, unrest was spreading amongst the Kurds and Persians who resented Arab domination, amongst the Shia who resented Sunni influence, amongst tribal leaders challenged by British power and amongst high-ranking officers and bureaucrats who had lost their status with the collapse of the Ottomans. Nationalism was stirring. Railway lines were cut, British officers murdered, towns besieged. It needed the application of terror by a nasty character like Saddam Hussein, just as Yugoslavia needed terror to hold it together after the Second World War by a character called Tito. The British reacted harshly and restored order, but it could not last.

The key men involved – Lloyd George, Curzon and Churchill wanted to keep Mesopotamia if they could, but they were fearful of the cost of doing so. The burden of having a huge army in the region was increasingly out of the question. The cheapest solution was to find a pliable Arab ruler – and walk away. Faisal, who had been betrayed, or at the best been abandoned by London in Syria, was still available. On 23 August 1921 Faisal was crowned King of Iraq, which was described as a 'well-rooted country'! Faisal's brother, Abdullah, was made King of Transjordan and to everyone's surprise became a successful ruler – and a friend of my grandfather, Lewis Nott.

Faisal did not prove to be as pliable as the British had hoped. He pushed for the independence of Iraq and in 1932 his new, cobbled-together country joined the League of Nations. Faisal's grandson succeeded to the throne in 1939.

On 26 July 1956 Faisal's grandson, by then King Faisal, was dining together with the Iraqi Prime Minister Nuri es-Said as the guest of honour of Prime Minister Anthony Eden at No. 10 Downing Street. During dinner it was announced that President Nasser of Egypt had nationalised the Suez Canal. King Faisal and Nuri of Iraq, which was Britain's staunchest ally in the Middle East, gave Eden some belligerent advice: 'Hit Nasser and hit him hard.'

Iraq and the Turkish government had entered the Baghdad Pact in February 1955 and they were joined by Iran, Pakistan and Britain. It was a mutual-assistance pact for protection against the Soviet Union, which was pouring assistance and arms into Egypt.

Eden saw the Baghdad Pact as a means of replacing the 'unequal treaties' signed after the First World War which had allowed British troops to be stationed in some Arab countries.

Nasser was violently opposed to the Pact and believed that it would prolong British influence in the Middle East. Nuri es-Said would have been delighted to see Nasser destroyed as he was pouring vitriolic propaganda into all the Arab countries of the region, especially against the rulers of Iraq,

Nonetheless, the Iraqi press welcomed Nasser's action, which won acclaim not just in Egypt, but throughout the Middle East. King Hussein of Jordan sent a congratulatory message; King Saud conveyed his unqualified support to Nasser for the Egyptian action; thanksgiving sermons were preached in the mosques of Damascus and throughout the Middle East. The divisions over Suez were opened and Nasser determined to bring down the ruling regime in Baghdad. Two years later he succeeded: in 1958 King Faisal was assassinated in a coup which led later to the murderous regime of Saddam Hussein.

Faisal's father, Hussein, who had hoped to found a great Hashemite dynasty to run the Arab world, lost his throne in the Hejaz in 1924 when Ibn Saud conquered it and created the kingdom which still bears his name. The only Hashemite kingdom to survive was Jordan, and Abdullah's great-grandson is now king.

The likelihood of Iraq remaining as a separate nation is remote. It has existed as a single entity for less than 100 years and the three Ottoman provinces, Baghdad, Basra and Kurdistan, have a far longer independent history than the nation of Iraq as we know it today. Of course, if Shia Basra unites with Shia Iran it will horrify the United States. Turkey will oppose the notion of an independent Kurdistan, and the Shia population will oppose Sunni domination of Baghdad. I fear that when this happens we could see the same tragic movement of people, with all the horror that accompanies it, that took place in 1948 when Muslim Pakistan split from Hindu India. But happen it will. And the United States, which has an extraordinary inability to intervene *anywhere* successfully, should keep out of it. Nation-building is not its thing.The scale of the catastrophe created by the US in Iraq is quite staggering. It is likely to set the whole Middle East alight when they depart – and there is nothing that we can do to avoid it.

It has cost the lives of nearly 3000 American soldiers, but that is nothing beside the number of Iraqi civilian deaths, which are estimated to amount to 50,000; according to a study in the Lancet it is nearer half a million dead but no one knows the true figure. Not surprisingly up to 40 per cent of the population is unemployed.

The strength of the insurgency has been growing and is thought to amount to around 30,000 men spread rather equally between militants from the Yemen, Syria, Algeria, Sudan, Egypt and Saudi Arabia. This is a massive recruiting ground for future terrorism in the West. Although Tony Blair has blocked an inquiry in the United Kingdom into the war with Iraq, he is hung by the Iraq Study Group (ISG) co-chaired by former Secretary of State James Baker in the United States which reported in December 2006. The report was a hopeless judgement based on a consensus amongst a disparate group. It spelt out the scale of the disaster but came to the feeble conclusion that the US should withdraw its contact troops but continue with a support group to train the Army and police. It makes no sense. It has to be either in or out.

The study group also recommended negotiations with Iran and Syria; only the British Foreign Office could suggest such a daft proposal. We have been part of a European group endeavouring to agree sanctions against Iran for its nuclear programme. Now it is suggested that the West should humiliate itself to get the assistance of its enemies. Take Basra. The effective power in the British sector is not the government of Iraq but the Mahdi army and the Badr Brigade, both under the influence of Iran. The British are forced to talk to the insurgents because the Iraqi police have been infiltrated by the terrorists. The British forces should not be asked to stay another minute – their presence merely exacerbates a chaotic situation on the ground.

The Arabs were definitely betrayed by the British between 1918 and 1920. High politics made them a scapegoat for the rivalries between France and Great Britain.

Faisal and his adviser, Lawrence, hated the French so they expected nothing from them. But they liked and trusted the British with whom they had allied themselves against the Turks in the Arab revolt. But the plight of the Arabs, which extends to the present time, is something of their own making. They cannot unite; instead they manoeuvre against one another, so well demonstrated by the rift between Hamas and Fatah in Palestine today.

The Mandate officials and the British Army in the Middle East were genuine friends of the Arabs – even if the Arabs did not want to be friends with them. Again and again the High Commissioner in Palestine, from the lukewarm Zionist Samuel to the Arabists Allenby, General Bols and Sir John Chancellor, attempted to give them real representative status, but they fell back on the bad, devious and corrupt Haj Amin el-Husseini, the Mufti of Jerusalem. He was particularly mistrusted by my grandfather, who had many dealings with him in Nablus, and in the end Husseini's judgement was distorted by hate and religious fanaticism.

In his diary Meinertzhagen wrote on 2 December 1917: 'The Arab is dominated by his religion. However much he appreciates the benefits of British rule and despises the serfdom of Turkish domination, he always remembers that we are unbelievers and as such must not be tolerated.'The Arab elite focus on the Balfour Declaration for all their troubles but Jewish immigrants into Palestine up to 1926 hardly numbered 20,000 men and women. Yet the rejectionist, nationalist and religious stance of the Arabs long pre-dates that time. It was just not possible to do business with them, in their own interest.

The irony of it is that the Arabs had far more sympathy from the British than the Jews who were admired for their energy, but quite distrusted. The present rallying cry in favour of the Palestinian Arabs in Europe is hardly supported, except in violent speeches, by Arab governments, who privately prefer the riffraff of the Arab world to be concentrated in Palestine, rather than in their own countries. In 1970–71 King Hussein, not without good reason, expelled the Palestinians from Jordan and they cannot move around the Arab world without restrictive permits.

Whenever the State of Israel has come to the negotiating table in a genuine desire for a peaceful solution, the Arabs have missed their opportunity, as Arafat did after his negotiations with Ehud Barak at the Camp David summit in 2001.

The behaviour of Israel during recent events in Lebanon was offensive to civilised opinion. I think the polite word is 'disproportionate'. The activities of the Jewish lobby in the United States and Britain can be extreme and ruthless. The New York Jews – and of course I generalise – can be a pretty nasty bunch. So my heart is certainly with the downtrodden Arabs, but my head is with Israel.

The West can certainly have friends in Jordan, Oman, Qatar, Oman and the UAE. The survival of the fragile regimes in Saudi Arabia and Egypt may prove short-lived. But the West needs a strong, determined ally in the Middle East and sadly there is nowhere else to turn but Israel. They say that alliances are temporary but interests are permanent. The United Kingdom only has one overriding interest – and that is its own security. It has been seriously jeopardised by the antics of Blair and Bush in the Middle East.

SUEZ AND DEFENCE POLICY

1956

I arrived in Cambridge in 1956, just before Suez, as a twenty-three-year-old undergraduate thinking that I might one day be interested in politics. Because I had no idea what career to follow I had earlier taken a regular Army commission in the 2nd Gurkha Rifles as a sort of extended gap year to avoid any decision about the future. No doubt the choice of regiment was influenced by the family connection with India, and, having had a rather conventional upbringing, I was looking for some adventure. The Gurkhas were involved in fighting the Communist insurgents in Malaya, so I gained some personal experience participating in a colonial war, not imagining that I could ever be involved, many years later, in what was probably Britain's last colonial war in the Falklands.

Before joining the Regiment I was sent in 1951 on probation, as it were, to the 1st Battalion the Royal Scots in Germany. Here I had the best of times, reminiscent of the sort of life that subalterns had spent in peacetime India. The majority of the soldiers in the Royal Scots were National Servicemen and I am reminded of that remarkable period in our military history.

These days when politicians send soldiers to war in Iraq, Afghanistan or elsewhere most of them have never experienced war, or even military life, themselves.

There is, it seems to me, a wide cultural gap between the fast-diminishing number of people who have served in the forces and the vast majority of the population who have not. Whereas Prince William has been to Sandhurst, you can tell, in so many ways, that Tony Blair and David Cameron have not.

Politicians grope around for some kind of National 'social' Service to direct young people into worthwhile activity, but that omits something called discipline which military service used to bring about.

Much of military discipline and training is, of course, completely pointless – cutting grass with scissors and painting boulders white – but it did force restless young men to knuckle down to someone else's orders and priorities. There is not much evidence of it in the symbolic 'hoodie' of David Cameron's acquaintance.

Right up until 1960 around 150,000 eighteen-year-olds were conscripted every year into the armed forces. No one who went through this experience will ever forget it. British male society today is divided into those who have experienced military service and those who have not. It remains a cultural divide of some significance. National Service probably did more good than harm to the youth of Britain, but some succumbed to temptation. Everything in military life is a mixture of intense activity, occasional excitement and prolonged periods of boredom. Inevitably, periods of inactivity and leisure led to what today would be the 'laddish' pursuits of booze and women. In those days most young men were virgins on enlistment, but service in the Far East, the Middle East and Germany did not extend their innocence for very long. Every young soldier was encouraged to equip himself with a prophylactic kit of condoms, cotton wool, antiseptic cream and instructions; and these provided limited safeguards, but also some encouragement to visit the brothels of Singapore, Berlin and Aden.

National Service began with a medical examination and an interview. With a mixture of extreme apprehension and some enthusiasm I reported early – only to founder at my first military hurdle through an inability to provide the urine sample. I could not fill the bottle. I was put to the end of the queue and, late in the afternoon, an impatient medical officer assisted me by turning on all the taps in his examination room. Humiliation No. 1!

Within six weeks of the interview, the buff envelope arrived containing an enlistment notice, a rail warrant and a postal order for four shillings, being an advance of pay. On Thursday, all over England, decrepit steam trains pulled out of stations delivering their quota of raw recruits to Inverness, Darlington, Preston, Worcester, Brookwood and Aldershot.

The first six weeks in the Army were traumatic for most young men, but not for the public schoolboys who were already inured to a life of humiliation, grilling, discipline and extreme discomfort. But for the majority who had never left home and had been indulged by a loving mother, it was a dreadful change. Suddenly all these young men were thrown together, in rowdy dormitories, with Brummies, Mancunians, Cockneys, Jocks, Geordies, borstal boys, graduates, illiterates and public schoolboys. The coarseness, vulgarity and language of the barrack room must have come as a real shock. Sex was the only unifying force – and was virtually the only topic of conversation; banter and the boasting of personal sexual achievement marked out the men from the boys. We had one recruit from Blackpool who boasted that he had 'f****d' hundreds of girls standing up against walls outside dance halls, and he was believed. He was the hero of our barrack room.

The horrors and absurdities of the first six weeks of Army basic training will live in the memory of everyone who did National Service – and, indeed, everyone who has subsequently joined the Army, because I do not think the shock tactics have changed very much.

I joined the Royal Scots in Berlin in 1951. The Berliners had suffered terrible atrocities at the hands of the conquering Russian soldiers in 1945 but, only six years later, it was already a recovering society, active and pleasure-seeking. The main square outside British military headquarters was known to the men of the Royal Scots as 'Gobblers' Gulch', and the most beautiful young German girls were available for a packet of five Woodbines. We young officers raced sailing dinghies on the Wannsee, took part in all the horse shows and spent several evenings a week on crawls around the proliferating nightclubs, which cost a tax-free half-bottle of gin and had all the vulgarity and perversions in which the Germans excel.

But what really endeared the Royal Scots to me was the character of the Scottish soldiers, whom we called the Jocks. Colonel Melville, at my request, agreed that I should take my platoon on a six-week camp into the Grunewald, the fairly wild park (as it was then) on the banks of the Wannsee. There I subjected my young men to a rigorous training programme during the day, so much so that I was told at the end of it that they were the best trained platoon in the battalion.

Isolated as we were from the rest of the battalion, I got to know the Jocks extremely well. Apart from the NCOs, they were all National Servicemen from Glasgow (although the Royal Scots was an Edinburgh regiment). Most of these young men came from the Gorbals; physically small but wiry and tough, they had an excellent sense of humour but only three consuming interests in life – alcohol, fighting and women. Each evening, although I pretended ignorance of their leisure pursuits outside the camp, they used to get themselves completely plastered before seeking out English soldiers for a fight. If they failed to find their chosen opposition, they returned to the tented camp for a punch-up amongst themselves. By this time I was tucked up in my tent and I ignored their antics. However late and drunk the night before, they were always on parade in time, often bearing the scars of the previous night's affray. It may seem all rather shocking in today's climate of opinion, but these were the immediate post-war days and I admired the fighting qualities of my soldiers. I have always believed that Scottish soldiers are the best for attack, but English soldiers for a dogged defence.

In due course, my time with the Royal Scots drew to an end. The battalion was posted to Korea, a really nasty conflict which was still in progress. My platoon sergeant, who had spent much of his early life in various civilian and military prisons, led a delegation of my Jocks to see me; they made the request that I abandon my transfer to the Gurkhas, and lead them as their platoon commander in Korea. They said it was wrong of me to desert the platoon. It was possibly the most flattering compliment I have ever been paid. However, I stuck to my decision to join the Gurkhas in Malaya.

After spending two years or so in the Malayan jungle with the Battalion I was recruited by two generals to act successively as their ADC, first the general commanding 17 Gurkha Infantry Division and then the Commander-in-Chief Far East Land Forces with whom I travelled to India and Nepal. It gave me an insight into the life and role of a senior officer. As ADC I was fascinated by strategy and the foreign policy issues which passed across my desk on their way to my boss.

I met in Malaya, albeit as a very junior officer, two men who were to play a prominent part in the Suez campaign: General Templar, who became the Chief of the General Staff in Whitehall, and General Stockwell, who commanded the land forces at Suez; they were High Commissioner and GOC Malaya respectively when I met them. I saw them frequently.

Familiarity with senior officers does not always fill young officers, or senior politicians, with the respect that these great men deserve, and I thought nothing of Stockwell. Nor, may I say, do senior officers show much respect for junior officers and politicians! Such is life.

***

It has been written that Suez was a military success and a political failure. In fact, it was a military failure and a political disaster. The plan for the invasion of the Canal Zone was called 'Musketeer'. It was revised seven times by General Stockwell and had five postponements, mainly in response to political prevarication. The French General Beaufre, who was constantly at odds with Stockwell, rightly believed in the need for speed and a rapid break-out from Port Said, but Stockwell, prompted by his immediate superior, General Keightley, had constantly to refer back to London. Beaufre was told that the air attack to neutralise the Egyptian air force must be extended beyond the forty-eight hours to eight days in order to break the Egyptian will to fight. This was revised again as a vast, slow-moving invasion force took five days to cross the Mediterranean, giving time for Egyptian resistance to stiffen and world opinion to grow in Egypt's favour. Stockwell and Keightley, with their experience of the European conflict against Germany, believed in overwhelming force as the only means of gaining victory with minimal losses. Beaufre urged a rapid move against Egypt with parachute forces, supported by elite infantry carried in fast ships. Too risky, said Stockwell, with his memories of Arnhem in 1944.

From the Downing Street dinner on 26 July 1956, when King Faisal and the Iraqi Prime Minister had been informed of Nasser's nationalisation of the Suez Canal, to 5 November, it had taken more than three months for troops to get ashore at Port Said. The first House of Commons debate, as famous as the later Falklands debate, took place on 2 August. The delays were not only the fault of the military planning; the Chiefs of Staff were divided, Mountbatten, the head of the Navy, being at odds with General Templar, the head of the Army. The House of Commons was in uproar, and as I describe it before, the bitterness spread throughout the country. President Eisenhower and John Foster Dulles, the Secretary of State, were deeply antagonistic and dealing with French and Israeli allies was, not surprisingly, very difficult.

The contrast with the Falklands in 1982 is stark. Margaret Thatcher was decisive from the outset and this, coupled with the determination and splendid readiness of the Royal Navy, got 100,000 men and women across 8000 miles of ocean, against 300 miles at Suez, in less than two months, from 2 April to the first landing at San Carlos Bay on 21 May.

When I arrived in Cambridge, I was something of an embryo politician, fascinated by world and military affairs. With memories of General Stockwell, I wrote:

My first term at Cambridge was the most interesting and intense of all the time that I spent there because it was the autumn of Hungary and Suez. Both events had a profound impact on me, but in rather different ways. When the Hungarian revolution began, it quickly divided my contemporaries between those who did not care to see an outside event distract them from their studies and their fun, and those who followed it with intense concern. A friend of mine, Charles Owen, and I met every day as the situation worsened. When the Russian tanks moved into Budapest and the newspapers showed pictures of young Hungarians pitching Molotov cocktails at the Soviet tanks, we discussed in all seriousness leaving Trinity, almost before we had arrived, to go and help the oppressed. It would have been a foolish gesture.

Chance then dealt me another lucky break. Visiting the Cambridge Union, in which I had determined to make my mark, I came across a strange character called Robin St John Shurley. He was a friendly, active 'groupie' of the Union and knew the then President, someone called Ken Post. As I poured out my misery about the lot of the Hungarians, he urged me to speak about it. Then to my astonishment I received a visit in my rooms in Great Court from Ken Post himself, urging me to propose an emergency motion on Hungary. I pleaded my junior status, saying that I had not yet spoken in a Union debate – but Post was insistent that he wanted to break tradition by having a freshman undergraduate, particularly one who had served in the Army, open the debate.

The motion I proposed on Tuesday 6 November was 'this House would risk a Third World War for the sake of a Communist Satellite in Revolt'. My speech began:

During the last two weeks we have seen a series of events in Eastern Europe that is likely to take its place in world history. For the first time we have witnessed the rising of a whole people against a modern totalitarian state. And just as the 1917 Revolution has already been acknowledged as a turning-point in world history, so must this first national uprising be accounted the same.

We must not delude ourselves that other events merit the same significance. The American election [that very day] and our actions in Egypt are indeed matters of some moment. But they will, I suggest, in future times be looked back on as events in history – matters which seriously disturbed the conscience of the world at the time, but which in themselves never diverted the pattern of history from its chosen course. The revolt in Hungary, Sir, short and tragic as it has been, is one of the most significant and momentous happenings of this century.

It is up to this House to decide whether we allow it to become a turning-point in the progress towards world happiness and peace, or merely a heroic story-book stand against a cruel tyranny.

The rest of my thirteen-minute speech placed a lot of emphasis on the word 'risk' – only by confronting aggression, with all the risk involved, would we ever sustain freedom and democracy. According to the press report of this 'serious-minded and often deeply felt debate on the dilemma of the West', my 'poise and general debating skills quickly won the support of the House'. When it duly divided just before midnight, we lost the motion (301–271), but my Union reputation had been established. I went on to become President two and a half years later.

Back in the autumn of 1956, as Charles Owen and I were exercising our consciences about the plight of the Hungarians and what we could do to help, the French and British governments invaded the Canal Zone. I do not think that we considered whether the Russians would have invaded Hungary anyhow, Suez or not – it just seemed to distract the world and to give them a free run. I was dumbfounded, stupefied, that this could happen at the very time when it was the moral duty of the West to bring military pressure on the Soviets to withdraw from Hungary. I did not quite see the Anglo-French action as an act of unprovoked aggression, as many socialist students did, but rather as an utterly foolhardy exercise distracting the world from the tragedy in Eastern Europe.

Cambridge was in turmoil. Suez galvanised opinion in a way that Hungary had not. Opinion divided mainly along party lines: the young Tories, represented mainly by the public school contingents at Trinity and Magdalene, took a strong anti-Nasser line, whilst the majority of the undergraduates, with their left-wing leanings, regarded it as an act of unprovoked aggression contrary to the Charter of the United Nations.

By the time of Suez, I had become a member of an institution called the Pitt Club. It consisted of two hundred or so rather preposterous young men – a collection of mainly wealthy and well-connected undergraduates of the Alan Clark variety. Most of them travelled frequently to London to attend debutante dances, and some would today be classified as 'Hooray Henrys'. The Pitt Club was founded and run on the principle of a London club, and there was a self-perpetuating committee which presided over the selection of its members.

The Pitt Club was a sort of haven for me away from the dreadful food in hall at Trinity, and I rather enjoyed the slightly louche culture with its emphasis on hunting, shooting and fishing. It was typical of my Cambridge way of life that I was a regular at meets of the Trinity Foot Beagles.

As the controversy over Suez grew, the Pitt Club organised a combined party, led by the Master of the Trinity Foot Beagles, to break up a massive protest meeting about Suez that was being held at the Union on Friday 2 November (four days before the debate on Hungary).The principal speaker was the Honourable Anthony Wedgwood Benn, as he then called himself, and to the ghastly young members of the Pitt Club he was regarded as a traitor to his class for not supporting Eden's absurd foray into Suez. As for myself, I attended as a protesting member of the Union rather than as a member of the Pitt Club.

Benn's co-speaker was another Labour MP, Kenneth Younger, and Benn's diary entry for that day vividly evokes a memorable occasion:

> The Union debating hall was absolutely packed tight, with crowds round it trying to get in through the windows and jamming the entrance thirty deep. We struggled to reach our places. The UN flag had been stolen and there were wildly noisy scenes and shouts. Great posters hung from the gallery reading, "Support Eden, not Nasser" and "We are now committed and must support our troops". The crowd of students laughing and screaming for war gave me an icy hatred of them. The uproar and noise and jolly funny remarks when the world was on the brink of disaster was completely revolting, disgusting and shameful.
>
> Kenneth Younger's speech was hardly audible, but he persevered patiently and quietly to the end. I decided to take it rather differently, by giving those people who took our view in the Hall something to cheer about and I therefore attacked the warmongers at once. Then I tried to buy silence by promising to answer questions. This was moderately successful though it meant my speech was prolonged to over an hour.
>
> My notes were carried away by a rotten tomato and stink bombs, and lavatory paper was thrown all over the place. One did not mind that but it was the flippancy on such a grave issue that was so completely horrifying.

As I recall, it was at a signal from a member of the hunt that the Trinity beagles were released into the debating chamber, accompanied by hunting horns and smoke bombs. Chaos indeed ensued. I remember Benn as incandescent with rage and the meeting being ruined.

I was appalled at the behaviour of the hunting set. To this day, whilst a supporter of hunting, I would do anything to avoid social intercourse with the horsey world and their ghastly noisy and drunken hunt balls. It bothers me to this day that I should have been associated with these ignorant public-school Tories. Possibly I fitted into this kind of undergraduate clique because we had in common a period of Army service. Somehow their company seemed more natural and congenial than that of undergraduates who had not served in the Army and who, as state school pupils, wisely kept themselves apart. They were known as 'trogs' by members of the Pitt Club and were identified by the fact that they wore college scarves.

Cambridge was thus divided somewhat down class lines, and the incident in the Cambridge Union was indicative of this. It was certainly touch and go as to whether I sought my political future in the Labour Party or swallowed my distaste for this section of the traditional Tory Party, something that I was forced to do for most of my subsequent political career. In fact, I joined the Tory Party because it was to become the radical party of the 1970s and early 1980s; and that is where I belonged. I am still a Tory Radical but the party is moving elsewhere without me.

If there had been a committee of privy councillors to examine Suez, similar to the committee which investigated the origins of the Falklands War, two key lessons would have emerged – the need to avoid divisions at the top in Whitehall and the necessity of carrying outside opinion, particularly the Americans. As it happened, the two generals – Templar and Stockwell – under whom I had just served in Malaya were key participants.

In later years I studied the whole episode, and it was very much on my mind when the Falklands crisis blew up. In 1956 Admiral Mountbatten and General Templar, the Chiefs of Staff for the Royal Navy and the Army, had strongly opposing views of the situation. When the invasion force was within four days of arriving at Port Said, Mountbatten wrote to Eden appealing to him 'to accept the resolution of the overwhelming majority of the United Nations to cease military operations' and begging him 'to turn back the assault convoy before it is too late'. Templar's letter to his minister, John Hare, could not have been more different: 'Whether this country was politically right in taking the action it did, is obviously not for me to say, but I can at least have my own personal opinion on the matter. Of course we were right, plum right, and I say it with certainty on strategic grounds.' Ironically, the position of the Service Chiefs at the time of the Falklands was reversed – the Navy Chief was the 'hawk', the Army Chief was the 'dove'. But on both occasions the Chiefs successfully concealed their differences, and courtesies and civilities were maintained.

So great was the muddle and the lack of coordination that even at the last moment the Chiefs of Staff, not knowing of the collusion with Israel, were concerned that under the Jordan Treaty we might have to go to war with Israel; accordingly, they were instructing their Air Force commanders to plan 'for air operations at maximum intensity to neutralise the Israeli Air Force'! Indeed, the devious nature of the whole Suez exercise destroyed the loyalty of the civil servants on whom all governments depend.

Above all, what was in my mind in 1982 at the outset of the Falklands War was the memory of an operation twenty-six years earlier involving more than 100,000 men being mounted for a war which lasted only a few days – and then being halted as it came within reach of achieving its objectives.

All of these events, of course, were unknown to me at the time in Cambridge, but I read of them subsequently with fascination and some horror.

No one who has served in the Forces can avoid a certain scepticism about military operations. If you know the Services, you are aware that things go wrong as often as they go right. Every second lieutenant has metaphorically led an armoured division into a suburban cul-de-sac without the ability to reverse, go sideways, or do anything but see the utter absurdity of it all. This is known in the vulgar parlance as GMFU – a Grand Military F***-Up – and you encounter many of them as a junior officer.

Suez became part of history. Ted Heath had been Chief Whip, and his memoirs have recently made clear that he was against the whole operation. To be fair to him, in politics you have to judge when to keep your head down and get on with the job. Personal conscience is a luxury to be indulged in infrequently and with discretion, and he is right to say that if the Chief Whip had resigned it would have destroyed the government. I discovered this kind of political dilemma myself as a Treasury minister during the so-called Barber Boom, when many times I wanted to resign – although, of course, the resignation of a junior Treasury minister would hardly have been noticed.

Suez would have a profound effect on me and greatly influence my future thinking. Sitting metaphorically at the feet of Enoch Powell, when I first became an MP ten years later, I came to believe that there could never be a full measure of economic and strategic independence for the United Kingdom unless we rid ourselves of a fixed exchange rate, which made Britain unnecessarily vulnerable to foreign exchange pressure. Since then I have always been a passionate 'floater'– and it remains an important economic argument against joining the single European currency. I am convinced that, had we had a fixed exchange rate during the Falklands War, the financial pressures on us would have been very similar to those during Suez.

Suez demonstrated that the world had changed forever. The lingering belief (or was it hope?) that Great Britain could still act as a world power was finally destroyed. The Defence White Paper of Duncan Sandys in 1957 not only ended conscription within three years, but sharply limited Britain's capacity for independent action; decolonisation now went ahead at a more rapid pace. Nostalgia for the days of Empire – great-great-great-grandfather William in Afghanistan, grandfather Lewis in

India and Palestine, the protection of the canal as the route to India – was no longer relevant.

The consequences of Suez were different from the predictions of both those who backed the operation and those who opposed it. Thus instead of the American alliance being broken, the British have never since been able to venture on a foreign policy independent of the United States. Instead, it was the entente cordiale with France that was destroyed. Suez was partly responsible both for the end of the Fourth Republic and for the Gaullist diplomacy that twice blocked Britain's application to join the Common Market.

***

Suez should have been a turning point in how we looked at the world, and our position in it. Nineteenth-century and early twentieth-century British history had revolved around the protection of our imperial possessions, particularly India, 'the Jewel in the Crown'. Lloyd George, Balfour, Curzon and Churchill in settling the future of the world in the aftermath of the Paris Peace Conference in 1918 were determined to protect the Suez Canal, especially from the ambitions of the French. It was the indispensable link with India, and all our policies in the Middle East saw Palestine, Iraq, Egypt, Arabia, Afghanistan and the Gulf sheikdoms almost as buffer states – a sort of neutral no-man's land – that protected the pride of all our possessions, India. It is quite hard to understand today how India was in the blood of Englishmen and Scots. The aristocracy had been despatched as Viceroys, and Governors of Bengal and Bombay. The second sons like Wellesley, the great Wellington, brother of the Governor-General Lord Mornington, had been sent to fight its wars. Generations of the landed gentry, the professional and middle classes had been educated at English public schools as future rulers of the Punjab, senior members of the Indian Civil Service and officers of the East India Company's Army.

And then, in 1947, India was gone. It was no longer ours. The Suez Canal remained valuable for British trade but its status as an integral part of our imperial possessions was no more.

Enoch Powell, who had a passionate love for India, became my mentor. I remember him saying when I first entered Parliament in 1966 – I believe in opposition he was Shadow Defence Secretary – that with India gone our defence commitments in the Middle East made no sense. He came up against the traditional Tory view in Parliament that having retained our links with the White Commonwealth, being possessor of the bomb, the holder of the sterling balances, a member of the Security Council, the principal ally of the United States – all this still made us a Great Power. If not a Great Power, at least we had great influence, prestige, status, standing as a Great Nation. It was our duty to carry the heavy burden of our great imperial past.

Nowhere was this view held more strongly than in the Foreign Office, still occupying the most expensive and prestigious sites in Paris, Tokyo, Washington and no doubt Addis Ababa and Khartoum. If we were not a Great Nation, why else should anyone join the diplomatic service? The idea of British foreign policy being dictated by a Thatcher or a Blair from No. 10 Downing Street was unthinkable. 'Prime ministers don't understand these things', or so they said amongst themselves.

This attitude was characterised in the person and attitude of that well-known Foreign Office official and Foreign Secretary Douglas Hurd, who stated that Great Britain still 'punched above her weight'. In other words, 'we think we are very important in the Foreign Service and don't you second-rate powers forget it'! As we shall see in the final chapter on Yugoslavia, this approach to foreign policy was to lead to Britain's 'Unfinest Hour' in the Balkans in 1991.

And the Cold War did not help. We were engaged with our wartime ally, the United States, in a genuine struggle to survive as a liberal Western democracy, against a bitter enemy, the Soviet Union. The bomb saved us. But more important, we were somehow able to cloak ourselves in the power of our ally. Everything we did, all our dispositions, were agreed within NATO, normally in private discussion with the United States. Certainly I saw myself in NATO Councils as British Defence Secretary, as the indispensable No. 2 to the United States. Britain, with some 5.4 per cent of her gross domestic product in defence, was the only European NATO country (with the exception of Greece, which had armed itself against its NATO ally, Turkey) making a full contribution to NATO targets. The so-called 'special relationship' was represented by an almost total pooling of intelligence and nuclear technology – something not shared by any other NATO ally.

In my memoirs I speculated about a future war of survival in a nuclear world. Reading it some twenty-five years later, I realise that, even if we were not a Great Power, I was thinking like one:

> My education into nuclear theology in the Ministry of Defence had been conducted by Michael Quinlan. He later became the Permanent Secretary at Defence and on retirement the Director of the Ditchley Foundation. We discussed the moral and ethical issues involved and whether what was described as the seamless web of nuclear response, strike and counter-strike was in fact more of a tangled web full of holes. I formed the view that whilst our nuclear deterrent was the first and most important of all our defence capabilities (we are truly independent; the Americans hold no veto over us) the whole nuclear debate had become stuck in a rut. It would need Reagan and Gorbachev to break down the barriers to a saner world.

My memoir went on:

It is nightmarish to speculate about what might have happened had some madman gained control in the Kremlin. Lying at the heart of my Defence Review was the appalling fact that, at that time, our forces on the Central Front had less than one week of ammunition stocks with which to resist a high-intensity assault by conventional forces over the German plain. My whole thrust was to rebalance the programme, so that we transferred resources away from ships, tanks and aeroplanes into weapon systems and into missile and ammunition stocks. In the Falklands campaign, a very minor skirmish compared to what we would have seen on the outbreak of a Third World War, we actually consumed almost the whole of our missile stocks. The shortage of ammunition stocks to meet a high-intensity conflict was a disgrace, partly brought about by cheese-paring at the margins each time the Ministry of Defence was asked to reduce expenditure.

If the Warsaw Pact had ever crossed the line and launched an assault on NATO forces, we might have held them for a time. But unless we had been able to interdict successfully the second echelon of their forces – and that was primarily a job for airpower – it would have been nearly impossible, in my view, to stop them reaching the Channel ports, such was their conventional superiority over NATO in tanks and men. Would we have released battlefield nuclear weapons? Who can say? We certainly did so in our exercises, and fortunately the Russians were aware of our intentions. But the world of exercises is different from the real world. The dilemma was: how in a real conflict would you stop nuclear escalation from battlefield to tactical to strategic nuclear weapons? The United States had no cause to defend Europe if that threatened the destruction of their own cities by a strategic strike from the Soviet Union. This was partly why our nuclear deterrent provided added security for Europe. But would we have chosen to defend Germany or France with nuclear weapons if the consequence was the nuclear destruction of the United Kingdom? I did not hesitate to say in every debate on nuclear weapons that we would release them, because that was what deterrence required. But would we have done so in the event? Fortunately for our survival, none of us were ever put to the test.

Today the debate on our nuclear defences has come round again. I cannot see how in a world of nuclear powers – and creeping proliferation – we could ever be so foolish as to abandon Trident. It is our ultimate defence – the last resort deterrent. Maybe we should reduce its yield and enhance its pinpoint capability. But its ability to strike a target with an accuracy of a few hundred yards, hidden from under the oceans of the world, surely provides uniquely for our safety in a dangerous world.

I am a follower of Correlli Barnett; he is the author of some great books such as *The Desert Generals* (1983), but it is his determined stance against so much conventional thinking in the defence establishment that I most admire.

In an article in the August 2005 *RUSI Journal* (the journal of the Royal United Services Institute) titled 'Imperial Overstretch from Dr Arnold to Mr. Blair' in which he challenged the whole post-war strategy of successive British Governments, Barnett wrote:

> How to explain the governing elite's nostalgic delusions? My answer is that almost all of them – politicians and mandarins, the opinion-forming intelligentsia, even the Chiefs of Staff – remained mental prisoners of Britain's very recent past as a genuinely first-class power. What is more the governing elite were also imbued with a high sense of moral duty towards our colonies and the world at large. For instance, in regard to the sterling area the words 'our responsibility' came up again and again as a justification for carrying on the burden

Our attitude to the sterling area, which was finally abandoned, abolished, dispersed, destroyed, in 1973, was indeed an excellent case in point.

I was Economic Secretary to the Treasury from 1972 to 1974 during the so-called Barber Boom when, in the midst of one of this country's recurring financial crises, we floated the pound sterling and thereby brought the sterling area to an end. It fell to me, a junior Treasury minister, to write letters to the holders of the largest sterling balances – Hong Kong, Kuwait and others – telling them that we could no longer guarantee the value of billions of pounds of their investments. The currency was to float. It was a great day for us, if not for them. The day we ceased to guarantee the sterling balances of our former colonies and dependent countries in the Middle East was as great a turning point as Suez – the one financial, the other strategic.

For years Enoch Powell had advocated setting the pound sterling free to find its natural level in the market place. But international politics had consistently claimed that fixed currencies were essential to world stability. It is one of the many nonsenses of the European Union today that a single exchange rate represented by the euro is said to be the best means of uniting member countries in prosperity and governance. It is proving, of course, to be the opposite of the case.

In October 1969 at the Conservative Party Conference, after Germany had floated the Deutschmark, Enoch Powell spoke as follows:

There is no secret about the cause of the 'cycle of stagnation, restriction and debt'. For a quarter-century we have been taught to believe that our livelihood depends on a pretence, on pretending that the £ is worth more in the world than it is. So we cling desperately to a fixed exchange. But so long as the price of anything is fixed, it will nearly always be wrong; for everything in the real world is changing all the time. The result has been either a surplus or a deficit and increasingly often a deficit. So we borrowed huge sums to keep up the fiction and accepted government interference in our lives in all directions. Once you have a wrong price fixed for anything, there is no interference by government that cannot be justified.

This being the cause, the remedy is plain. We have to do what we were on the verge of doing after 1951 but unhappily did not. We have to set the rate for the pound free to behave like any other price and keep supply and demand in balance. A fortnight ago this would have sounded like theory. For ten days now it has been fact. The pound has been floated, at least against the mark, and, contrary to expectation, the world has not come to an end ...

The truth is better; the truth is safer; and the truth is freer. In this, as in so much besides today, our fears are our own worst enemies. Let us dare to face reality: it is the road to freedom.

Britain's prosperity today is compounded by three factors: North Sea Oil, the City of London and our floating exchange rate. I regard the latter as the most important of all. Only our post-imperial delusions in defence policy stand in the way of further progress in the future.

In his August 2005 article Correlli Barnett also said: 'In my belief, the elite remained prisoners of their indoctrination at public school and "Oxbridge". There they had been programmed to be house prefects to the world.'

Anthony Eden, Foreign Secretary for most of his political career, exemplifies this type. Eden could no more imagine Britain giving up her inheritance as a Great Power because she was hard up than, for a similar reason, having to exchange his Savile Row suits for ready-made reach-me-downs from the Fifty-Shilling Tailors. In Eden's view 'our worldwide commitments are inescapable'. Under ruthless American pressure Blair would say the same today.

It was the same American pressure that forced us into the Korean War, involving a three-year rearmament programme costing £4.7 billion on top of the existing Defence Budget. It caused a massive balance of payments crisis with our then fixed exchange rate. Whilst Germany and France were leaping ahead in the 1950s invading our markets and updating their infrastructure and private industry, we were held back by the delusion that our 'worldwide commitments were inescapable'.

I quote from my own experience as Defence Secretary in 1981:

What, of course, upset the Chiefs of Staff was that the annual 3 per cent real growth target in defence expenditure was not what it seemed. Every year the Treasury allocated cash limits which eroded the real volume, resulting in an out-turn which was less than the NATO commitment. In 1981–2 the volume of defence spending, at 1980 prices, was £9.7 billion – but the real cash spend was £12.3 billion. As a great protagonist for cash limits, I could hardly complain if real money, cash, took precedence over 'funny money' volume. I was faced by a group of highly intelligent men feeling that real growth in expenditure of 7 per cent over three years was a disappointing let-down, and this at a time when the economy was hardly growing at all and unemployment was rising to three million. In relative terms the military was basking in the Elysian fields, but they could not accept it. 'Ah, but the Soviet threat,' they would say – as if there was not a different threat to the country in poor schools and hospitals, and the riots which were being exacerbated by high unemployment.

So I take the view that, masked by the exigencies of the Cold War, attitudes had not much changed by the time I joined the Ministry of Defence in 1981. I tried to prioritise our expenditure away from our overseas commitments and obligations to concentrate on the immediate threat from the Soviet Union – the immediate threat to the United Kingdom itself. But the Royal Navy, in particular, rebelled against this notion because it came right up against their concept of the 'blue water navy' – with its worldwide mission to police the seas. The shift in British military strategy that I attempted might have been successful had not the Falklands intervened. It made a change inevitable back to the traditional worldwide concept of naval-based worldwide forces. It could only have been avoided if we had ditched the Falklands – and quite rightly Margaret Thatcher was having none of that. Her government was threatened and she reacted with great courage and determination. The Falklands was a very great success and raised the prestige of the country immeasurably but it convinced the British Establishment and the opinion-forming classes that, in an emergency, we were still a Great Power.

Given our respective roles and rather different view of life, it may seem odd that I have considerable respect for Dwin Bramall – Field-Marshall Lord Bramall of Bushfield. He was, as I have already said, Chief of the General Staff during my time as Defence Secretary and the Colonel of my old Regiment, the 2nd Gurkhas. I have often noted with astonishment and admiration his way with people. His man-management skills are impeccable. He knows everybody's name; the names of their wives, brothers, aunts and uncles! Margaret Thatcher had some of these qualities, and it is an important attribute to leadership.

I mention Dwin Bramall again because after I had left politics he became Chief of the Defence Staff and played an important role with Michael Heseltine and George Younger as my successors in shifting the equipment and flexibility of our forces back towards a worldwide role, an ability to respond at the request of government to emergencies in places like East Timor and Sierra Leone. His 2005 biography by Michael Tillotson sets out his views very admirably. The point is made that, whilst there is no obvious threat at present to the security of the United Kingdom from external sources, it is impossible to predict from where a future threat may come. And what are our forces to be doing in times of relative peace? They cannot be confined to exercises among the gorse bushes around Aldershot, or tied up in Portsmouth harbour. The forces need a role to keep them viable and alert.

We need 'balanced forces', I was told, to meet whatever contingency may come along. The military is the servant of an elected government and no one, certainly not the Chiefs of Staff, can be sure what prime ministers and cabinets will get up to next.

So going back to Bramall's time – and I do not think that successive Defence Secretaries really questioned this approach – we developed a policy now known as 'expeditionary warfare'...

In the *Spectator* Diary and subsequently repeated in the journal of the the Royal United Services Institute in 2005, I wrote the following letter, somewhat in jest, I must admit:

One day we will no longer have an evangelist as Prime Minister and the passion for neo-imperialist do-goodery – joining with the Americans to bring democracy to Johnny Foreigner, pre-empting threats by taking war to the enemy as a subsidiary of the Pentagon – all of this will fall out of fashion. Someone will say that high-cost, high-technology warfare as a small reinforcement to the massive resources of the US is beyond our means. We should spend more on the police, the security services, the poor old British infantry and our reserve forces.

Instead, huge financial resources are to be deployed over a ten-year period into making us into a rather under-equipped global policeman (PC Plod Inc.). If we go down this road I fear an accelerating financial and political nightmare. The problem is that ministers are not in charge; the defence establishment has taken over.

We keep on coming back to the politics of Suez. We may be equipped for 'expeditionary warfare', but we cannot succeed in an emergency without the political and logistic support of the United States – and it is difficult to refuse to support the United States, even if it sets out on a misconceived adventure like Iraq.

Again I resort to my letter in the *RUSI Journal*:

Iraq is in the process of becoming a national humiliation, but more relevant to Defence policy, Iraq is likely to sharply reduce recruitment to the army and increase the threat of terrorism here at home. Maybe after 9/11 we had cause to support our American allies in hammering the Taliban, but now Iraq and Afghanistan are in a far worse state than before. Unlike the Americans we have our own history to teach us the realities of intervention, a generation spent unsuccessfully trying to pacify Palestine under the Mandate and several generations attempting to pacify Afghanistan.

I have memories of Somalia, Lebanon and even Vietnam. Expeditionary warfare may keep our troops occupied in times of relative peace but it hardly ever results in a happy outcome, normally it is counter-productive and marks us out as an unjust aggressor. Indeed as Dr Paul Robinson wrote in a thought-provoking article (*RUSI Journal*, August 2005) it makes us weaker because expeditionary warfare provokes us into 'wars of choice' rather than 'wars of necessity'.

During the Cold War the prevailing model in most Western defence ministries was 'threat-based' planning. You hit us and we will retaliate in self-defence with all we've got. It was called deterrence. 'If you want peace, you must prepare for war' etc. When the threat to the United Kingdom's survival disappeared with the collapse of the Soviet Union, we might have expected a fundamental rethink of defence policy but, in fact, 'Options for Change', as it was called, hardly touched the underlying strategy. Instead of 'threat-based' planning the defence model became 'capabilities-based' planning. Whereas previously capabilities were the end process in planning, now we started with the assets and worked backwards to find a role for the ships and planes and guns that we had inherited from our deterrence stance in the Cold War. It was not hard to alight on 'expeditionary warfare' as the means of keeping servicemen and assets fully employed.

Where this policy is at its most absurd is in the plans to build two new aircraft carriers and order the Joint Strike Fighter (JSF) from the Americans at a capital cost over ten years of something around £12 billion. The two carriers are estimated to have an in-service cost over thirty to forty years of £35 billion. These carriers have nothing whatsoever to do with the defence of the United Kingdom. In the opening of the chapter on Iraq I commented on how 'deterrence' had been superseded by 'pre-emption'. As Paul Robinson said in his article, the policy, advocated by the neo-conservatives in Washington, is predicated on controlling and pre-empting trouble from 'rogue' and 'failed' states, as well as transnational terrorists. The argument goes that 'if we leave these wasps overseas untouched, the wasps will shortly be buzzing about our ears'.

In contrast, the traditions of 'just war' theory suggest that war is only justifiable in conditions of extreme emergency. A key criterion for a just war is 'last resort'. We know from bitter experience that war invariably does more harm than good. If we permit the exercise of wars to do good – do-goodery, as I have described it – everybody will have an excuse to fight whenever it takes their fancy. Self-defence is the only justification for war – and preparation for it.

Of course, 'just war' theory does not always help us to decide what are 'wars of choice' and what are 'wars of necessity'. Did we intervene in the Bosnian war, which is covered in the next chapter, to do good or in self-defence? Not an easy one. It depends on a judgement as to whether a conflagration in the heart of Europe could spread outwards into confrontation between the Russians, as supporters of the Serbs, and the rest of NATO. Would three million displaced persons have seriously undermined the stability of central Europe? Would we have been justified in confronting Hitler when he marched into the Rhineland? Would that have been deterrence or pre-emption? A war of choice or a war of necessity? It could be argued, at a stretch, that the Falklands War was fought in self-defence under Article 51 of the United Nations Charter because it involved an unprovoked attack on British citizens – that is an easier one than intervention in former Yugoslavia. But coming to the heading of this chapter, by no possible argument could it have been said that Suez was justified in self-defence, especially when India had already achieved her independence.

Intervention in the First Gulf War was certainly necessary in self-defence. Saddam Hussein had to be stopped from gaining control over a major proportion of the world's oil supplies. Maybe we had to remove the Taliban from power, not to do good for the poor people of Afghanistan but to prevent them harbouring al-Qaeda. But what are we doing there now? We cannot police Afghanistan indefinitely – and history teaches us that our presence there can only end in humiliation and retreat.

Surely we want our military to be a 'force for good'. Yet in both Iraq and Afghanistan we are uniting the people of these countries in hate against us. Pre-empting trouble has caused no end of trouble. The whole concept of pre-emption is misconceived; surely we must learn from our mistakes?

So coming back to home, our defence policy needs to be redefined. Instead of equipping the forces for expeditionary warfare, which stems from 'capability-based planning', we should return to 'threat-based planning', and the threat is staring at us in the face: home-based terrorism. We should rely on deterrence and abandon the concept of pre-emption. The £12 billion estimated cost of building the new carrier force should be removed from the Defence Budget and reallocated to the police, our reserve forces and the security and emergency services. If recruitment and retention can be restored, a fair proportion of the money should be returned by the Treasury to the Defence Budget but only on condition that it finances 'boots on the ground', the police, the infantry and our reserve forces, not on equipment, like the carrier force, which simply fortifies our ability to indulge ourselves in 'wars of choice'. The Ministry of Defence, which nowadays runs on a consensus among the Chiefs of Staff – 'if you will agree to a new tank, or a new fighter aircraft; we will agree to a new carrier' etc. – cannot be trusted. The new Prime Minister or the

Treasury must intervene, on both financial and strategic grounds, if the Defence Secretary fails to do so.

Such a shift in policy would cause howls of outrage, especially from the Royal Navy, which is understandably fighting for survival and a role in the twenty-first century. In fact, the Navy can survive and prosper without its carrier force. Its valuable frigates are being mothballed to make room for a carrier force that we do not need. It is an extravagant folly that will lead us into endless trouble.

So I come back to the Suez drama. Suez was a defining moment. We failed to hold the canal, which had been a lifeline of the Empire, but it was no longer so. We were quite able to succeed in our military objectives within a few days but the Americans brought us down. They humiliated a Great Power, or what was left of one. They were able to do so because the pound was a fixed currency and our imperial obligations to the holders of the sterling balances made us baulk at devaluing the pound. We had a devious Chancellor, Harold Macmillan, who, having been a major hawk, then persuaded his Cabinet colleagues that devaluation was not an option. With the sterling balances under threat and an overwhelming vote against us in the United Nation he voted in Cabinet for withdrawal – or was it surrender?

In a later financial crisis in 1972, Edward Heath had the courage, against all his instincts, to float the pound, which should go down, in his record, as an equally far-sighted move beside our reluctant entry into Europe. Because of the sterling balances, devaluation was the great unmentionable. In my view Macmillan had as much responsibility for our humiliation at Suez as Eden.

Suez meant that we were never able independently to go for a 'war of choice'; our dependence on the United States, as a strategic ally, became complete. It served us well in the Cold War when that alliance enabled us to defeat the 'Evil Empire'.

But now, with a floating pound, we are free. We might not have succeeded in the Falklands imbroglio had we had a fixed currency – speculation against the currency might have been intolerable. We are free but our leaders choose not to use our political freedom. We must change our strategic outlook and regain our independence, judgement and action as a rich nation acting again as a bridge between our traditional ally, the United States, and Europe.

YUGOSLAVIA
1992–96

Like Iraq, Yugoslavia was an artificial construction but it was created in 1918 at the urging of the south Slavs themselves. The British, looking to Empire, were largely indifferent to what happened in central Europe so long as their interests were not affected. Only a handful of specialists had made it their business to study the area. What the British knew then (and later forgot) was that the Balkans were dangerous to Europe; they had caused trouble for decades as the Ottoman Empire disintegrated and Austria-Hungary and Russia vied for control.

Austria-Hungary had been defeated by 1918 but it was already imploding before the Great War under a bloated bureaucracy. We would be wise to study how a large, intrusive and stifling bureaucracy can destroy the freedom and creativity of a thriving society. It's happening right here in Britain.

Serbia, which had fought on the side of the Allies in the Great War and had only been released from the Ottoman yoke not many years before, saw an opportunity to create a Greater Serbia. Belgrade, the capital, sitting at the confluence of the Danube and Sava rivers was not very large. Indeed, in 1918 it had a population of only 20,000 people. The Serbs were peasant soldiers and farmers living in the countryside and occupying a series of small towns and villages, largely isolated from the culture of European civilisation. Before Serbia emerged on the right side as an ally of the Western powers it had been defeated by the Austrian armies comprising Croat, Slovene and Bosnian troops; and Belgrade had been reduced to ruins. The Serbian government had gone into exile and the Austrian armies had raped and brutalised the civilian population. It was never proved conclusively that the Serbian government had been complicit in the murder in 1914 of Archduke Ferdinand in Sarajevo, but Serbia paid a heavy price for triggering the start of the First World War.

As Austria-Hungary stumbled from one military disaster to another, its south Slav people, the Croats, Slovenes and Bosnians, turned with reluctance towards some kind of federation. The Serbs, chastened by defeat and by the collapse, in the Bolshevik Revolution, of their great protector, Russia, became receptive to some kind of alliance with the remnant countries of the Austrian Empire. It was a strange alliance because the only thing that the south Slavs had in common was a language. In most other respects they were ill suited to the creation of a viable and stable nation. The Croats and Slovenes were Catholic and looked to the West and European culture. The National Hero of Slovenia (France Prešeren) is a poet! The Serbs were Orthodox and looked north and east with envious eyes on the disintegrating Balkans, like them not long released from five hundred years of Ottoman rule. Serbia took the view that if Croats and Slovenes were to join them in the creation of a new country called Yugoslavia, they would do so on Serbian terms with Serbian leadership. The Serbs did not really see Yugoslavia as a new country but more an extension of Serbian territory, whilst the Croats and Slovenes thought in terms of a federation. Although the Serbs made up less than half of the population of Yugoslavia, they ran the country. The Serbian Army, the forerunner of the Yugoslav National Army of President Milošević, became the Yugoslav Army; Croatian units from the old Austro-Hungarian Army were disbanded. In the bureaucracy, the Serbs held all the important posts. Belgrade was to be the capital and the King of Serbia became King of Yugoslavia.

No one was much concerned with the Bosnian Muslims and how they would fit into this new creation. They were Muslims, after all, and had deserted the Catholic and Orthodox faiths in order to retain their land and privileges under the Ottoman Turks. Moreover, unlike the Serbs and Croats, the Bosnian Muslims were essentially passive people. When a Serbian government official was asked in 1918 how the new people of

Yugoslavia, enemies in the recent wars, might be brought together, he replied that the Bosnian Muslims would cause no problem. 'The Serbian Army would give them 24 hours, no, perhaps even 48 hours, to return to the Orthodox faith.' Those who refused 'will be killed, as we have done in Serbia'! He was serious.

When the delegation from the southern Slavs arrived at the Paris Peace Conference in 1919, it was almost one hundred-strong. It consisted of Orthodox Serbs, Catholic Slovenes and Croats, and Muslim Bosnians. There were university professors, soldiers, former deputies from the Parliament in Vienna, diplomats from Belgrade, lawyers from Dalmatia, radicals and monarchists. Many of the members did not know one another and had fought on opposite sides. By the time they all arrived in Paris they had agreed to create Yugoslavia but the boundaries of the new state were in dispute. The Croats and the Slovenes were frightened of Italian ambitions over their territory. Italian nationalists were quick to cast Yugoslavia as their main enemy in the role left empty by the collapse of Austria-Hungary. The Serbs rummaged through their history, made their defeat by the Turks at the Battle of Kosovo in 1398 a great national victory; and used that period five hundred years before to bolster their claims for a greater Serbia stretching from the Black Sea to the Adriatic. Fortunately for the Slovenes and Croats, the Italians made themselves so unpopular at the Peace Conference that Britain, France and the United States rejected most of their claims.

The Yugoslav delegation was led by Nikola Pašić. He had been Prime Minister of Serbia and was in his mid-seventies. He had a long white beard down to his waist. Just like Milošević, he was a devious and dangerous man. Because he spoke in a slow and deliberate way – and knew no English – he had a reputation for great wisdom. Lloyd George described him as one of the 'craftiest and most tenacious statesmen in Eastern Europe'. He impressed his Western visitors with his charm and deluded them, just as Milošević deluded a succession of Western statesmen – Carrington, Hurd, Vance, Owen – some sixty years later. Few of his colleagues trusted him but he was adored in the countryside where most Serbs lived. 'He only loved two things, Serbia and power.' Every night he used to sing Serbian songs and dream about Serbia's great history. The Ottomans had left behind in Serbia their customs, their cooking, their corruption – and a particularly Balkan state of mind. Nothing much has changed. The Serbs are world champions at deceiving diplomats, especially British diplomats, who have a strong inclination to believe what these charming people tell them. The dream of creating a Greater Serbia, hopefully with the support of the Russians, is as strong today as it had been in the days of the fall of the Ottoman Empire.

The Croat delegation was led by Ante Trumbić. Whilst Pašić had been dreaming of destroying the Austro-Hungarian Empire and grabbing as much of its territory as he could, Trumbić had sat in its parliaments. He came from the Dalmatian coast and regarded the Serbs as barbarians, scarred by their long years under Ottoman rule.

'You are not going to compare, I hope,' he said, 'the Croats, the Slovenes, the Dalmatians who have had centuries of artistic, moral and intellectual communion with Italy, Austria and Hungary with these half-civilised Serbs, the Balkan hybrids of Slavs and Turks.' Trumbić complained bitterly that Pašić and the Serbs refused to commit themselves to an alliance of equals. Indeed it was never an alliance of equals, right up to the dissolution of Yugoslavia in 1991.

The alliance broke down in the Second World War when the fascist Ustasi movement, which supported the Nazis, murdered large numbers of Serbs, and the Serb Chetniks, some of whom re-emerged in the 1990s, murdered thousands of Bosnian Muslims. It was Tito, supported by the British, who stopped the sectarian killing and at the end of the war he forced a peace among the warring factions. Tito, half Croat, half Slovene, made no attempt to negotiate anything with them, but he did allow them the lion's share of government, majority control of the Yugoslav Army; and in factories, schools, universities and the foreign service Serbs were given ultimate authority. The Slovenes and Croats who generated the wealth of Yugoslavia were never going to accept second-class citizenship after Tito died.

One of the first of many misjudgements by the British Foreign Office was to oppose the independence of Slovenia and Croatia when it was proposed by Hans-Dietrich Genscher, the German Foreign Minister. Carrington believed that it had undermined his negotiating position with these countries. There had been a plebiscite in Slovenia when 92 per cent of the population voted for independence from the Communist government in Belgrade. The reaction of Belgrade was to despatch the Yugoslav National Army to seal off the borders of Yugoslavia. Resistance by Slovenia was resolute and it succeeded. The conscripts in the Yugoslav National Army were deceived into believing that they were defending Slovenia against an outside attack but when they discovered the truth they were unprepared to fight. All Communist politicians lie and there were no better liars than the Communist regime in Belgrade.

Throughout Europe after the breakup of the Soviet Union one Communist regime after another had thrown out its Communist dictators with the tacit support of the West. How the Foreign Office and Carrington argued that it was morally defensible to deny freedom to Slovenia and Croatia from the repressive Communist regime in Belgrade when it had supported freedom in the rest of Europe is unexplained. Retired diplomats still nod their heads sagely and say that the disintegration of Yugoslavia was partially brought about by German support for secession. In fact, in the Yugoslav constitution there was a right of secession to any republic that voted over 70 per cent for independence; this is never mentioned. Nor is justice, or an understanding of how the Slovenes and Croats were treated by Communist Belgrade. The attack on Slovenia should have been a warning to the West that Serb nationalism was about to go on the rampage again.

When the first Bosnian refugees fled from the Serbs in 1992 my wife, who is Slovene, met them to hear their story. She spoke their language, unlike the vast majority of British advisers and diplomats. Some 80,000 refugees crowded into the camps in Slovenia, all of them having lost their homes and land, and most of them having lost husbands, fathers, brothers and sons at the hands of the murderous Bosnian Serbs. It was the beginning of the twentieth-century's second Holocaust, instigated by the nationalist policies of Milošević and implemented first by the Yugoslav National Army and then carried on by the Bosnian Serbs with weapons and supplies provided by Belgrade.

One of the big lies disseminated by Foreign Office propaganda was that it was a civil war. Certainly Serbs, Croats and Bosnians were fighting one another but if one country invades another and the victim attempts to defend himself it is hardly a civil war – a civil war implies guilt on every side. Another lie, often used in British propaganda, and stated by ministers in Parliament, is that all sides were guilty of atrocities and 'were all as bad as one another'. It was a theme often sounded by Lord Carrington. There is no doubt that Islamist radicals in Tehran sent parties to Bosnia to defend their Muslim brothers, and the Bosnian army lost control of them. But the balance of savagery was all one way – huge swathes of Bosnia were razed to the ground, every house destroyed, virtually every Bosnian family suffering murder, rape or torture, in an attempt to ethnically cleanse the Bosnians of non-Serbian extraction, as the Nazis had destroyed the Jews.

***

Before continuing with this unhappy story I think it is relevant that when I published my memoirs my wife explained in her own words what had happened to her as a child in Yugoslavia. It explains the turmoils of that country and how she came to take up the cause of the Bosnian Muslims. Similarly, in this context, it may seem surprising that 95 per cent of the money my wife raised for her charity, which I describe below, came from Jewish funds and individuals who themselves had suffered from racial cleansing of the most horrific kind.

These are my wife's own words:

I was born in Maribor, the second town of Slovenia, about ten miles from the Austrian border. We were very much part of the old Austro-Hungarian Empire. There was a family problem, so I really grew up with my father. But just before the Nazis invaded I was put on a farm for protection, so that the Germans didn't connect me with my father, who didn't know if he was safe with the Germans or not. He would come and collect me, and we would spend weekends together.

I loved the farm. I was freer, I could run about; they didn't dress me up in stiff collars and things. I have nothing but very happy memories of it. The family had four boys, who were all older than me, and one daughter. We were completely self-sufficient there – the only things we had to buy were coffee and sugar. They killed all their own pigs and cattle and preserved meat for the winter in pigs' fat. They had a small vineyard and made their own slivovitz. I still remember all the ways that we fed ourselves – I could survive today if we ever had to go back to subsistence agriculture; but I don't know how the urban population of this country, which has lost its knowledge of basic farming skills, would ever survive.

When war broke out, the Germans came to the farm quite often, although there were no roads up to it. My hairstyle had to be changed because I had a fringe, and that would have shown that I was not a farmer's daughter. So I had to have two plaits, to make it appear that I was their daughter. I think the boys started to believe that I was really their sister. Every day I walked to the village school, which was several miles there and back, and in the winter there was a lot of snow. Slovenia is very cold in the winter.

My father's family had plenty of land and they had a good deal of businesses. My grandfather had made a lot of money – he had provided the grain and fed all the horses for the Royal Yugoslav Army. My father loved music, and he didn't really work for his living. He had a hotel in Maribor, and the Gestapo and SS would come to eat in its restaurant. And so the waitresses always knew who was due to be deported – they apparently had a tunnel under an old cemetery, and so people were smuggled away. As well as my father, there was a professor and some other people who dug this tunnel. They would hide the people who were intended to be deported to concentration camps for three or four days in this tunnel – and when the Germans stopped looking for these people, then they would get them up to the Pohorje Mountains, and they were safe there because you couldn't find anybody at all in the mountains. So this went on until around 1944, and then the professor was caught, and apparently he was tortured and mutilated by the Gestapo, and people think he gave my father away. I don't know exactly what happened when my father was taken to Dachau in 1944 – nearly at the end of the war.

In Dachau people had seen him. But they had so many stories. Some say that when the Americans bombed Dachau he was running with some other people over a bridge and this bridge was bombed. Then the other story, which is persisting still, is that he survived and that he came as far as the border and then the Communist partisans killed him. They killed many people who came from the old 'capitalist' families in Slovenia and they killed a lot of people returning from concentration camps because they did not understand how they had survived the Germans. But we have no proof, we don't know where he died, and there are many stories.

After the war I finished elementary school and wanted to go to further education. So I walked to Maribor by myself – it was about ten miles from the farm. I was nearly ten years old; the Nazis had gone and the Communists had taken over. I had no family to go to – my father was dead and my aunts were in concentration camps in Croatia – so I was taken to a privileged sort of students' home where some of the children were orphans and others were children of famous heroes of the resistance to the Nazis. It was run by the Communist Party. I can't remember how I finished there. I was taken to an office and told that I could sleep the night there. I told them who I was, also that the farmer's wife who had looked after me during the war had died and that the boys were coming back from war but now they were grown up. And then I had some sort of intelligence test and I was allowed to stay.

At this school I was brainwashed completely into Communism. I was made into the most enthusiastic eleven-year-old Communist that you could find. I presented a bouquet to Tito when he visited Maribor – funnily enough, Tito was a distant relation of my family.

Our patron at the school was the Red Star Army, the Yugoslav Army. We got everything from them. We were very privileged. It was rather like a Communist Eton in a way, and I was very happy there. We had a political afternoon, but basically our education was the same as anybody else's. Once at New Year – we didn't have Christmas ourselves, because we were Communists – we had to recite partisan poems in the officers' house, and the interesting thing was that the heroes were always Serbs. Drago, a schoolboy friend of mine, and I were invited by the Army officers to play the guitar and sing partisan songs. Evidently Drago had said somewhere 'the officers are eating like pigs and the people are still queuing for bread'. Then a few days later I got called by the secret police, asking 'Did you tell anyone what Drago had said, did you tell anyone outside, and what else was he saying?' and they went on and on and on and for the first time I got frightened about the secret police. I actually got frightened of the system. I got worried. I had switched off from my own background. I wanted to be either a peasant's daughter or a hero's daughter; one thing I did not want to be was from the type of family that I came from, because that was shame. We had in this school a big picture of a fat, fat capitalist with a boy who was begging for food, and this capitalist takes a whip and he's going to hit him but not give him the bread. Every capitalist was bad; there were no good capitalists. Everything in the Western world was exploitation. One per cent of the population was very rich, that's how we were taught, and the rest were all poor and starving. Of course, I believed every single word they said. You were not really a private person; you were the child of your country, and they were preparing you for your country.

I had never known my mother because of the family dispute. Eventually I found a relative of hers who said that she remarried in '43 – that she went to Split and was an interpreter because she spoke a lot of languages, and that then she married this chap from Rome and had gone to Italy, and that she knew how to find her. So I went to Zagreb to see the Italian consul. The school said that I could go to Italy to find my mother – the director rather liked me, he was very nice and he let me go.

I had not seen my mother since I was two months old, so it was quite difficult. I wrote to her and I got a very strange letter back. And I then remembered that I needed a passport. Somebody told me that a friend of my father was now Minister of Culture in Tito's government, I think, and he would see me. By this time I was sixteen and a half. He gave me a passport. He organised a passport for two weeks during my school holidays.

So then I wrote to my mother and said I'm coming. She said she would wait for me in Milan at the station, which she did. We went home and my mother just went out. The maid looked after me and my stepfather was kind to me, but she was never there. I was there two months and I wanted to escape.

I did escape – I escaped to the Yugoslav consul in Milan and he brought me back because I was a minor and then I escaped again three days later. But I remembered that the Italian consul in Zagreb had said something funny – he must have known that my mother didn't really want me to come. The Italian consul had said, 'I want you to take this address. If you have any problems, ring.' I rang this person, who said, 'Come to Como, and somebody will be waiting for you.' This was a princess from Naples, an old lady from an Italian royal family, and she talked to my mother and said, 'This girl will go back to Communism if you are not interested in her.' That was the last time I saw my mother.

The Italian princess became my guardian; she was very religious and, as a passionate Catholic, she wanted to save me from Communism. From that time on I never wanted for money or anything. She arranged for me to attend a convent school in Milan. I had a private tutor for the Italian language. I started at university. I really wanted to read medicine, but because I knew so many languages I thought the easiest thing was to read languages. I wanted to take Russian again, but I had already done Russian for seven years, so she organised the Italian ambassador in Germany to arrange that I go to the Goethe Institute.

What I have not mentioned yet is that I had a terrible problem. When I came to Italy, I was looking for all these poor people and I couldn't find any, and I realised that everything I was told by the Communists was a lie. And now I couldn't understand how these people that I had trusted so much, who were more than my parents, who were everything to me over all those years – how they could lie so much? Also, some nuns in the convent school were not much different from the Communists; although they were good to me they were also trying to brainwash me. There was a priest who was continuously telling me that I should talk on the radio against the Communists. But I had this fear of the Communists and what they could do to me, even outside Yugoslavia. I wouldn't talk against Communism. Anyhow, I felt the nuns were similar to the Communists – they were both trying to ruin me. And I developed a high temperature and loss of weight. They started to send me a very attractive Jesuit. At this time I was seventeen, he was around thirty-five. He was always sitting at the bottom of my bed, and one day he said they were confiscating some books on philosophy or something that I'd bought. He said to me, 'Miloska, forget the nuns, forget the brainwashing of the nuns, you have enough in the Communist system.' Also all this religion they were pumping into me. And he said, 'Love is God and God is Love'. And that I think is what cured me in the end. Because if you have any love for humanity, it's OK; and if God exists, and has love for you, you will have love for him. It was so simple.

In 1992 my wife returned from Slovenia and sought an interview with Douglas Hurd, the former Foreign Secretary. His diary secretary explained that he was a very busy man, going from one summit to another, but she would try and arrange a meeting in about three weeks' time. It was not meant as a put-down but it certainly had that effect on both of us. I could not conceive that if a former colleague had approached me to see his wife on an urgent matter I would not have fixed it within a few days. My wife saw Margaret Thatcher, who said that it was no use talking to the Foreign Office – they took no notice of anyone's views but their own; she recommended forming a charity, which was done. Margaret Thatcher became the patron. Since then, with her support, my wife has raised more than £3 million for her charity, The Fund for Refugees in Slovenia.

As I have said, nearly all of it came from Jewish sources. My wife has built fifty-nine houses, many schools and a medical centre in the area around Srebrenica, the scene of the massacre of 8000 men and boys by Bosnian Serb General Ratko Mladić in 1995. Mladić is still free today. There are still thousands of destitute Bosnian Muslims in the Srebrenica area who, up until five years ago, had hardly been helped to return to their land by any official European body. My wife, who has worked in Bosnia unceasingly for fourteen years, says that 3000 houses are urgently needed in the Srebrenica area. Catholic and Presbyterian charities have been active with her in the area, but it is a struggle because Serbian propaganda promotes the view in Europe that the Bosnian Muslims do not really want to return to their land; this monstrous lie is actually believed by gullible members of the European Parliament and sections of the Foreign Office – both of them prattle on about reconciliation when the surrounding area is overrun by war criminals who move around freely with no sign of justice being exercised by anyone.

Paddy Ashdown, whilst he was European High Representative in Sarajevo, did his best to rein in the Serb police and organise justice but he lacked support from the European Union. The merry-go-round that is the European Union has moved on – and, in so far as this area is given any attention it is to discuss the candidature of Serbia to the European Union. This is totally unjustified. In the meantime, there are 7000 troops from Europe, deployed throughout Bosnia, whilst arms smuggling, police harassment and illegal logging of the forests goes on unabated in the rural areas of Republica Serbska.

In November 1999 Kofi Annan released a 155-page report on the Srebrenica massacre of July 1995. He pointed the finger directly at the Serbs and 'their central war aim: to create a geographically contiguous and ethnically pure territory'. Above all he criticised the 'prism of moral equivalency' through which the conflict was seen by 'international observers and actors'. The UN arms embargo, the pride of British diplomacy, imposed against the internationally recognised government of Bosnia-Herzegovina, did little more than freeze in place the military balance within the former Yugoslavia, which was heavily in favour of Serbia. It was Serbia that controlled and equipped the Bosnian Serb army. Moreover, the various mediatory efforts sponsored by the UN, the European Community and the five-power Contact Group 'amounted to appeasement'. Annan argued that neither humanitarian assistance nor a peacekeeping force could solve a problem 'which cried out for a political-military solution'.

John Major, the Prime Minister at the time, apparently horrified at the appalling television footage of mass murder, rape, torture and concentration camps, agreed with the Foreign Office to send a humanitarian mission to alleviate the suffering. The soldiers who were despatched to Bosnia were given feeble rules of engagement and had to witness shocking sights without the power to intervene. By agreeing this form of government intervention, the soldiers were liable to become victims of hostage-taking by the Serbs – and since they and the United Nations were scattered indiscriminately over the whole country it made it impossible to take firm action against the perpetrators of the outrages without hazarding the safety of the troops. One air strike after another was cancelled at the last moment by UN officials on the ground. The soldiers were ordered to restrict their activities to peacekeeping when the proper function of the military in peacemaking, which may well involve the use of force. The soldiers found themselves in the middle of war in which they were powerless to take action.

I had no desire at the time to attack individuals like Douglas Hurd, the Foreign Secretary, who is a perfectly decent, well-meaning man, but I regret that he was inbred with the attitudes of the Foreign Service.

When my wife, who was intimately involved from the outset in the troubles of the country, spoke the language and could communicate with the victims, tried to explain what was happening, she was simply patronised by ministers and officials who apparently knew it all. I have never been able to understand how so many charming and intelligent officials can be seduced by the culture of this organisation which is 'institutionally wedded to appeasement' and holds the extraordinary belief that diplomacy is the answer to every intractable problem. Unfortunately the Serbs did not play cricket – and the notion that this was never a 'civil war', as Hurd described it, never seemed to filter into the minds of those concerned. It was a grab for territory by the Serbs, who were straightforward, unprovoked aggressors.

The definitive study of this crisis is by Brendan Simms, a Cambridge don, in a book called *Unfinest Hour: Britain and the Destruction of Bosnia* (2001). It was well-reviewed but has never received a full response from the Foreign Office, which conducted an internal review of their actions and attitudes but never published it. If they had done so, it would have shown how Britain obstructed every effort to aid Bosnia militarily. It then tried, and ultimately succeeded, through the Dayton Agreement, to be accomplice to pressure upon the Bosnian government in Sarajevo to accept an unjust peace. It would show, according to Simms, that

Britain's standing in the world 'plummeted … to levels not seen since the Suez crisis'. And relevant to today's problems with Islamic terrorism, it showed to the world that, in a crisis, Europe was unwilling to take a stand to protect oppressed Muslim people. So many of the fierce denunciations from Arab sources against the West stem from the treatment meted out to the Bosnian Muslims during the Bosnian war.

In so far as it is possible to attribute blame to individuals, the ultimate responsibility must rest with John Major. But he quite openly admitted that foreign policy was not his thing, and he handed over day-to-day decision-making – and policy formation – to Douglas Hurd and Malcolm Rifkind, the latter Defence Secretary at the time. Both these men are personally decent, highly intelligent and undoubtedly motivated by the desire to do good. But at the time they somehow convinced themselves that the proper course was non-intervention and, worse still, that intervention by others should be obstructed whenever possible.

Here it is relevant to interpose a short post-mortem on the Major government. It suffered from a vacuum of leadership. The lack of it at the top from 1992 to 1997 is excused by the exigencies brought about by a slender majority in the House of Commons, leading to endless tacking and jibbing to hold the Conservative parliamentary party together. In fact, Tory backbench MPs are a flock of sheep, broadly uninterested in policy issues; they will follow a strong shepherd that offers them prospects of a return to Parliament at the next election.

This is exemplified by their apparent support today for the liberal policies espoused by David Cameron. He is showing leadership along consistent liberal lines and the flock of sheep will follow him to any "focus group" policy that seems to give Tory MPs a chance of re-election.

The Major government was all over the place, unable to take a firm line on anything substantial. The Cabinet seems to have been dominated by three determined men, Hurd, Heseltine and Clarke, and this comes through in Douglas Hurd's memoirs. These men, joined by other Cabinet members, frustrated Major's several attempts to take a firm line in the wars in former Yugoslavia.

I have read and reread Douglas Hurd's own memoir and the chapter headed 'Croatia and Bosnia'. I reviewed his book (*Memoirs*, 2003) very favourably in the *Guardian*, only qualifying my support for this episode in his long and distinguished career. He singled out my wife, Miloska, for particular praise for her work in Bosnia, which makes my criticism all the more unfortunate! I commend his chapter to interested readers as an antidote to my invective against the Foreign Office; the pressures and conflicting voices are all there. But reading it again I am left with one strong impression.

John Major never gripped the issue as Margaret Thatcher would have done. She might have got it wrong but she would never have handed over policy decisions of that nature to the Foreign Office, nor to endless fruitless meetings of the European Union. It is a sad episode in recent history.

However, with the benefit of hindsight it is quite possible to construct an intellectual argument in favour of such a policy. It would go like this: 'This is a European problem, not a distinctly British one. We have few British interests in this part of the world and there are greater humanitarian problems elsewhere which are engaging our attention. We have a strategic interest in stopping a local war spreading across central Europe but, if we can engage the Russians (as supporters of the Serbs) to take a neutral stance, then the best course of action is to let the combatants fight it out, without our taking a moral position. We have an interest, as a member of the European Union, to broker a peace, but peace in these circumstances overrides the need for justice, particularly when we do not possess the forces or the conviction to bring about a settlement by military means.'

Such a policy is impractical in the circumstances of today for several reasons. Whilst it is feasible to reject 'wars of choice' encouraged by a policy of 'expeditionary warfare' in distant parts of the world where British interests are largely unaffected and do-goodery is the principal motive for action; it is just not possible to remain neutral when wars break out on our own doorstep. Sarajevo is nearly as close to London as Rome. Of course, 'closeness' is more psychological than geographic, and that is the problem with the Balkans – they are strange and unstable and have drawn us into a terrible war in the past.

But in a media world, where the media has more immediate power to influence opinion than ministers, it has to be central to policy formation.

John Major had 'to do something'. Doing nothing in politics is always the hardest policy of all. The media will always close in on a story to fill tomorrow's newspapers or television programmes. And murder, rape and torture on our doorstep is a great story for the media. The fact that governments can resist media interest is evident with today's crisis in Darfur, where horrors comparable to those in Bosnia are daily perpetrated. But it is somehow far away.

Given that ministers had not the power to intervene militarily in Bosnia, what was to be done?

Surely the answer had to be, as Europe always does in a crisis, to turn to the United States for help. The new Europe, as of January 2007 with twenty-seven members, is one great unending committee meeting. It is institutionally incapable of action. It is simply world class in formulating opinions, writing reports and arriving at a consensus but ministers must accept Europe for what it is – a huge, overweight bureaucracy running a gravy train to enlarge its own institutional influence. With the exception of France, the original core members of the European Union – Germany, Holland, Belgium and Italy – are neutralist by inclination and hobbled by electoral systems that make positive action extremely difficult; so are the Scandinavian members. It may be that some new members from central Europe will tip the balance against the neutralist consensus but it seems improbable. So Europe in a crisis has nowhere else to turn but the United States.

And the extraordinary fact is that in the Bosnian crisis Britain sought to sabotage any kind of international political – and later military – intervention to curb Serb aggression and ethnic cleansing. I take the course of events from Brendan Simms: 'In 1991 it was Britain which decisively opposed the French idea of a Western European Union interposition force in Croatia. At the crucial and bad-tempered emergency meeting of EC Foreign Ministers at The Hague, Douglas Hurd warned his colleagues that the dispatch of such a force would lead Europe into a 'quagmire without an exit.' British officials briefed the press that 'there is no peace to keep. It would mean sending a force to keep the parties apart. Public opinion isn't ready for it yet. It is too drastic.'

Six months later, in early July 1992, Britain was alone in opposing the idea of armed intervention to safeguard the passage of humanitarian aid, thereby humiliating the soldiers who were engaged in this task. In this same period my wife was taking lorries of vital medical equipment to Tuzla hospital in northern Bosnia, where she was often shelled by Serb forces. Britain dismissed US plans for aid flights to isolated Bosnian government enclaves as mere gimmicks likely to provoke the Serbs into yet more retaliation, thereby endangering the whole aid effort. Britain abstained on a UN General Assembly resolution in December 1992 comparing ethnic cleansing to genocide. And so it went on, culminating in the disgraceful arms embargo, obstinately advocated and defended by Britain, which crippled Bosnia's ability to resist armed aggression and ethnic cleansing by Serbs.

When I left politics in 1983 to return to business I tried to put all these great policy issues behind me. For several years I said very little about political issues and I had resigned from all my political posts. I realised from my time in government that there is nothing more tedious for ministers than retired politicians and military officers sounding off from the touchlines. You are no one in the eyes of Whitehall and Westminster when you leave the Westminster village. But affected by my wife's knowledge of the day-to-day horrors in Bosnia, which she was personally experiencing, I returned to the political fray as an occasional newspaper and television commentator. My exasperation exploded in several leading articles in the *Evening Standard*, a newspaper that I knew caught the attention of the London-centric politicians. On 21 February 1994 I wrote:

British foreign policy is in disarray. Last week the Russians announced that they would move their troops to Sarajevo. This city is now totally surrounded and besieged by the Bosnian Serbs, supported by their Russian allies, Russian soldiers will presumably take their place on the hills around Sarajevo; these are the same troops who showed no impartiality whatsoever as peacekeepers in eastern Croatia. In the meantime, and perhaps indefinitely, the United Nations will be responsible for feeding the 300,000 citizens of Sarajevo. This development has been welcomed by the Foreign Secretary. But what is the endgame, as they say?

Elsewhere in Bosnia, where several Muslim enclaves are still besieged and starving, the Serbs are increasing their military strength. The tanks and guns for Sarajevo will simply be moved to meet the next Serb military objective.

Astonishingly, the British have moved two infantry companies with Warrior vehicles to Sarajevo away from the warring areas in the east. As a palliative to public dismay over Sarajevo we have now diminished our ability to protect supplies in central Bosnia. We have shown no resolve to reopen Tuzla airport to alleviate the suffering in that area.

Encouraged by the moral support of the Russians, the Serbs have now achieved virtually every one of their objectives, not least because of the gutless and all too corrosive policy of the British Foreign Office.

The Greeks, the third member of this Orthodox alliance, have meanwhile closed the trade routes into Macedonia against the policy of the European Union which they chair. The objective is similar to the Serb annexation of Kosovo. The Turks, Bulgarians, Albanians and Hungarians look on in dismay. So should we.

What is the British national interest? We hear from many members of the Conservative Party that none of this is anything to do with us. At least the British press is aware of pending danger and one British political leader, Mr. Paddy Ashdown, held in contempt of course by the Conservative administration, has taken an unequivocal stance.

When the Balkan crisis began and Yugoslav troops invaded the newly independent republic of Slovenia, we were told that this did not affect the British national interest. The same was said when the Serbs committed the most appalling devastation in Croatia. After the British had trumpeted our policy of non-engagement on every news programme, and we were then chairman of the European Council, the Serbs invaded Bosnia. There are now around four million refugees from this region in the heart of Europe. Any respect that the British might have retained in the Muslim countries of the world has gone. Rightly, they see us as having naively encouraged the aggression.

When the United States administration advocated a moral and humane alternative to Western military engagement, namely a lifting of the UN arms embargo against the Bosnian Muslims, the British Foreign Secretary was in the vanguard of the opposition. It was all going to be solved by diplomacy, we were told. We must not destabilise the peace process under Dr Owen, we were told. One moment we are sending British troops, the next moment we are disengaging them.

One disagreement after another has led to a post-war low in our relations with the United States. Publicly announced transatlantic telephone calls and visits to Washington do not constitute a working and positive alliance.

Now the Russians are newly active in the Balkans imbroglio and with near access to the Adriatic for the first time; confidence has collapsed between ourselves and the United States; we have been wrong-footed by the French and seen to be one of the weakest links in the resolve of NATO; and our unwillingness to provide the means for the Bosnian Muslims to defend themselves means that we are held in increasing contempt by the Muslim world.

The best-case scenario is that the Russians and Americans will elbow the British and other Europeans aside and jointly stabilise the situation, leaving us to solve the humanitarian crisis in Europe. The worst-case scenario is that the Europeans continue to argue, prevaricate and appease, diminishing the United Nations and NATO, leading to ever more chaos and wider European conflict.

Did someone say that the problems of former Yugoslavia do not engage the British national interest?

That invective was written at the beginning of 1994 but worse was to follow.

By early 1995 British policy had reached a dead end. Douglas Hurd continued to argue that the lifting of the arms embargo, or any military support for the Bosnians by the United States, would endanger the British and other troops engaged in humanitarian work. Whilst he argued that there was no British national interest in supporting the Bosnians against Serb ethnic cleansing, there was, apparently, a considerable national interest in preventing the Americans from doing so. To the frustration of the British and its negotiators, the Bosnians refused to see sense and agree to the truncation of their country in which they had a majority of the population.

In the meantime things were hotting up in the United States. President Clinton did not wish to create a major breach with the British because it would mean that the United States would have to step in and sort out the mess the Europeans had created. But Congress was getting stroppy. Since 1994 the congressional campaign to lift the embargo and strike the Bosnian Serbs with air power had been growing.

In May 1995 the rearmed Croatian Army in the west had a series of military successes against the Croatian Serbs in the east. At the same time the Bosnian Serbs started shelling Sarajevo once again in provocation against a NATO ultimatum which had been agreed the previous year.

General Rupert Smith, the new Commander of the UN protection force (UNPROFOR), responded with the first two major air strikes of the war and destroyed Serb ammunition dumps in Pale, not far from Sarajevo. The Bosnian Serbs then shelled the town of Tuzla in the north, where my wife conducted much of her humanitarian work, and killed more than seventy-five youths who were gathering in front of a café to celebrate their high-school graduation. At the same time they overreached themselves by taking British and UN personnel hostage, placing them around potential NATO targets, and stepping up their threat to the UN safe areas.

In mid-July Mladić pushed aside the feeble Dutch peacekeepers in Srebrenica and overran the enclave. Tens of thousands of Muslim refugees, who formed the overwhelming population in Srebrenica, were bussed into Tuzla. Some 8000 men and boys were murdered, constituting far and away the worst crime since the Second World War.

In Britain the hostage-taking and the Srebrenica massacre provoked public outrage but no fundamental change in British policy took place, although an Anglo-French rapid reaction force was despatched to bolster the humanitarian and peacekeeping effort.

The British press, in general, supported this squalid policy and *The Times* proclaimed 'no government has an electoral mandate to go beyond the present humanitarian operation, however much the American Congress and the Moslem side urge a partisan military response'. The newspapers urged on by Foreign Office 'spin' took a strong anti-American stance.

But the joint impact of the Srebrenica massacre and the hostage-taking had a seismic impact in the United States. Rifkind, with his skilled dialectic, appointed himself the chief advocate against the 'siren voices' in America, thereby widening the transatlantic rift and damaging further the fragile unity of NATO.

By the time Congress had passed a 'lift and strike' resolution, which Clinton could not veto, the US administration was forced to change from a restless but neutral stance to a position in direct opposition to the British.

Around this time in France the devious President Chirac broke ranks with London. Speaking on Bastille Day in Paris he condemned the West's reaction to the fall of Srebrenica as 'a bit like the talks that Chamberlain and Daladier had held with Hitler at Munich'. Failure to act, he said, would make the UN 'accomplices to ethnic cleansing'. Rifkind responded by saying that 'President Chirac has so far given a lot of fine words but no proposal'. Rifkind liked taking everyone on – he became a liability.

Britain had become well and truly isolated. Although the British were contemptuous of Chirac's posturing, toughing it out was no longer an option. Breaching the Atlantic partnership was bad enough but now, horror of horrors for the Foreign Office, Britain now found itself confronted by a Franco-American alliance, the ultimate nightmare for British foreign policy.

The Americans too had an ally in General Rupert Smith, the NATO commander in Sarajevo, who saw that there was no coherent strategy in place, merely a series of palliative devices. Smith took the view, against the mood in London, that it was necessary to break the vicious cycle of appeasement, vulnerability and inaction which had dogged the operation from the start. Unlike the advisers in London, Smith had a realistic view of the fighting power of the Bosnian Serbs – and believed that NATO could destroy it. He stuck his neck out very bravely and when the hostage crisis erupted he was effectively disowned by London.

Pauline Neville-Jones, the political director in the Foreign Office who had been a chief appeaser and subsequently destroyed her reputation by trying to do banks business with Milošević, began to gravitate towards enforcement. Smith was then able to do the job which should have been undertaken by his predecessor, General Sir Michael Rose.

Things began to move quite fast. The rearmed Croatian Army, and the Bosnian Muslims, began a push against the Serbs. The tables were turned and the Croatian Serbs were outnumbered; they turned and fled. Within a short period of time, 150,000 refugees, most of them innocent Serb women and children, who feared retribution by the Croats for the terrible devastation that Serbs had wreaked in Vukova, fled east, forced there by the retreating Serb army. Those who remained were subjected to terrible abuse by the Croatians. The Croatian successes led to further transatlantic recrimination as the British accused the Americans of facilitating the ethnic cleansing of the Serbs by rearming the Croatians.

Shortly afterwards, the Serbs fired a shell into the centre of Sarajevo, which killed large numbers of innocent civilians. Taking advantage of the new Franco-American alliance – and largely ignoring the feeble voices in London – General Smith struck. In Operation Deliberate Force, Serb artillery around Sarajevo found itself under sustained attack both from the rapid reaction force on the ground and from the air. Great damage was done to the Serb ammunition dumps and its communication infrastructure. 'I just stood and gasped, unbelieving,' said Martin Bell, the BBC journalist. 'This was the option that for three and a half years the policy-makers had told us was inconceivable ... the road they could not go down.'

Croatian and Bosnian forces now attacked on several fronts. Large areas of north-west Bosnia snatched by the invading Bosnian Serb forces were taken back. The Serbs were in disarray and had been bombed to the negotiating table. The siege of Sarajevo was lifted. The Russians kept out of it. 'Lift and strike' had worked – and it had all been achieved on the strength of the existing UN mandate. The press began to turn. Many commentators who had implicitly supported the British line switched their leaders and wrote articles suggesting that 'anything less than this approach would condemn the Balkans to further war and provide a green light to ethnic cleansers in other parts of the world'. The *Guardian*, a long-time sceptic, conceded that NATO air strikes 'will be seen to have worked and a further threat to employ air power will acquire greater credibility'.

President Clinton appointed Richard Holbrooke to negotiate a solution backed by the threat of force. Unfortunately for domestic political reasons in the United States he was charged with bringing about 'the quickest possible resolution of the conflict, which does not necessarily mean a lasting peace'. It was cynically suggested by journalists in the United States that it was 'about getting Bosnia off the front page ... and getting Bill Clinton re-elected'.

Holbrooke had been a long-standing critic of Western appeasement in Bosnia, which he had described as 'the greatest collective security failure of the West since the 1930s'. He had taken the measure of the Bosnian Serbs, 'headstrong but in the end essentially bullies when their bluff was called'. He elbowed aside the Europeans, in particular Major and Rifkind, and enforced the Dayton Agreement which brought the war to an end.

He was urged by British diplomats in Belgrade 'not to push the Serbs into a corner' and that simple adage has been the position of the Foreign Office ever since. Of course, a welter of justification for the opposition in Europe to 'lift and strike' then, and still does, fill the memoirs. It is claimed that the air bombardment called down by General Rupert Smith, with the assistance of NATO air power, was much less the cause of the defeat of the Bosnian Serbs than the renewed power of the Croatian and Bosnian armies. It doesn't really matter. What is clear is that the Croat, Bosnian and Serb forces on the ground all agree about the tremendous impact that the air campaign had on the control systems of the Bosnian Serbs. In all such issues one must expect Major, Hurd, Rifkind, Owen, Carrington, Neville-Jones, General Rose and others – the authors and the implementers of the old policy of negotiation and appeasement – to stick to their guns. Never mind; the weight of evidence heavily indicates that this terrible war was stopped by the Americans, aided by one of the heroes of the affair, the British General Rupert Smith, who for a variety of reasons did not go on to lead the British Army.

I must say in passing that I met many generals in my time in Whitehall and very few of them would I have charged with responsibility for a major campaign in war. Generals Smith, Bagnall and Chapple had the intelligence and courage to do so but they were regarded by the system as 'awkward sods'; but so was Montgomery.

**

So where are we now? In the doldrums, I fear. The eruption in the former Yugoslavia which shocked the world, and Serb nationalism and ambition which brought it all about, has not been lanced. Since the time that the Crusaders avoided Serb territory as full of trouble nothing much has changed. The Serbs are a charming, brave and persuasive people and they have been good allies of the West in two world wars. They are hugely expert propagandists and the British are gullible, believing what these people tell them. Dayton was a retreat from the principle of creating a unitary state and an ethnically diverse Bosnia. Maybe it was impossible.

'1995 had seen not only the triumph of a sound American military strategy but the acceptance of a deeply unsound European political strategy', says Simms in his book. Instead of allowing Bosnian and Croat forces to retake Bosnia up to the River Drina, Richard Holbrooke, much to the bafflement of all on the ground and to his own subsequent regret, threw away the military advantage gained. He forced the Bosnians to settle for less than their entitlement. The Croats and Bosnians who had been on the verge of capturing Banja Luka and other towns, in most of which the Bosnian Muslims had the majority population, were forced to settle for the sake of peace. The Serbs who were on the verge of defeat were able to extract a partitionist, ethnically exclusive and Serb-dominated state within a state called the Entity of Serbska Republica, previously heavily populated by Bosnian Muslims. Since then they have placed every obstacle in the way of the return to their homes of the Bosnian Muslim people. Serbska Republica is a European disaster in the making. It should be merged into Federal Bosnia-Herzegovina, a recognised state, where the rule of law can be administered for all ethnic communities.

Is this a recipe for future trouble in the powder keg of the Balkans? The Bosnian Muslims who have been disgracefully treated have no militaristic attributes like their neighbours, the Croats and the Serbs. They are a docile people, lacking the organisation and ability to speak loudly for their cause. But in spite of his sterling efforts to bring the Bosnian Serbs in Serbska Republica into the twenty-first century and hunt down the war criminals who move about quite openly, Paddy Ashdown failed. The British Foreign Office promotes the cause of reconciliation, but there can be no lasting reconciliation in an area where justice has not been done. The resentment of the new generation of Bosnian Muslims is growing – and the hate of the Serbs for the Muslims has not diminished.

Travelling around the territory of Serbska Republica, as I have done, is a shocking education. Everywhere there is still destruction; everywhere Serb occupation is evident on previously owned Bosnian land. Thousands of new homes are required. The European Union claims that it has financed a large rebuilding programme in Serbska Republica but the funds appear to have been diverted into rebuilding Serb property and towns, normally on Bosnian Muslim land. And European Union financial accounts are of course worthless. Beside Sarajevo, the capital of federal Bosnia-Herzegovina, where massive reconstruction has taken place, Serbska Republica seems derelict and very many Bosnian Muslims within it are still destitute and are harassed by the Serb police. It is a recipe for trouble. But the world has moved on and no one has the interest or the energy to put it right.

What conclusions can we draw from the Bosnian crisis? Certainly the British government was right to be cautious about the dangers of involvement in a war in Central Europe. We did not possess sufficient ground forces to go it alone in support of one side or another – that was never an option. The British could have examined with France in 1991 their proposal for an intervention force in Croatia but it was rejected out of hand by Douglas Hurd.

Several other opportunities were considered in a European context for limited peace-making moves but each one was rejected vehemently by Hurd as 'leading to a quagmire without an exit'. It was the British, in the early stages, who insisted to the Americans that this was a European problem and that Europe should be left alone to sort it out; that was foolish. All these crises should engage the West collectively even if one party, as should have been the case in Iraq, firmly rejects the judgement of another and refuses to participate. The Americans were only too glad initially to be told to stay away and leave it to the Europeans.

The first major error, well illustrated in Kofi Annan's report to the United Nations, was the choice of humanitarianism as the sop to public protest at the scenes of horror on the television screens. It called for a political military response, said Annan, rather than a peacekeeping and humanitarian mission. No one is denying that humanitarian supplies were well conducted and that they saved hundreds of thousands from starvation – after Serb aggression brought about at least three million displaced persons. But the troops who could have been ordered in as peace*makers*, as they conducted humanitarian supplies, were ordered to restrict their role to peace*keeping*, an almost impossible task in the middle of a vicious war. The military were let down by the politicians but also by the attitude of their own general, Sir Michael Rose. I knew him, albeit briefly, as the Commander of the SAS in the Falklands, and in spite of many disagreements with the Task Force Commander he handled that task brilliantly. He was the wrong man for the job in Sarajevo. His successor, General Sir Rupert Smith, was a brilliant success, took many personal risks and brave initiatives, which helped to bring the war to an end. He should have led the Army as Chief of the General Staff.

Surrounding it all was an unsustainable and narrow conception of the British national interest. Britain cannot be active everywhere, as we are finding out today. Bosnia was not as straightforward as the Falklands or the Gulf – and it is certainly easy to be wise with hindsight. The feeling that Britain must avoid being drawn into a partisan war without an exit strategy was held by the Conservative government with passion. What was not grasped was how an apparently 'civil war', as they described it, could lead to a wider conflict in the heart of Europe. The fault was initial hesitation, something that Margaret Thatcher never suffered from; with her, it was often a frightening ride but she had the instinct and judgement to get it right. Just how different it might have been was demonstrated by Tony Blair after 1997. Madeleine Albright's memoirs make clear the determined way in which the Labour government handled the Kosovo problem in 1999. It became obvious that the diplomats and military personnel were capable of decisive action under a new management. The wider lesson is that foreign policy must never be left to the Foreign Office.

Among the huge panoply of eccentric advisers gathered around the new Conservative leader, David Cameron, are two of the leading players in the Bosnia affair. Douglas Hurd and Pauline Neville-Jones are advising David Cameron on foreign policy! Their appointment remains a mystery.

Miloska 1968

Miloska distributing aid to Bosnian refugees in Slovenia, 1992

POSTSCRIPT

POSTSCRIPT

Where does all this leave us? It would be quite possible to say: absolutely nowhere!

I have written a series of essays, commentaries based on historical events around the experiences of my family. As a result, I make one dire but hesitant prophecy. We are heading for a dreadful conflagration in the Middle East and only the nations of that region have the chance of mitigating its potential horror. We are somewhere on a timescale of where we found ourselves in the mid-1930s after the rise of Nazi Germany. It is still conceivable that the good offices and cash of Saudi Arabia, with the support of the leadership in Egypt and Jordan, can find some way to neutralise the ambitions of Iran and Syria. There is so much danger of the Sunni–Shia conflicts spreading outside Iraq.

The reputation of the United States is so tarnished that an essential precondition for progress is for the Americans to get out and stay out of the Middle East, confining its presence to the narrow task of upholding the security of Israel. The leadership of the United States is so compromised that restraint and self-abnegation would be the most constructive course for the Americans to follow. Maybe there is some sign of that, now that the neo-cons are in retreat and disarray.

In one respect the European Union might be judged a huge achievement. Jaw-jaw is better than war-war – and never in history has jaw-jaw been so exercised as in the Councils of Europe. But Europe, concerned with its own selfish interests, has been dependent on the goodwill and selflessness of the United States for too long. When America suffers an aberration at the hands of a group of right-wing Republicans Europe has nothing to offer in its place. It is true that the French led a revolt against the Iraqi intervention, but France's reputation as an anti-American troublemaker reduced its influence. Jacques Chirac had already compromised the integrity of France – if integrity can be acknowledged as a characteristic of French diplomacy! Whilst it is possible that the troubles in the Middle East might have engulfed us anyhow, there is no doubt that the author of the current chaos is Bush, most oddly supported by Blair.

If Blair's support of Bush was based on a very honest sense that stability in the world depended on the health of the Anglo-American alliance, then he might be excused for his misjudgement. But the suspicion remains that lurking in Blair is a feeling that he must impose his own personal sense of Christian justice on other nations in the world. He seems to suffer from a misplaced urge for do-goodery which a more cynical, worldly wise statesman might have avoided.

As the world's attention is focused on Iraq, no one thinks anything about the Balkans. If the West becomes distracted by a Middle East conflagration, the nationalists in Serbia will make another move for Greater Serbia – and the Balkans will fall apart again. The flashpoint will be Kosovo and Serbska Republica, almost forgotten at the present time. Certainly the security of Bosnia-Herzegovina is being held together solely by the presence of 7000 troops from Europe, whilst nothing is done to curb the rearming of criminal elements in that region. Following the recent elections in Serbia and the known ambition for independence on the part of Serbska Republika, it will be a huge misjudgment for the EU to withdraw the office of the High Representative in Bosnia Herzegovina.

So I return to Rupert Smith, the former general in the Bosnian imbroglio. In 2005 he published a modern classic, *The Utility of Force: The Art of War in the Modern World*. It is something of an academic treatise and, although quite brilliant, its counsel of perfection in planning for the use of force makes a cynical old politician like me gasp in some incredulity. He correctly illustrates the necessity of full coordination among all the organs of the state, political, diplomatic, legal and economic, in deciding upon objectives. But, given the tribal nature of policy-making in Whitehall and Washington, this counsel of perfection seems normally unattainable.

I return to the Falklands experience because I suspect that the authority and leadership of a Margaret Thatcher is needed to bash heads together in striving towards better policy formation; since committees, coordination, consensus, textbook procedures will always be second best to the prejudices, judgement and will of a single man or woman. I think in the persons of Margaret Thatcher and Admiral Lewin, the Chief of Defence Staff in the Falklands campaign, we had a uniquely successful combination which it will be hard to emulate again.

As a senior politician I observed, with surprise, on more than one occasion the inability of the competing organs of government in Washington to come together in formulating policy, just as I found tribal rivalries in Whitehall similarly wanting. The success of policy formation in the Falklands was simply because everything happened so fast that no textbook procedures were possible, Whitehall was struck down by a blow to its solar plexus, and the Prime Minister's decisiveness was the only policy around. What General Sir Mike Jackson described in the Dimbleby Lecture in 2006 as 'process' is a stumbling animal. It removes 'the springs of action'.

The European Union, a committee of twenty-seven member states, can only arrive at a consensus based on the lowest common denominator of its members. Most European electoral systems are geared against any decisiveness in policy-making. I found it surprising, in view of the ghastly mess which Smith inherited in Bosnia, that he seemed to have some faith – or was it hope? – for a European Defence initiative. Lord Vincent, formerly Chairman of NATO's Military Committee, described meetings in Brussels as consisting of 'a hotbed of cold feet'.

Anyhow, to return to *The Utility of Force*, it is excellent because it is radical. Its theme is that 'industrial war' no longer exists. We are now engaged constantly and in many permutations in 'war amongst the people'. We must adapt our approach and organise our institutions to this overwhelming reality if we are to triumph in the confrontations and conflicts that we face.

The Utility of Force opens like this:

> War no longer exists. Confrontations, conflict and combat undoubtedly exist all around the world, most noticeably, but not only in Iraq, Afghanistan and the Palestinian territories – and States have armed forces which they use as a symbol of power. Nonetheless, war as cognitively known to most non-combatants, war as battle in a field between men and machines, war as a massively deciding event in a dispute in international affairs; such war no longer exists.

If Rupert Smith is correct, and industrial war of the kind that took place in the huge tank battle at Kursk in 1943, is no longer relevant to the threats we face today, what is the lesson for British policy? You don't achieve victory by military means anymore; all you can do is buy time. Fighting can not create security or stabilisation.

When aircraft can take off from the central United States to bomb Baghdad; when flight refuelling can sustain fighters in combat; and when the United States has five carrier groups, what is the justification for our spending £12 billion on carrier-borne aircraft at a time when the British Army is strapped for men and equipment, and the police and security services are our front line at home?

Expeditionary warfare is a nonsense.

I have written a book of history based on personal and family experience and if it illustrates anything it is how very difficult it is to get things right in the affairs of men. One would think that a benign dictatorship would be the best form of government to achieve order, the rule of law and the greatest happiness for the greatest number. But history prompts us otherwise. Even in our tolerant democracy prime ministers seem to have a shelf life of only two administrations before everything starts to crumble.

I am well aware that I have not answered any fundamental questions. Judgement of those in authority is what matters in the end. There can be no formula. I believe we were probably right to intervene in the Falklands, in the Gulf War, initially in Afghanistan to support an ally, and possibly in Kosovo. All these episodes more or less achieved their objectives. In my judgement we should have intervened earlier in former Yugoslavia, and the end result, namely the Dayton Agreement – a short-term amelioration to achieve peace at any cost – will prove a huge disaster. The Balkans powder keg could explode again.

I have no neat prescription for the future, although a study of Rupert Smith's interesting book should bring dividends. We should certainly abandon 'capabilities-based' planning which will mean limiting our ability to intervene here, there and everywhere. 'Threat- based' planning will teach us where our national interest really lies – here at home. We have to put our own fractured society, including our disaffected young Muslims, back on the right road before we intervene to remedy the ills of others.

PRAISE FOR JOHN NOTT'S TITLES

Here Today Gone Tomorrow:
Recollections of an Errant Politician
Published by Politico's Publishing Ltd – 1st April 2002

"A model political memoir"
Anthony Howard – The Sunday Times

"Its candor makes this book an excellent read."
John Biffen, The Spectator

"Nott has composed one of the best political memoirs of the era. It is likely to become an essential source for future historians"
Simon Heffer, Literary Review

"Riveting"
Matthew Parris, The Sunday Times

"Lively, informative and amusingly self-critical"
Peter Weston, Western Daily Press

Mr. Wonderful Takes a Cruise:
The Adventures of an Old Age Pensioner
Published by Ebury Press – 10th June 2004

"provocative, hilariously funny and the most explicit diary to have been written by a retired politician"
Frances Hardy, Daily Mail

"Politicians aren't meant to be this witty and rebellious... Has there been a more droll comic persona since Henry Root or Wallace Arnold?"
Daily Express

"one of the funniest books for years... a revelation".
Evening Standard